"For the Purposes
of Defense"

"For the Purposes of Defense"

The Politics of the Jeffersonian Gunboat Program

Gene A. Smith

DELAWARE

Newark: University of Delaware Press
London: Associated University Presses

Associated University Presses
440 Forsgate Drive
Cranbury, NJ 08512

Associated University Presses
25 Sicilian Avenue
London WC1A 2QH, England

Associated University Presses
P.O. Box 338, Port Credit
Mississauga, Ontario
Canada L5G 4L8

The paper used in this publication meets the requirements
of the American National Standard for Permanence of Paper
for Printed Library Materials 39.48–1984.

Library of Congress Cataloging-in-Publication Data

Smith, Gene A., 1963-
   "For the purposes of defense" : the politics of the Jeffersonian gunboat program /
Gene A. Smith.
      p. cm.
   Includes bibliographical references and index.
   ISBN 0-87413-559-1 (alk. paper)
   1. Gunboats--History--19th century 2. United States--Politics and government--1801-
1815. 3. United States--Foreign relations--1801-1815. 4. United States--Military policy--
19th century. I. Title.
   V895.S63   1995
   359'.03'097309034--dc20   94-33735
                                                                              CIP

*To my mother
for her love and unwaivering support,
and to my wife for understanding*

Contents

List of Illustrations

Preface

This book originated when a young graduate student decided to create an interpretational hole "in the fence of consensus." Explaining the gunboat program instituted by Thomas Jefferson allowed youthful idealism to confront established naval historians and anti-Jeffersonians alike. Moreover, the writings of navalists such as Alfred Thayer Mahan, as well as the presence of American expansionism in the late nineteenth century, had relegated the gunboat program to the shadows of American naval history. Virtually all who had discussed the subject contended that Jefferson was wrong and his gunboat program without merit.

Surprisingly, this long-standing interpretation had never been challenged in book-length form, and it appeared to be beyond reproach. But could such a program have been as worthless as posterity had indicated? Why would the nation have accepted such a detrimental program? Why would Jefferson or Congress have gambled the nation's defense solely on these untrustworthy diminutive craft? What role did Jefferson or Congress expect the gunboats to play? Questions such as these originally prompted the desire to investigate this difficult topic.

This project took shape just as Professor Spencer C. Tucker was undertaking his study of gunboat construction and operations before and during the War of 1812. Fortunately, when I learned of his tactical and operational focus, I was able to redirect my research towards the politics and ideology of Jefferson's program. Tucker's subsequent book, *The Jeffersonian Gunboat Navy* (1993), provides a detailed description of the construction, provisioning, and uses of the vessels. It also contains information concerning the craft's service in the Mediterranean and during the War of 1812. Although it is a valuable reference work, Tucker's study concentrates on the characteristics and employment of the vessels rather than on the political and ideological motivations that lay behind the program.

Several other works detail the larger Federalist-Republican, navalist-antinavalist, or "white water" versus "blue water" debate over naval policy, most notably Craig L. Symonds' *Navalists and Antinavalists: The Naval Policy Debate in the United States, 1785-1827* (1980). Yet neither Symonds nor others focus on the gunboat program. Instead, the craft simply become immersed in the waves of controversy and accusations. For this reason, I have chosen to examine the gunboats from a political and ideological perspective.

This work views the program simply as a means to a political end, and chapter 1 raises the historiographical arguments that surround Jefferson and the craft. Chapter 2 is the most controversial, as it examines Jefferson's theory of defense in relation to the gunboats. Chapters 3 and 4 explore the domestic and foreign events which precipitated legislation regarding the program and the congressional debates which followed. Chapter 5 deals with related legislation that impacted the development and direction of the program, while chapter 6 analyzes the political motivations of gunboat construction. Chapters 7 and 8 trace the gunboats as they uphold political policy before, during, and immediately after the War of 1812, concluding with the craft's legacy. Anyone who anticipates a detailed gunboat-by-gunboat description, or an in-depth analysis of the craft's service during the War of 1812, will probably be disappointed. Instead, what one will find is an attempt to place the gunboat program in the larger picture not only of naval history but of early American democracy.

Far more people contributed to the preparation of this manuscript than can be mentioned, and for those who are omitted, my oversight does not diminish the support they rendered or the appreciation I feel. I am immeasurably indebted to my mentor, Frank L. Owsley, Jr., who took me under his wing as an undergraduate and ultimately surrendered one of his "pet projects" to an untested, but ambitious, graduate student. This single acknowledgment cannot truly express the gratitude I feel. Bill Trimble, a modern navalist who continually suggested I defect to the twentieth century, taught me more about writing and rewriting than I can say. Other faculty within the Auburn University History Department, including Donna Bohanan, Hines Hall, Gordon Bond, and Allen Cronenberg, provided support and encouragement while I finished the dissertation. Junius Rodriguez, Chris Blackburn, Dixie Dysart, and Buddy Sledge of the Friday afternoon "Momma Goldberg's" group amicably debated the merits of my work as well as other issues. The Auburn University

History Department Milo Howard Scholarship provided financial assistance to defray research expenses.

Spencer Tucker of Texas Christian University unselfishly shared his ideas about the gunboats long before they appeared in book-length form. James Bradford, of Texas A & M University, and Craig Symonds, of the United States Naval Academy, offered useful suggestions and provided professional encouragement. Bill Dudley, of the Naval Historical Center, helped secure microfilm source materials which, according to the National Archives, did not exist, and my former colleagues at Montana State University–Billings demonstrated that hard work and perseverance is rewarded in numerous ways.

This book, when combined with Tucker's study, should answer most questions concerning the Jeffersonian gunboats. Because this volume analyzes Jefferson's ideological motivations and their political consequences, both of which are constantly open to changing interpretation, it will probably raise more questions and disputes than it answers. Nonetheless, it opens another historiographical door to the subject and may well encourage additional research. Finally, any mistakes and misinterpretations that may exist in the text are solely my responsibility.

"For the Purposes
of Defense"

1

Introduction

Thomas Jefferson was a complex man who invites conflicting theories about nearly every aspect of his public and private life. Because of the complexity, it should be remembered, according to noted historian Merrill Peterson, that Jefferson is "one of those men about whom the last word can never be said.... [H]e demands continual restudy and re-evaluation."[1] Just as Jefferson's life demands reevaluation, so do his views on gunboats, defense, and the navy's role in national security. When evaluating his naval policy, some believe that because of his affinity for gunboats, the navy "had always been ... his abhorrence."[2] This is as ridiculous as claims that once Jefferson, a Deist, assumed the presidency, he would destroy all established religious institutions.[3]

Just as Jefferson did not detest religion, neither did he abhor the navy. He did not philosophically oppose the navy, nor did he intend to eliminate the fleet. In fact, Jefferson realized, as did Thomas Gautier, commander of the Wilmington, North Carolina, gunboat flotilla, that the eyes of the "people must be opened sooner or later ... [to] the necessity of a navy."[4] Jefferson even supported a seagoing navy, especially since he expected it to be an integral part of a comprehensive strategic defense program. Had Jefferson opposed the navy and persisted in eliminating it as president, he would not have sent four consecutive squadrons to the Mediterranean to face the Barbary pirates and restore American honor and dignity. What becomes apparent is that Jefferson was not the "impractical pacifist he has so often been depicted," but that he had a complex yet flexible naval policy determined by time and world events rather than by ideology.[5]

The Jeffersonian gunboats were not large, heavily armed, seagoing vessels. They were generally forty to eighty feet long, fifteen to twenty feet across the beam, four to seven feet in the hold, and usually armed with one or two long 24- or 32-pound cannon plus assorted smaller guns. They were one- or two-masted, shallow-draft vessels designed to maneuver and fight in coastal waters, and they were considered defensive rather than offensive craft.[6] Because of their limited sailing abilities, they have become the focus of the "white water" versus "blue water" controversy as well as the navalist-antinavalist debate of the Jeffersonian period.[7]

The composition of the navy during the Jeffersonian era reflected Republican theories of defense. Ships-of-the-line and frigates were necessary only if a country were protecting trade and projecting its offensive power. During Jefferson's years as president, 1801–9, the United States focused predominantly on internal concerns, of which security was paramount. It was a country preoccupied with preserving its independence and protecting its own territorial integrity from the uncertainties of a world at war. Furthermore, geography was more important than machines or weapons during this period; thus, national defense meant protecting the nation against invasion rather than following the directives of the modern concept of the offensive defense.

It is true that gunboats were defensive weapons that were unlikely to become involved in provocative incidents on the open seas. But, more precisely, they were a calculated defensive measure and were not intended to be the nation's only protection. Harold and Margaret Sprout, along with other historians, charge that the gunboats "repudiated the idea of maintaining a navy." Yet a careful analysis of the gunboat program demonstrates that Jefferson preferred a balanced defense consisting of ships-of-the-line; frigates; smaller vessels, including gunboats; floating, stationary, and moving batteries; as well as coastal fortifications — all working in unison to ensure the nation's security. While it is true that the gunboats were obviously designed for defensive service, they also had unadvertised usefulness in revenue enforcement, the suppression of piracy along the coastal frontier, the elimination of the illegal slave trade and smuggling, and even limited offensive operations.[8]

Because of the duties to which gunboats were assigned, and because of their physical characteristics, they did not in themselves constitute a naval policy but rather were a program set within a sophisticated political-military context. While the craft were theoretically designed for port and harbor protection, in reality they were used as an adjunct to the seagoing navy in upholding political policy. Their construction and service during the period before the War of 1812 reinforces this concept.

Although Jefferson initiated the gunboat program, his secretary of the treasury, Albert Gallatin, and his secretary of the navy, Robert Smith, played conspicuous roles in the formulation of the policy. Gallatin, the economy-minded Swiss from western Pennsylvania, had attained public service experience as state representative (1790–92), Republican senator (1793), and congressman (1795–1801). Moreover, Gallatin and Jefferson had similar ideological convictions, as both viewed "debt, taxes, wars, armies, and navies ... [as] pillars of corruption" needing to be restricted. After Jefferson assumed the presidency, he naturally chose the devout, like-minded Republican to head the important treasury department.[9]

GUN-BOATS.

Gunboats such as these, depicted in Benson J. Lossing's *Pictorial Field Book of the War of 1812* (New York: Harper and Brothers, 1869), were to be a primary component of Jefferson's defense system. Photo courtesy of the Naval Historical Center.

Gallatin influenced the gunboat program through his fiscal policies. He viewed the navy as an unnecessary drain on the country's resources and regarded gunboats as a way to reduce the navy department's expenditures. The secretary's fiscal plan advocated reducing government spending so that the size of the public debt could be decreased. Once the debt was reduced, the tax burden could be lessened and a balanced budget attained. Viewing the navy as "unproductive, wasteful, and destructive," he preferred its elimination but understood that Jefferson was not going to dismantle the fleet completely. That being the case, gunboats became Gallatin's way of reducing government spending, or his means to an end. The treasury secretary constantly argued with Smith about Jeffersonian policy in general as well as the amount of money that should be expended on the gunboat program.[10]

Robert Smith, a Baltimore admiralty lawyer and brother of the influential Republican senator Samuel Smith, assumed the post of secretary of the navy on 27 July 1801 as Jefferson's fourth choice for the position. While Smith had little nautical knowledge or practical experience at administering such a department, he did, according to Charles Oscar Paullin, have "in considerable measure the lubricating qualities of the politician." This was essential for maintaining the integrity of the navy against the desires of an antinaval Congress and penny-pinching treasury secretary. While Smith was not particularly well trained for the job, he had the foresight to appoint Charles Goldsborough, who exerted considerable influence as chief clerk for more than forty years and on several occasions even ran the department.[11]

Among Smith's attributes were his political savvy and general ability to understand what the president wanted. During 1804 and 1805, Smith avidly supported the gunboat program, but by 1806 he wanted to diversify the navy and build some larger ships. This idea reflected the president's opinions but was overshadowed by an antinaval Congress, which refused to support measures for the development of a seagoing navy. Smith's suggestions did not sway Congress, but his ideas about the number of gunboats needed and where they should be deployed were important in formulating the program.[12]

Jefferson's gunboat program attempted to provide the country with such a pluralistic defensive policy. But the president encountered many obstacles while trying to ensure the country's security, and the gunboats became part of a much larger political argument. They were no longer simply a naval program, nor were they solely defensive weapons pitting navalist against antinavalist, Federalist against Republican, and East against West. Gunboats were a part of Jeffersonian Republican philosophy, and the program's victory or defeat reflected the political and diplomatic course the country followed during the early nineteenth century.

The gunboat program has been misjudged by historians who have measured Jeffersonian naval policy against the great expansion of the fleet during the late nineteenth and early twentieth centuries. The gunboat policy was a means of meeting the challenges of the era, and it enjoyed some success. Yet once the Napoleonic wars, the conflict with Britain, and the immediate need for small naval vessels ended, the demise of the gunboats came quickly. The remaining vessels were sold, creating a legacy of opposition to small vessels and a prejudicial view of Jeffersonian military policies that has lasted well into our own century. For our time, as for Jefferson's, both small vessels and a flexible, pluralistic military policy have their place. Walter Millis expressed that belief succinctly when he wrote, "while the 'battlewagons' might determine the broad question of 'control,' it has always been discovered (and usually belatedly) that light craft of shallow draft, able to work close in, were an essential requirement" for gaining complete command of the seas. Once the gunboat program was dismantled, that concept was forgotten.[13]

2

A Means to an End:
Gunboats and Jefferson's Theory of Defense

The American military experience in the twentieth century has produced a mentality reflecting the belief that defensive preparedness can be achieved only by offensive capacity, which equates to the amount of damage one can inflict upon the enemy. This is not a view unique to this nation or this century. Hermocrates of Syracuse, fearing an Athenian naval expedition against his city in 413 B.C., advocated a similar policy.[1] Naval historian Alfred Thayer Mahan, more than two thousand years later, made this view universal. When Mahan exclaimed, "every war must be aggressive" or the enemy will not "yield to your contention," he laid the foundations for what we have accepted as naval and military policy. This is a view easily understood in an age of mechanized war, nuclear weapons, and high-technology, quick-strike capability, but the Jeffersonian era was not such an age.[2]

At the beginning of the nineteenth century, the location of the United States provided natural defense and unparalleled national security.[3] Jefferson recognized that the Atlantic Ocean was a blessing separating the young republic from the turmoil of Europe. He had outlined his attitude concerning the country's location and its defense in his *Notes on the State of Virginia*. "It will be enough," he had written, "if we enable ourselves to prevent insults from those nations of Europe which are weak on sea, because circumstances exist, which render even the stronger ones weak as to us," for "Providence has placed their richest and most defenceless possessions at our door." And, as Jefferson well knew, "to assail us, a small part only of their naval force will ever be risqued across the Atlantic." "A small naval force," Jefferson wrote, was therefore both "sufficient" and "necessary" to protect what Providence had ordained.

Thus, a small naval force served double duty: it satisfied Republican opposition to large permanent establishments and helped reduce the national debt.[4]

Jefferson, although supportive of a seagoing navy, understood that the security offered by the ocean did not preserve the country's national honor. Only offensive capacity could spare humiliation abroad. Though the United States cherished the mythical tradition of its militia gloriously saving the country from British redcoats, it quickly became apparent that the image of the citizen soldiers of Lexington and Concord meant little when the American flag was flying in the harbors of Tripoli or Jamaica. Respect for the U.S. navy had to be earned on the seas rather than by defending the ports of North America. Jefferson's defense policy ensured a degree of security, but it provided the navy with only limited opportunities to gain respect because the president disliked a navy that went beyond the realm of protection. He did not want the navy "in search of adventure which contributes little to the protection of our commerce and not at all to the defence of our coast or the shores of our inland waters."[5]

The navy, born in the midst of the American Revolution, dwindled nearly to extinction in the years following the war, despite the continuing need for protection of the coast and avenues of seagoing commerce. After the Revolution, economic and political circumstances necessitated that the navy be deactivated. Only fifteen years later, the country's naval force was reactivated because of French marauders who infested the Caribbean, challenged neutral rights, threatened American economic interests, and insulted the country's honor. The result was an undeclared naval war with France, the Quasi-War of 1798–1801, which provided the first tests for the reborn navy. Historians generally agree that although there were no epic victories, the navy proved itself useful, emerging under Federalist direction as a respectable cruising force.[6]

But with the end of the Quasi-War, public events once again necessitated reducing the navy. On 3 March 1801, the day before Jefferson's inauguration, Congress passed an act "Providing for the Naval Peace Establishment." The Federalist majority in Congress, fearing even harsher measures from the new Republican administration, preserved the fleet while discharging all but forty-five officers and selling more than twenty frigates. The navy retained only thirteen ships, and of these, six were to be "kept in constant service in time of peace" and the others placed "in ordinary" — laid up out of service. In other words, the Federalists actually began what anti-Jeffersonians and pronavy supporters credit Jefferson with. While it is true that the rationale given by some Federalists for the passage of the 3 March 1801 naval reduction bill was stimulated by fear that Republicans would totally disband the navy, that concern was unfounded. Jefferson had no intention of eliminating the fleet or converting it, as many have maintained, to a white-water or gunboat navy.[7]

The phrase "Jeffersonian gunboats" incurs scorn almost universally from navalists and historians alike. Mahan wrote with disdain that "Jefferson with his gunboat policy ... proclaimed by act as by voice his adherence to a bare defensive."[8] It was true that Jefferson attempted to foster a defense, yet it was not intended to be as bare as Mahan charges. The gunboat policy was a well-formulated plan, considering the international tension of the era, and it had the added benefit of meshing with the principles of Jefferson and the Republican party.

Others argue that Jefferson did not have a real naval policy at all and that gunboats were used for specific objectives rather than for satisfying the requirements of a full-fledged naval policy.[9] That is a valid argument if one defines the duties of a navy as an instrument to protect the nation's overseas interests. But if one accepts a broader definition of the navy as a part of an overall defense program, then Jefferson had a valid naval policy and gunboats were a useful component within that policy.[10] Charles Goldsborough, chief clerk of the navy department during Jefferson's terms, accepted the president's definition and in 1824 published his *Naval Chronicle* "to show the intimate connection, between a defensive navy, and every essential interest of the nation."[11] Ultimately, Jefferson's naval doctrine emphasizing defense coincided well with the needs of the country and its citizens.

There were also domestic needs that had to be considered. Jefferson knew that the rabidly antinavy Republican Congress did not support seagoing vessels but rather embraced gunboats as an alternative for maintaining the country's security. Because Jefferson was the leader of the Republican party, he has been accused of making the navy dependent on gunboats. Noted Jeffersonian historian Dumas Malone exclaims that, despite Jefferson's leadership of his party, he was unable to overcome congressional opposition to a seagoing navy. Thus, the president was forced to reconcile the defense problem in the only way Congress would approve — the gunboat program. What becomes apparent is that Jefferson's attitude towards the navy has been stereotyped, just as his gunboat program has been erroneously over-simplified.[12]

While Jefferson was not ardently pronavy, he did desire a modest blue-water force to complement coastal fortifications, gunboats, and other defensive works. He understood that war, as the "greatest scourge of mankind," could never be eliminated, and that national leaders must

Thomas Jefferson. Portrait by Asher B. Durand after Gilbert Stuart. Photo courtesy of the Naval Historical Center.

bolster a country's defense to preserve the freedom and the security of its citizens.[13] Jefferson wrote, "although our prospect is peace, our policy and purpose is to provide for defense by all those means to which our resources are competent."[14]

The gunboats' perceived economic benefits strongly appealed to Jefferson, Republican congressmen, and a country whose resources were extremely meager. This was especially true because the reduction of the national debt was such an integral part of the country's survival. Jefferson considered the "fortunes of our republic as depending, in an eminent

Secretary of the Treasury Albert Gallatin. Engraving from the portrait by Gilbert Stuart, 1803. Reproduced from the frontispiece of Henry Adams's *Life of Albert Gallatin* **(Philadelphia, PA: J. B. Lippincott and Company, 1879).**

degree, on the extinguishment of the public debt." In other words, he was obsessed with debt reduction because of his personal situation as well as his observations of debt-ridden Virginia. He also understood that Britain's financial problems produced the American Revolution, and that similar woes in France spawned the French Revolution.[15]

Should America not settle her fiscal problems, Jefferson feared his country would be "committed to the English career of debt, corruption and rottenness, closing with revolution." This concerned him, because he understood that revolutions produced "a host of admirals, generals and other officers ... having more pride than property" and who drained the country's resources or overthrew its government. Even after the wars or revolutions ended, the expenditures continued, leading Congressman Nathaniel Macon of North Carolina to proclaim, "the war of killing prepares the way for a war of taxes, which never ends." Jefferson knew gunboats would not stop the war of taxes, but he believed it would lessen the drain on the nation's resources, and that strongly appealed to Republicans.[16]

Treasury Secretary Albert Gallatin concurred with Jefferson's assessments and regarded the navy as the prime candidate for budgetary cuts. Gallatin argued that the navy was unnecessary because "the bravery of the mass of the people" was sufficient to repel any invader. During the last year of John Adams's presidency, naval expenditures totaled almost $3.5 million, due primarily to an undeclared naval war with France. Gallatin proposed to apportion less than $2 million to the army and navy together, and in 1802 the navy received only $946,213.24. Both Jefferson and Gallatin were opposed to a navy that "by its own expenses and the eternal wars in which it will implicate us, will grind us with public burthens, and sink us under them." The country could, Jefferson believed, make large savings by reducing the navy, and it would do so without sacrificing national security. [17]

Although Jefferson wrote isolated statements about the country's defense throughout his lifetime, the most complete exposition of his defense theory was his "Special Message on Gun-Boats," presented to the Senate and House on 10 February 1807. In it, he reported that the nation's defense should be based on a combination of land batteries, moveable artillery, floating batteries, and gunboats.[18] This message, coming near the end of his second term, did not truly do justice to his defense doctrine. All implements called for in this report were solely defensive, and there was no reference to a seagoing navy. Through most of his years in office, Jefferson carefully avoided such statements because he was a consummate politician and realistic statesman who understood, especially after the *Chesapeake* incident of June 1807, that the construction of a seagoing navy had diplomatic as well as domestic ramifications.[19]

Jefferson's message to Congress did not reflect his true ideas concerning security. He preferred a more complete defensive arrangement; but as always, his naval and military policy was determined by circumstances or, more simply, a calculated reaction to events.[20] Throughout Jefferson's administration, war — whether with Spain, Britain, or France — seemed imminent, and national defense was a paramount concern. Jefferson could, to some degree, determine the course of action the United States should follow, but he was unable to prevent other nations from threatening the country. Therefore, passive military preparation provided security, despite the actions of other nations.

Jefferson's system, formulated piecemeal over many years, attempted to create a balanced defense for security. It included not only a navy of seagoing ships and gunboats but also a system of coastal and harbor fortifications stretching from Maine to Louisiana. Jefferson was not the first to recognize the defense needs of the nation's seaports. Congress had authorized a system of simple and inexpensive earthwork forts as early as March 1794. By contemporary European standards, however, these works were simple and weak, and they quickly fell into disrepair after 1800. There were other attempts to complete works at locations of primary importance, but the building appropriations were always negligible. It was not until November 1807, after the *Chesapeake* disaster, that the country embarked on another major program of fortress construction. These works, consisting of open batteries, masonry-faced earth forts, and all-masonry forts, did much to prepare the country for the ensuing conflict.[21]

While the construction materials may have differed, each fort reflected a similar idea — to protect the larger harbors from "more serious attacks as they may be exposed to."[22] Secretary of War Henry Dearborn realized that harbor forts protected the port from serious attacks but could not prevent enemies from landing.[23] Not even the fortress at New York, which Jefferson claimed mounted 438 guns and was "adequate to the resistance of any fleet which will ever be entrusted across the Atlantic," would be sufficient. The president concurred with Dearborn's observations and remarked that fortifications could become "bridles for an enemy to put into our mouths," especially if they were the country's sole defense.[24]

To supplement the system of fortifications, Jefferson wanted "land batteries, furnished with heavy cannon and mortars." Although he believed these would not foil enemy vessels from entering a harbor, they would do much to prevent a port town from being damaged. Stationary land batteries prevented a vessel from passing a fort without tacking under some guns, be it the fort's or the battery's.[25] John Shaw, naval commander of the New Orleans flotilla 1806–8 and 1810–14, recognized the importance of a fixed land battery for the protection of Mobile harbor on the Gulf of Mexico. He argued that fifteen cannons on Mobile point working in cooperation with gunboats were "the best mode of defense that can be devised, against maritime invasion."[26] Working as a part of the overall system, stationary land batteries limited an enemy's approach and provided a more defensible position.

For locations that did not warrant a fixed battery or a fort, Jefferson advocated the use of "moveable artillery" consisting of "heavy cannon on traveling carriages." He argued that cannon and mortars could quickly be moved to the bank of a river or beach to frustrate an enemy's landing or to drive a vessel back to sea. Additionally, these weapons could be lent to seaport towns and their citizen soldiers trained in their use, thus perpetuating the militia tradition while lessening defense costs for the federal government.[27] Moreover, they could serve in conjunction with harbor forts and stationary batteries to create a virtually invincible position.

"Floating batteries" were to be another integral part of Jefferson's maritime defense. Cannon on floating platforms, he argued, stationed to prevent enemy vessels from penetrating a harbor or to drive them out once they had entered, could create difficulties for an attacker. Jefferson believed that cannon, mortars, rockets or "whatever else could ... destroy a ship," blocked the approach to a harbor and forced the enemy to sacrifice valuable resources to remove the obstacle before assaulting the target.[28] This, in turn, limited the resources the enemy could bring to bear on the port.

Other statements illustrate that Jefferson's theory of defense did not exclude a seagoing navy. He believed seagoing vessels were required to harass and demoralize the enemy before they assaulted the defense. "Brigs and schooners," he wrote, should "be free to cruise," especially "in time of war," because they could serve as a disruptive factor.[29] Frigates were also an important feature of the nation's sailing force. "The wooden walls of Themistocles" were necessary for the country's protection and were not to be supplanted by gunboats. Rather, seagoing ships would complement coastal vessels.[30] In 1806, Jefferson half-heartedly remarked that "building some ships of the line" should "not to be lost sight of." For, as he understood, "a [seagoing] squadron properly composed" was necessary "to prevent the blockading [of] our ports."[31] He acknowledged, however, that construction of larger vessels depended on congressional approval rather than on any action he alone could take. This became apparent early in 1806, when Congress overwhelmingly defeated legislation for building capital vessels.[32] An antinavy Congress was responsible for the seagoing navy's setback.[33]

The notion of brigs, schooners, frigates, ships-of-the-line, and gunboats working in unison with Jefferson's harbor defenses challenges the common assertion that he wanted to eliminate the navy. In fact, as early as 1785, Jefferson supported the navy and hoped that "our first attention ... will be to the beginning of a naval force of some sort."[34] Navies did not "endanger our freedom, nor occasion blood-shed," he professed, but were a guard against foreign incursions.[35] Yet the navy he advocated in 1806 was much different than that of 1785. In 1785, Jefferson supported an offensive navy to deal with incursions of the North African pirates. In 1806, he preferred a defensive navy or "such a naval force as may protect our coasts and harbors from ... depredations."[36] As such, Jefferson did not want to replace the "blue water" fleet with "white water" gunboats but rather to integrate all into a defense system predicated on national security. Gunboats fit nicely into this scheme. "In fact," as Craig Symonds claims in his *Navalists and Antinavalists*, "coastal defense was always the complete raison d' être for the gunboats."[37]

Gunboat-type vessels were not novel to the Jeffersonian period but had been around virtually as long as there had been armed sailing vessels. Demosthenes, perhaps the greatest Greek orator of antiquity, wrote of an intermediate type of vessel, called myoparones, which served as a naval auxiliary in much the same manner as Jefferson intended for the gunboat.[38] The first American gunboats, however, did not appear until 1775 for use in the defense of the Delaware. During their service on that station, they drove *Roebuck*, a British man-of-war, aground before withdrawing to the secure confines of Philadelphia.[39] Other galleys and gondolas were instrumental in Brigadier General Benedict Arnold's defense against the British at the Battle of Lake Champlain in October 1776. During the 1790s, even the Federalists, who were critical of Jefferson's program, built gunboat-type vessels for the defense of "harbors, bays and inlets," demonstrating that these craft were not exclusively in the Republican domain but were widely valued for defense purposes.[40]

Although gunboats played a limited role in American naval activities before Jefferson's presidency, they achieved noteworthy success in foreign navies. The French used them successfully during the British attack on the St. Lawrence River during the Seven Years' War.[41] Moreover, the British had seen the value of using them for an assault on

Mobile in 1760. In fact, Britain had used them, as Jefferson vividly remembered, "for ravaging the rivers" during the Revolution.[42]

But it was Sweden and Russia who made the most extensive use of the diminutive craft, with the Russians proving the vessels' effectiveness against ships-of-the-line. On 28 June 1788, a flotilla of twenty-two Russian gunboats in the mouth of the Dnieper River defeated the celebrated Turkish captain Pacha Hassan Aly. Hassan's attempt to besiege the city of Kimburn with sixteen ships-of-the-line and several frigates proved fruitless and resulted in the loss of nine vessels. The remainder of the Turkish fleet fled to the protection of the fortified city of Ocrakow. It is possible to attribute the Turkish loss to Hassan's decision to split his forces and attack piecemeal, but the gunboats nonetheless demonstrated defensive effectiveness.[43]

By the time the gunboat program was implemented in the United States nearly all of the countries of Europe, including several Mediterranean maritime nations, employed similar craft "for the purposes of defense."[44] Gunboats obviously were not novel; they had proven their worth and had carved out a complementary role in naval operations. They did not and could not replace larger vessels, but in certain situations their strengths were self-evident. If that were not true, gunboat-type vessels would have quickly disappeared from the world's fleets.

For Jefferson's administration, the "great desideratum in building gunboats [was] to prepare them well for fighting."[45] They were "for home defense," whereas "ships [were] for distant expeditions."[46] The president admitted that gunboats were "proposed merely for defensive operations," and for that reason they were ridiculed by those "who wished for engines of offense."[47] A gunboat's offensive potential was limited. Many maintained that the most gunboats could do, whether working alone or in groups, was to be an "annoyance."[48] They could not scour the open seas waiting for their prey, for on the open seas they themselves were prey. As long as they protected the coast, gunboats escaped the possibilities of potential conflicts, thereby saving the country money as well as human lives. If the gunboats worked within the confines of Jefferson's passive coastal defensive system, they were, he wrote, "the humble, the ridiculed, but the formidable gunboats" which ultimately made our harbors "hors d' insulte."[49]

While gunboats were built for defensive reasons, they had other qualities that strongly appealed to Jefferson and Republicans. Building gunboats, he believed, was economical, while navies were inherently expensive, and Jefferson could ill afford additional debt, especially since the Republicans had inherited a $82 million debt, or "moral canker."[50]

The price for building gunboats, originally estimated at about five thousand dollars each, was extremely attractive when compared to larger ships, such the frigate *Constitution*, which cost $302,718.84, or the brig *Syren,* which cost $32,521.[51] In time, Jefferson found that gunboats armed with two cannons cost twelve thousand dollars, whereas those carrying one cost nine thousand, but by the time this discovery became apparent, Republican congressmen were blinded by the perceived short-term fiscal advantages of the craft.[52]

Gunboats, according to Jefferson, had other economic advantages. Navies, admittedly, were not only expensive to construct but even more costly to maintain. He repeated this belief to John Adams later in life: "A navy is a very expensive engine.... [As such,] a nation who could count on twelve or fifteen years of peace would gain by burning its navy and building a new one in time."[53] In his *Notes*, Jefferson had professed that the annual maintenance expense for the British navy was $1,280 per gun, or more than $2,304,000 for the entire fleet.[54] Utilizing gunboats lessened the amount needed for maintenance because the vessels could be taken out of commission and placed under small sheds when not in use.[55] Likewise, repairs could be made more economically because deepwater shipbuilding facilities were unnecessary.

Navy Secretary Robert Smith confirmed Jefferson's ideas about the economical attributes of the vessels when he reported that the *Constitution*'s annual upkeep amounted to $113,618.25 and the *Syren*'s to $41,880.20, whereas the 2-cannon gunboat's expense was only $11,039.46.[56] While it was true that the gunboat's annual expense was exorbitant on a per-gun average, those costs could be reduced to $2,147 per year when the vessels were out of commission.[57] Because only a limited number were needed for service during peacetime, the annual costs for the gunboat fleet would be less than those of one frigate.[58]

Additionally, Jefferson planned for the gunboats to be manned by a naval militia, which would spring to arms at the appearance of enemy sails.[59] Using the citizen sailors, Jefferson visualized three scenarios for gunboats. The first was when the country was at peace. Under these conditions, only six or eight vessels were necessary, while the rest were placed in ordinary — incurring expenses only for the sheds to protect them and the sentinels to ensure that no mischievous damage occurred.[60] The second situation presupposed that the wars in Europe continued. If so, Jefferson deemed that about twenty-five vessels, afloat but with only enough men to navigate and care for them, were necessary. The last situation anticipated that the United States would be at war. In this case, the number of gunboats needed depended on the "character" of the war itself, but regardless they were to be fully manned and ready for action.[61] Using these simple criteria, Jefferson expected that the navy's annual expenditures could be considerably reduced.

The defensive and economic attributes of the gunboats were impossible for Republicans to ignore. But there were other advantages not so obvious. Gunboats had political considerations that also made them attractive. Because they were small vessels, their construction did not require deepwater shipyards or a large pool of trained labor. Instead, they could be built on any river or beach where a supervisor could be procured and materials amassed.[62] This appealed to the predominantly Republican South and West, where shipbuilding facilities were few and skilled labor limited.

Ship construction traditionally occurred in the maritime region of the Northeast where building facilities already existed. Not requiring large shipyards, gunboats would be contracted for in many areas of the country, thus becoming a powerful piece of political patronage for the Republican party.[63] Ultimately, no fewer than forty-five different gunboat contracts were distributed to eleven states and the District of Columbia, which helped perpetuate the Republican idea of government for the people, rather than the Federalist government for the elite.[64]

Another reason Jefferson supported gunboats was because he remembered some of the reasons his dry-dock proposal had failed. In the fall of 1802, Jefferson supported the construction of a dry dock aimed at mothballing up to twelve of the nation's frigates. His rationale for this project, to be discussed later, was to eliminate costly naval expenditures by economically preserving the vessels under cover. But when the issue was debated, Jefferson was charged with wanting to eliminate completely future naval appropriations and contracts while concentrating the navy in one location, under the watchful eye of the government.[65] These suggestions struck fear in the pronavy faction and threatened their commercial livelihood. Gunboats, however, should theoretically have ameliorated those fears. Built at various locations, their construction ensured the Northeast a share of future ship-building appropriations rather than the "feast or famine" that went along with big-ship contracts. The vessels were also to be distributed to any location where there was a perceived threat. This countered the charge that the navy would be concentrated at any one location.

Because many gunboats could be constructed for the price of a single frigate, the money expended for the small craft served double duty. For example, a $300,000 frigate could only be at one place at a given time and then only operate from deepwater ports. This left many areas undefended. For the same amount expended on a frigate, numerous gunboats could be built and distributed to several locations, providing perceived security to many areas simultaneously. Additionally, gunboats were not restricted to deepwater ports but were even "serviceable to the headwaters of nearly all rivers."[66] This provided each locale, regardless of importance, with its own defense and helped to further the idea of equality, because each threatened region warranted some protection. In this respect, gunboats calmed fears concerning possible attacks and, although they were not frigates or ships-of-the-line, their ability to make a presence was a strong argument for Jefferson's overall defense program.

Another advantage of the gunboats was that they were not limited solely to defensive operations but could serve in an offensive or preventive capacity. In August 1808, Jefferson professed that gunboats could strike "the shore in an instant" to seize land from Spain "as a reprisal for spoliations." Jefferson also declared they could be used against pirates and smugglers, their shallow-draft construction making them ideal for that purpose. These lawless adventurers evaded larger ships by slipping across shoals, where they could not be followed. Gunboats could, however, continue the chase and confront those vessels carrying on illegal activities. As such, Jefferson comprehended they would keep the "West India pirates in order" and limit the activities of privateers in coastal waters.[67]

Once Congress passed the Non-Intercourse Act, the Embargo, and the Non-Importation Act, the gunboats' principal duties were to enforce revenue laws and suppress "illicit trade," or smuggling.[68] They also attempted to prevent other nations from violating American neutrality. But Jefferson did not want needlessly to provoke a conflict with the British, so he concealed that the vessels were to be used against ships violating American neutrality.[69] Gunboats, working in conjunction with revenue cutters, became essential in attempting to uphold the country's antitrade manifestos.[70] While frigates and ships-of-the-line tried to perform these duties, because their draft prohibited them from coming near shore and their locations were usually advertised, their success was limited. That violators could avoid larger ships provided an additional rationale for the gunboats' existence.

The flexibility of the gunboat's size and design allowed the craft to serve in several nontraditional roles. Because they could easily maneuver among the numerous inlets, bays, and rivers of the South, they became increasingly useful after Congress abolished the African slave trade in 1808 as a means for suppressing the illegal act.[71] Not only did they hinder the successful importation of slaves, but in one instance their presence was invaluable in preventing a slave insurrection from succeeding.[72] Although gunboats did not eliminate the illegal activity, their presence on the American coast provided an obstacle that could not be overlooked and helped to establish a precedent for the navy's involvement in suppression of the slave trade.

Probably the most unique duty that gunboats were considered for was their role in Indian uprisings. Jefferson was well aware that protecting the western frontier was a major concern. In 1803, the year of the Louisiana Purchase, he estimated that the number of Indian warriors in the territory amounted to 26,286.[73] The combined army and navy for the entire United States numbered less than 5,000 men. Because the United States was, as the president believed, so "miserably weak" in the Louisiana territory, maintaining friendly relations, especially with the "powerful nations" of the Osage and Sioux, was crucial.[74] But if relations did not remain amiable, gunboats could supplement the meager forces stationed on the frontier. They were viewed as indispensable agents for "defending the Mississippi and Illinois Rivers ... from the approach of any hostile party of Indians." The vessels were "well calculated for the defence of ... rivers against Any force that attempt[ed] to descend." This was crucial because rivers were the principal avenues of communication and transportation. But gunboats served as more than a visible obstacle against hostile Indians: their reported presence was also a deterrent that exhibited the power of the white man's government.[75] The gunboats' distinctive design and size made them suitable for this uncommon role.

Gunboats also functioned in other roles to which larger ships were not well suited. Their size made them ideal for performing simple logistical operations such as convoy duty, or transporting men and materials from one port to another.[76] Although larger ships could perform these functions, they were much more cumbersome and expensive. Gunboats, because of their shallow draft, were also suitable in supporting land operations and invasions, as they could sail up rivers or onto beaches.[77] The vessels even provided a way to train numerous men simultaneously.[78] This was especially attractive because the number of men on larger ships was fixed, and their prolonged cruises provided few opportunities for duty rotation.

The gunboat's size and design allowed the craft to serve in various capacities. Their shallow draft provided mobility and accessibility unmatched by larger ships, which made them ideal for coastal and riverine service, especially in the Gulf region. They were to operate virtually at all times because they were supposed to be equipped with both sails and oars. This meant that lack of wind did not hinder their movement. In contrast, larger vessels were forced to retire until favorable winds prevailed.

The gunboats did, however, have their drawbacks. They did not provide young men with the chance to learn seamanship, a naval environment for training professional officers, nor the opportunity to gain a naval "mentality." Some felt the craft provided little experience in intricate fleet tactics and combat maneuvers, while others believed they produced derelict seamen. Still others disliked the vessels because of the difficulty in recruiting seamen. Gunboats generally did not provide the opportunity for glory or prize money that bigger ships offered.[79]

Their size and seaworthiness allowed other complaints as they were "very wet," and "almost uninhabitable in a sea-way."[80] Henry Adams characterized the gunboats as "not wide enough to lie straight in, with the certainty of oversetting or running ashore or being sunk, in case of bad weather or hostile attack."[81] Furthermore, a gunboat's efficiency decreased in direct proportion to how far it sailed into the open seas, and when at sea, the vessels generally had to stow their guns in the hold in order to maintain seaworthiness.[82] In fact, a gunboat under Stephen Decatur's command capsized in a brisk wind and sank in only six fathoms of water. This prompted him to ask a fellow captain, "What would be the real national loss if all gunboats were sunk in a 100 fathoms of water?"[83] Obviously, gunboats could not adequately handle rough waters and would never be decisive on the open seas. On the other hand, they were not intended as such. They were proposed for defensive purposes, which made any additional service they rendered an added benefit.

There are valid reasons to condemn Jefferson's gunboat program as it developed, and it can be viewed as a failure in light of the president's original conception of how the vessels were to be integrated into the nation's defense. On another level, the craft did not inspire confidence from commanders, crews, or the people. They were generally ridiculed, and few people placed much emphasis on their capabilities.

But just as Jefferson's gunboats are viewed with contempt, so is his theory of defense. Few accept what Jefferson wanted to accomplish with the gunboats. They were not to be a replacement for a seagoing navy but instead an adjunct to the regular fleet within a multifaceted defense system. This is difficult to understand because the United States has since become a world maritime power. Moreover, the country has not been invaded since the War of 1812, and few Americans have feared territorial encroachment by other nations.

When discussing Jefferson's naval theory, one cannot condense his policy into a black-and-white dichotomy between seagoing vessels and gunboats. Such an assertion is groundless, as evidenced by Gallatin's statement that "federal papers" were trying to spread the idea that gunboats were "intended as a substitute to the navy."[84] Others charge that Jefferson was "prepared to let the nation's magnificent Humphreys frigates rot at the wharves and ... build a 'mosquito fleet' of gunboats in their place."[85] These assertions are far from the truth, as even John Adams recognized that, although not ardently pronavy, Jefferson did believe in a navy.[86] As president, however, Jefferson was concerned with maintaining the country's security, and a sophisticated defense policy was his response. He wanted a navy oriented to defense rather than to offense.[87] Had Jefferson wanted to eliminate the navy, there would have been no reason for him to have advocated a fleet at all, whether it consisted of gunboats or any other type of vessel, and he certainly would not have sent fleets to the Mediterranean. As one component in an overall plan, the navy was essential to the country's defense, and above all Jefferson wanted to provide security for his countrymen in what he believed was the best possible way. For Jefferson's comprehensive strategic concept of defense, gunboats were a means to that end.

3

The Emergence of Policy:
First Term, 1801–5

Sir Isaac Newton argues, in his *Principia Mathematica*, one of the basic laws of physics: that for every action there is an equal and opposite reaction.[1] Although Newton's law refers to the world of science, it also applies to human nature. People act and accordingly react to events that have a bearing on their lives. This especially applies to the world of politics and government. Statesmen play the game of world politics with chesslike precision while trying to navigate the ship of state through the turbulent waters of international affairs. No country can live completely isolated from these events. In some periods, international strife is more intense, thus requiring a more drastic response to the actions of others. The period of the Napoleonic wars is an example of one such era. The conflict's ramifications permeated every aspect of American political life and ultimately had a bearing on the decisions made by the country's leaders.

When Thomas Jefferson assumed the presidency in 1801, world events necessitated that the country keep one eye focused on Europe and the other on American domestic problems. The country could not ignore European events as long as the turmoil continued. Jefferson realized that actions across the Atlantic determined, to some extent, the policy his country followed. His realization was obvious in the formulation of what has been called "Jefferson's gunboat policy." Craig Symonds, recognizing the president's dilemma, wrote in his book, *Navalists and Antinavalists,* that Jefferson's naval policy was always ruled by circumstance. Yet, in the formulation of the gunboat program, those circumstances were as much foreign as domestic.[2]

The problem Jefferson faced during the summer of 1802 concerned navigation of the Mississippi River, the lifeline of the West. As long as this avenue of transportation and communication remained open, the farmers and frontiersmen west of the Appalachian Mountains were satisfied, but tempers flared whenever there was a possibility of closing the river. In 1785–86, during the Confederation period, American Secretary of Foreign Affairs John Jay negotiated a treaty with Spanish Foreign Minister Don Diego Gardoqui, proposing to close the Mississippi for at least twenty-five years in return for favorable commercial concessions. Once Jay learned of western opposition to the agreement, his better judgment prevailed and no commercial treaty was agreed upon; thus the Mississippi River remained open. This incident demonstrated the American attitude concerning the importance of the river.[3]

In 1802, the problem of the Mississippi was equally distressing, but this time there were more characters involved, including Napoleon Bonaparte and France. Revolution on the island of San Domang (Haiti) threatened the stability of Louisiana and the Mississippi River. The Treaty of San Ildefonso of 1 October 1800, drawn up between France and Spain according to Napoleon Bonaparte's wishes, underscored the uncertainty by making Louisiana the French breadbasket for what appeared to be a western empire. The formal transfer of Louisiana from Spain to France, however, did not occur until after the Peace of Amiens in 1802, which left plenty of time for other complications.[4]

Before France was able to take possession of the distant province, a more urgent event occurred. On 16 October 1802, Juan Ventura Morales, Spanish intendant at New Orleans, closed the port to all American commerce descending the river. Despite this blatant violation of the 1795 Pinckney Treaty between Spain and the United States, Jefferson stubbornly refused to admit in his annual message of 15 December 1802 that any problem existed. But there was a problem, and a precedent was being set, because the actions of another nation determined the course the United States was destined to follow.[5]

Only two days after Jefferson's annual message, the House of Representatives requested all information concerning Morales's actions. Majority leader John Randolph of Virginia led the attack at Jefferson's behest. The president waited until 22 December before answering the House's call for documents, and only then sent papers, most of which had already been printed in newspapers. On 30 December, Jefferson followed up by sending the House a letter from Spanish Governor Juan Manuel y de Salcedo to William Charles Cole Claiborne, governor of the Mississippi territory. In the letter, the governor vehemently denied the

Spanish government's involvement in closing the port. But in reality, a royal order on 14 July 1802, had directed the intendant to terminate the right of deposit at New Orleans and instructed him to claim that the action had been taken independently of any royal decree. This order placed responsibility for closing the port squarely on the shoulders of Morales.[6]

Accepting Salcedo's note at face value, the House debated behind closed doors for the following week. Before reemerging, the body concluded that the government should assert the rights and vindicate the injuries of the United States whatever the reason for Morales's actions. Jefferson quieted opposition and satisfied westerners by appointing James Monroe as minister extraordinaire empowered to negotiate with both France and Spain to settle the Mississippi question.[7]

On 11 January 1803, Samuel Smith of Maryland moved that the House go into special session. Two days later, the Senate confirmed Monroe's mission to Europe, acknowledging Jefferson's attempt to settle the problem peacefully. The president realized that Monroe's appointment did not guarantee success, yet his only alternative, should Monroe fail, was "to get entangled in European politics," which obviously meant war.[8]

Because Jefferson's attentions were not "confined to the Eastern states alone, but ... to the western states also," war was a viable alternative for the president.[9] War became even more of a possibility when it was discovered that Spain had transferred Louisiana to Napoleon. Once it became apparent that France controlled the region in question, Jefferson's critics asserted that Monroe's mission was doomed to failure. Republican John Randolph charged that the Mississippi question was providing certain Federalists with an opportunity to divide the country. Federalist Senator James Ross of Pennsylvania retorted that the French might be willing to negotiate only "if they found us armed, in possession, and resolved to maintain [Louisiana]."[10] Ross argued that 50,000 militia from the states of Kentucky, Tennessee, South Carolina, Georgia, and Ohio could ensure the American claim to the region and prompt Napoleon to make a settlement. Should Monroe's mission fail, however, Jefferson understood that "war cannot be distant" and as such "it behooves us immediately to be preparing for that course." Secretary of the Navy Robert Smith asked Congress to begin those preparations by constructing a gunboat flotilla.[11]

The groundwork for a defensive war came in the form of section three of "an act to provide an additional armament for the protection of the seamen and commerce of the United States." Robert Smith had suggested to DeWitt Clinton, chairman of the Senate Committee on Naval Affairs, that Jefferson wanted eight gunboats and four small vessels of war for the country's defense. The committee ultimately responded by approving a proposal for fifteen gunboats and sent it to the House, where it passed only after some debate. To ensure protection of commerce, especially on the Mississippi River, the act provided the president with $50,000 for the construction of fifteen gunboats to be "employed for such purposes ... the public service may require."[12] On 28 February 1803, events dictated that these vessels were necessary to settle the Mississippi question, especially if war was required.[13] Congressman John Stanly summed up this legislation: after this measure, it was obvious "that acts may be efficacious where words will fail; and that waiting with perfect confidence for negotiations to 'vindicate our injuries' may be beautiful in theory but dangerous in practice."[14]

When or where Jefferson conceived the idea of using gunboats is unclear. He apparently knew of their use by both the British and colonials during the American Revolution, and their construction under the Federalist administrations of the 1790s. He was also well aware of a plan for a gunboat assault across the Channel presented to the French Directory by Thomas Paine in 1798. Jefferson would have known about Paine's proposal because the author stayed with James Monroe, the American minister to Paris and Jefferson's intimate friend. Perhaps Jefferson remembered Paine's proposal and envisioned the political, economic, and military possibilities gunboats offered for the United States. Regardless of the source of Jefferson's inspiration, he knew of the existence of gunboats or similar types of vessels used by other countries.[15]

Gunboat construction was to begin immediately to force a quick settlement to the Mississippi problem. A month before the legislation received congressional approval, Robert Smith wrote to consul John Gavino at Gibraltar, asking him to procure a model of the gunboats being used at Algeciras. On 24 February, Smith even went so far as to request Captains Samuel Barron, William Bainbridge, and Edward Preble to supervise gunboat construction. Smith apparently believed that the legislation's passage was imminent and wanted to have the vessels ready for action as soon as possible. Because timing was important, he considered Pittsburgh at the head of the Ohio River as the best place to construct these vessels. Pittsburgh's strategic location, on a major tributary of the Mississippi, would allow the craft to be speedily delivered to the troubled area while at the same time bolstering the defenses of the western country.[16]

Fortunately, the difficulties with Spain were short-lived. By spring of 1803, the Spanish king, Charles IV, had disavowed Morales's act and renewed the right of deposit. This magnanimous gesture made little difference because France and Napoleon controlled the region's destiny. Even so, Jefferson took steps to ensure that such an event would not occur again. James Monroe traveled to Europe to try to purchase the entire territory east of the Mississippi River, including New Orleans. The president hoped that negotiations would produce the desired results. "Peace," he said, "is our passion," yet if peaceful negotiations were not successful, then "we would recur to war." Passage of the gunboat legislation demonstrated the defensive posture Jefferson and the country would take.[17]

While Congress prepared for a defensive war, Robert R. Livingston, minister to France, negotiated one of the nation's greatest diplomatic coups. Jefferson received news on 3 July 1803 that the Louisiana question had been settled by Livingston, Monroe, and François Barbé-Marbois, French minister of finance. In the settlement, Americans agreed to buy the region for $15 million, thereby bringing an end to the Mississippi saga. The gunboats were no longer needed to protect American rights on the river. Henry Adams asserted that no other treaty gave the United States so much for so little in return. "It was unparalleled, because it cost almost nothing." True, it was a diplomatic victory, but the entire episode demonstrated that Jefferson supported the use of military force, including gunboats, to defend the country's territorial integrity. That idea became much more important during Jefferson's second term.[18]

Once the Mississippi question had been settled, Jefferson remarked that "this removes from us the greatest source of danger to our peace."[19] This prophetic statement, however, was unfounded, for events in the Mediterranean Sea had already proved the president wrong. Whereas expropriations for the gunboats had resulted from the difficulties on the Mississippi, their subsequent construction was due to events occurring in the Mediterranean that had been ongoing since the founding of the Republic.

Relations between the United States and the Barbary powers had resulted by 1800 in the American payment of more than $1 million in tribute to the North African states. To compound matters, the piratical states had a long history of using threats, insults, and torture of hostages to ensure that blackmail was paid. The United States was not alone in its humiliation; all countries with Mediterranean commercial interests suffered likewise.[20]

One example of the atrocious conduct perpetrated by the Barbary states was the humiliation afforded the U.S.S. *George Washington*, which arrived at Algiers in September 1800. Tribute to Algiers was three years in arrears, and the dey was becoming restless. His intolerance resulted in an order to Captain William Bainbridge to transport passengers and cargo to the sultan at Constantinople or be fired upon. The dey exclaimed, "You pay me tribute, by which you become my slaves. I have therefore a right to order you as I may think proper." Bainbridge realized that his failure to comply with the Dey's order meant war and that America's Mediterranean commerce, which totaled more than $12 million annually, would suffer. The only sensible choice was his reluctant agreement to carry the passengers, animals, and tribute to Constantinople.

Meanwhile, Yusuf Karamanli, the pasha of Tripoli, made his own declaration of war on the United States. Karamanli believed his tribute should equal that of his more powerful neighbors, Tunis and Algiers. The negotiations that followed proved that the pasha was not truly interested in settling the affair but preferred war. In May 1801, the pasha had the American consulate's flagpole chopped down, which was the North African equivalent of a declaration of war. Events such as these exacerbated relations between the young republic and the North African pirates and ultimately brought Jefferson to the conclusion that war was inevitable.[21]

The president was caught between using the navy to force the issue in the Mediterranean, and buying peace, which in reality was ad hoc support of the lawlessness he so despised. Jefferson thought that in the long run paying blackmail was much more expensive than the two frigates he originally felt necessary for the Mediterranean force. Secretary of State James Madison suggested, much to Jefferson's pleasure, that it would cost little more to maintain the fleet in the Mediterranean than in American waters. Additionally, American officers and men would acquire invaluable training which coastal maneuvers did not provide. Jefferson became determined to pursue a limited offensive action in the Mediterranean, dictated by money — not desire, pacifism, or constitutional limitations. [22]

The administration sent the frigates *President, Essex,* and *Philadelphia,* and the schooner *Enterprise* under Commodore Richard Dale to deal with the situation in the Mediterranean. Upon Dale's arrival, he learned that the U.S. consul at Tunis, William Eaton, had proclaimed a blockade of Tripoli. For the remainder of 1801 and until May 1802, the Mediterranean squadron attempted to enforce Eaton's blockade. Dale's replacement, Commodore Richard V. Morris, who served from June

1802 until July 1803, had an enlarged squadron of five frigates, but he was unable to achieve any substantial results during his tour. Jefferson callously referred to Morris's tour as the "two years' sleep" in which the Tripolitan campaign dragged on.

A truly effective blockade was impossible to maintain because American warships were unable to prevent shallow-draft vessels from escaping into the coastal shoals. Despite Robert Smith's suggestion to Morris that he procure a "few gunboats" to aid his squadron, the commodore did not heed the secretary's advice. Morris also cruised the Mediterranean rather than devoting his forces to close-in blockading duties. Morris's apparent disregard for a clear-cut policy objective resulted in a presidential recall and a court of inquiry that dismissed him from the service for his "inactive and dilatory conduct." Morris was replaced by forty-two-year-old Captain Edward Preble, who, upon his arrival in the Mediterranean in September 1803, quickly saw the need for gunboat-type vessels.[23]

Once again, the actions of other far-away countries prescribed the course the United States would follow. In his annual message of 1803, Jefferson confessed that the $50,000 appropriated by Congress for gunboats remained unexpended. The quick settlement of the Mississippi question made the fulfillment of the 28 February 1803 act unnecessary. But now, even Virginia Congressman William Branch Giles, one of the bitterest of the antinavalists, agreed that the augmentation of the navy was necessary and that gunboats were needed in the Mediterranean to achieve Jefferson's peace without tribute. Congress had authorized other small vessels to confine the Tripolitan cruisers within their harbors, but they were not the shallow-draft gunboats. Had the president or Congress foreseen the events of 31 October 1803, the gunboats might already have been constructed and placed in service in the Mediterranean, possibly saving *Philadelphia* from her ultimate humiliation. In any case, the disaster revealed the need for small vessels to perform shallow-draft service near the shore.[24]

William Bainbridge, the hardluck commander of *George Washington*, received command of the frigate *Philadelphia* on 21 May 1803, with orders to join Dale's squadron in the Mediterranean and carry on the struggle against the Barbary pirates. Bainbridge, upon his arrival at Gibraltar in mid-September, received additional orders to proceed to Tripoli to renew the blockade. While chasing a corsair back into the harbor on 31 October, *Philadelphia* ran aground on an uncharted reef at an unusual angle. The ship was left defenseless because she was unable to bring her guns to bear on the Tripolitan gunboats that soon swarmed around. After four hours of unsuccessful attempts to refloat the ship,

Bainbridge threw over his ammunition, disabled his guns, destroyed his signal books, and had holes bored in the ship's hull before striking his colors. That evening Bainbridge and over 300 crewmen were paraded through Tripoli, signifying the young republic's greatest indignity thus far. Months later, Stephen Decatur partially redressed the nation's honor by heroically setting fire to *Philadelphia* under the walls and guns of the harbor fort in an act English Admiral Horatio Nelson called "the most bold and daring act of the age." The loss of one of the nation's few frigates made Jefferson even more determined to bring the Mediterranean matter to a victorious conclusion. [25]

Jefferson decided before the *Philadelphia* disaster to expedite the gunboat appropriation of February 1803 "in order that ... our force might begin on models most proved by experience." By late December, Robert Smith instructed John Rodgers and James Barron to each begin building a gunboat based on a forthcoming Neapolitan model. Although these vessels were themselves to serve only as examples of what the craft would resemble, they provided a good illustration to Congress of what a gunboat actually was. [26]

The loss of *Philadelphia* emphasized the need for shallow-draft vessels for inshore work. The American agent at Leghorn, Italy — James Leander Cathcart, former consul at Tripoli, Algiers, and Tunis — understood Preble's position after the loss of his valuable frigate. "Eight or ten gunboats," Cathcart told Preble, "with the force under your command is sufficient to reduce Tripoli to ashes." Preble acknowledged Cathcart's assertion and requested him to procure such vessels, of which six were ultimately obtained. The commodore, in return, informed the administration of his plans to obtain gunboats "on loan" from Naples. On 26 March 1804, six days after learning of the loss of *Philadelphia*, Jefferson authorized Preble to "hire or accept on loan" as many gunboats as was necessary to "enter the harbour of Tripoli, destroy their marine" and bring about "a lasting peace." Gunboats were, Jefferson felt, essential for a victory. As he saw it, thus far the Tripolitan conflict "tho[ugh] a small war in fact, it [was] big in principle" and had resulted only with the United States being "humble[d] ... in the eyes of Europe." [27]

Borrowing gunboats was necessary because the experimental models ordered by the secretary of the navy would not be launched until July and August 1804. Jefferson, without reports on the unfinished gunboats, nonetheless decided to expand the experiment and ordered eight additional vessels for the Mediterranean service. Of these first ten American-built gunboats, eight traveled to the Mediterranean, but none saw combat in the Barbary wars, even though that was their primary reason for being built. Joseph Henrich, in his dissertation "Triumph of Ideology," disagrees. Although he does not provide a rationale for their construction, Henrich claims that they were not built due to the Tripolitan War because they were not seagoing craft. The lack of progress in the North African conflict, however, combined with the *Philadelphia* disaster, revealed a necessity for shallow-draft vessels that cannot be ignored or underestimated. [28]

During the summer of 1804, the United States sent, under the command of Commodore Samuel Barron, a fleet to the Mediterranean consisting of virtually the entire navy except the frigates *Chesapeake* and *United States*. Smith and Jefferson wanted to bring a quick conclusion to the conflict. Yet, while the navy was making "our flag dreaded by the barbarians of Africa" the American caldron was beginning to boil.[29]

Difficulties began soon after the rupture of the Peace of Amiens in May 1803. The revival of hostilities between England and France once again placed the United States in a precarious position, prompting Jefferson to decide that the country should follow a policy of neutrality. In the summer of 1803, shortly after the renewal of European hostilities, Jefferson believed that if the administration was "sincerely friendly to both" belligerents, the country could maintain its neutrality and not "have as much to swallow from them as our predecessors had." Neutrality, however, did not prevent encroachments on American rights. Infringements, such as impressment, the seizure of neutral ships, and violations of American laws in coastal waters as well as in the harbors of the United States, not only threatened national security but also produced public outrage which neither Jefferson nor Congress could ignore. [30]

Because the president realized the problem the country faced, he decided American economic interests had to be protected. In July 1804, Jefferson presented his ideas to Republican Massachusetts Congressman Jacob Crowninshield. "We must be authorized to refuse our ports to belligerents," he said, especially because keeping hostile powers out of American waters diminished the possibility of dragging the United States into an unwanted war. Jefferson understood, however, that it took more than threats to ensure obedience to the laws. To assure compliance, the president suggested that "we must have a force of gunboats sufficient to compel obedience in every sea-port." Jefferson was judicious enough to solicit professional opinions on the subject before presenting his ideas to Congress.[31]

Jefferson requested the opinions of Generals Horatio Gates and James Wilkinson before going public with his plan. Gates contended that gunboats were "the most proper defence for large harbors that has hitherto been imagined." Gunboats, he argued, "co-operating with small batteries of heavy guns ... are much better ... than fixed and large fortifications." He proposed that by using these vessels "a paltry frigate dare not then to insult us, as has been, and now is."[32]

General Wilkinson was not as verbose. He admitted that the president's "proposition could not be better ascertained" than by comparing it to the defense system already adopted in the towns and harbors of the country. Instead of belaboring his point, he presented an essay by the Marquis of Santa Cruz, a respected military author of the early eighteenth century, who held gunboat-type vessels in high esteem. Months later, Wilkinson wrote Edward Preble a long discourse in which he concluded that gunboats, working in conjunction with heavy movable batteries, formed the "most economical, durable, and effectual means of defense and afforded the best security to the objects to be protected." Although Wilkinson's letter to Preble was not immediately used to sway Congress, it became the "administration's official justification" for the gunboat program. Although neither Gates nor Wilkinson were sailors, both understood the meaning of national defense and presented Jefferson with arguments supporting the president's conclusions.[33]

Before Jefferson released his annual message, he asked his cabinet members to present their suggestions. Gallatin agreed that gunboats should be used to uphold the laws of the United States within the country's harbors, but he was not as eager as Jefferson to begin their construction. The secretary of the treasury felt that because gunboats could be built on short notice, it was not necessary to provide for them before they were warranted. Postponing their construction until times of emergency would, he argued, eliminate maintenance costs and aid in further reducing the national debt. Although Gallatin's arguments were economically sound, they did not influence Jefferson, nor did they prevent the president from going to Congress with the program.[34]

Secretary of the Navy Robert Smith was supportive of the gunboat program. During 1804 and 1805, Smith even placed more emphasis on the gunboats than did Jefferson himself. Smith's backing, however, was not unusual because he consistently towed the administration's line in regard to all naval policy. The secretary agreed with Gallatin that gunboats were a cheap alternative to a large seagoing navy; but, like Jefferson, he felt they would not unnecessarily "become the instruments of involving the United States with foreign powers." They could, as Smith asserted, provide an adequate defense as well as prevent the country from being humiliated. Throughout, Smith remained loyal to Jefferson, and his position reflected his political astuteness. Smith's attitudes

ROBERT SMITH
JULY 1801 — MARCH 1809
ARTIST: U. D. TENNEY

Secretary of the Navy Robert Smith. Portrait by U. D. Tenney. Photo courtesy of the
Naval Historical Center.

about the gunboats generally mirrored the president's, and they changed as Jefferson's policy evolved.[35]

Jefferson's ideas became public with his fourth annual message presented to Congress on 8 November 1804. In it, Jefferson mentioned the peculiar irregularities that affected neutral commerce in American waters, while demanding that they "called for serious attention." Some civilians, he admitted, had taken matters into their own hands by arming merchant ships, but he confessed that could "not be permitted in a well-ordered society."[36]

Jefferson's solution was simple and straightforward. "A number of gunboats," he contested, "offer [defense] for our seaport towns, their utility toward supporting within our waters the authority of the laws." Jefferson, however, was a consummate politician who realized that his statement regarding insults, combined with the request for additional gunboats, would challenge Great Britain. To remedy this, he tried to place the subjects "as far apart as the frames of the message would bear," so "that they might not appear inconnection as a menace." This, he argued, would not "bring the measures into collision with the pride of Great Britain." Jefferson believed that the gunboats "may well stand in a bill by themselves ... as a continuation of the former act on the same subject." It was apparent that Jefferson wanted Congress to consider gunboat legislation during the next session.[37]

Shortly after presenting his message, Jefferson contacted Joseph H. Nicholson, chairman of the select committee appointed on 12 November, concerning "the defence and security of ... ports and harbors." During the previous summer, several seaports had suffered serious insults, including defiance of peace officers, smuggling, and even impressment. Jefferson felt the time had come for action; even Federalists would not act "on any principle of duty or patriotism." The opposition party wanted ships or forts rather than gunboats, which they viewed with disdain. Recognizing the attitude of his own party, Jefferson stated that ships would "not be built in our day, and would be no defense if built," and forts "will never be built or maintained." Despite Federalist opposition, Nicholson's committee decided, on the last day of January 1805, that "a sum of money" should be appropriated for building gunboats. The opposition provided little hindrance as the bill passed the House and was sent to the Senate on 8 February.[38]

In the Senate there was little overt opposition to the House resolution, even though there were some who opposed the philosophy of Jefferson's naval policy. William Plumer, New Hampshire's Federalist senator from 1802 to 1807, criticized the gunboat plan because he felt "this whimsical phylosophic President" was spending money for vessels "incapable of sailing on the rough sea or of being of use to us." To emphasize his point, Plumer recalled the experience of gunboat *No. 1*. This vessel, built at Washington under the supervision of John Rodgers in 1803–4, had been relegated to harbor duty at Savannah because of her poor sailing qualities. A hurricane subsequently tore the vessel from its moorings and tossed it into a cornfield on Whitemarsh Island. The senator, as well as antinavalists alike, used the misfortune of *No. 1* to ridicule the entire gunboat program. Even though Jefferson's "philosophism" had, as historian Merrill Peterson claimed, run amok, Plumer still had "a certain partiality" for the president that later evolved into friendship and admiration.[39]

The gunboat legislation easily ran its course through the Senate, with only token opposition. Republican Senator Samuel Smith guided the proposal through its third reading and passage on 28 February. Less than two months had expired since the legislation's introduction. On 2 March 1805, Congress appropriated $60,000 for the construction of twenty-five gunboats "for the better protection of the ports and harbors of the United States" and to augment, not replace, the seagoing navy.[40]

What becomes obvious in the gunboat legislation of Jefferson's first term is that each appropriation was in response to other countries, whether Spain, the Barbary states, or Great Britain and France. Viewing the legislation in such light, it is apparent that the program was not, as many have deemed, Jefferson's sole naval policy. It also becomes obvious that, despite being supervised by the navy department, the gunboat program was not just naval policy but a political-military defense program. Moreover, each situation resulting in gunboat construction had political as well as military implications, whether it was defending the western country from the actions of a misguided intendant, protecting maritime interests from the piratical activities of the Barbary states, or safeguarding the Atlantic seaboard from the degradations resulting from renewal of the Napoleonic wars. The gunboats were more than just naval implements; they were tools by which the administration conducted policy, be it domestic or foreign. Their use in administering policy became greater and certainly more controversial during Jefferson's second term.

Another interesting and unique point about the gunboat program was its reception in Congress. During his first term, Jefferson enjoyed a Republican majority but was uncomfortable because there were still enough Federalists to block his programs. Despite the potential contentiousness of the issue, the gunboat legislation provoked little debate or noteworthy discussion. A review of the *Annals of Congress* and personal papers reveals little, if anything, concerning congressional atti- tude about gunboats during the first term. The resulting votes also have little significance except that policy was being made that dramatically affected Jefferson's second term. During his second administration, Jefferson had a much larger Republican majority, but his policy was still not accepted unquestioningly. This time, factionalism within his own party resulted in heated debates concerning national defense and the gunboat program. Even though Jefferson still controlled the party, his attitudes were not accepted uncritically and his approach concerning gunboats and foreign policy divided Congress. Nonetheless, the gunboat program continued as part of political-military policy ultimately dictated by external events. William Lynch succinctly presented the same argu- ment when he wrote, "The plain truth is that the world situation pre- sented a hard problem to the American Government, a problem for which no degree of preparedness could have provided an easy solution." Jefferson's second term aptly illustrates Lynch's premise. [41]

4

The Failure of Ideology:
Second Term, 1805–9

Shortly after Jefferson took his second presidential oath, it became apparent that the tranquillity and political successes of the first term were nothing more than the proverbial calm before the storm. Jefferson found that domestic tranquillity could not be maintained while the tiger and shark wrestled for European supremacy, and especially as long as British and French warships stopped American merchantmen, seized seamen as deserters, and condemned cargo as contraband. Moreover, the United States could not allow the country's honor to be continually violated. The unpredictable events of Jefferson's second term forced the country to emphasize defensive preparedness.

Jefferson needed to preserve honor while at the same time ensuring national security. This task seemed insurmountable, as international hostilities escalated into a general European war, resulting in numerous encroachments on the country's neutrality during the summer of 1805. Jefferson responded to the trouble by immediately increasing the country's naval establishment. In July, he decided that the frigate *Adams* and the brig *Hornet* should be finished without delay to suppress piratical activities. Moreover, believing that extra gunboats should be constructed to "secure our seaports from hostile attacks," Jefferson turned to his cabinet for guidance. [1]

Robert Smith used the opportunity to expound his ideas of augmenting the fleet. The navy secretary understood the need for offensive as well as defensive capabilities and recommended the recommissioning of all existing frigates. He also wanted to build the six seventy-fours for which materials had already been amassed as well as six additional capital vessels, for a total of twelve ships-of-the-line. He hypothesized that these twelve ships, added to the frigates and gunboats, would provide the United States with "a commanding attitude."[2]

Surprisingly, Albert Gallatin agreed with Smith. The penny-pinching treasury secretary who constantly fought additional appropriations for the navy succumbed to Smith's argument. Gallatin accepted that, without a seagoing fleet, the United States would "perpetually be liable to injury and insults, particularly when there is a war in Europe." His remedy was an appropriation of one million dollars a year for building capital ships and an immediate expenditure for frigates. This, he believed, would "impress other nations that we are in earnest" about protecting American rights.[3]

Jefferson welcomed his cabinet's suggestions and may have drafted an appropriate response for inclusion in his annual message. On 21 October 1805, however, less than a month and a half before the presentation of his fifth message, news arrived of the Battle of Trafalgar. The British victory solidified supremacy of the seas and perhaps persuaded Jefferson that a tiny American fleet could serve little purpose in deterring English aggressions. Until this point, Jefferson considered using an American navy as a diplomatic counter to ensure benevolent treatment. Thereafter, "a lonely, microscopic American fleet would have been gold cast into the sea ... with fatal consequences to morale, even to survival as a republic." Jefferson conceivably realized the significance of the British victory and concluded that his idea of a defensive system ensuring national security had been correct all along.[4]

When Isaac Coles, secretary to the president, presented Jefferson's annual message to the Ninth Congress on 3 December 1805, Henry Adams claimed, it was "received with applause as a proof of vigor." In the message, the president assailed the lawless pirates who infested American coastal waters. Private armed ships, he said, had the audacity to capture friendly vessels coming to trade as well as merchantmen of the United States. Furthermore, foreign warships had acted in a similarly atrocious fashion. Jefferson asserted that the offenders should be brought to trial as pirates, whereas the belligerent powers should be dealt with by the "moderation, the firmness, and the wisdom of the Legislature." This rhetoric, nonetheless, did not provide a practical solution to the problem. His remedy was a declaration that these injuries "are of a nature to be met by force only."

Jefferson was reluctant to place the country on a war footing despite the offenses committed. He believed that amassing armaments would possibly incur the wrath of the British, and he preferred "a peaceable remedy." Yet preparations had to be made just the same. Jefferson had already assigned artillery to harbor towns, since his first priority was "to place our seaport towns out of the danger of insult." For additional support, he believed, "it is desirable to have a competent number of gunboats," and the competent number, he argued, "must be considerable."[5]

The president recommended "such preparations as circumstances call[ed] for." Some argue that he was doing just the opposite because he was not protecting trade outside coastal waters. Jefferson had, however, already equipped a cruising force to protect trade "within our own seas." He had also advised Congress that the government still possessed materials to build ships-of-the-line for use on the open seas. Despite his suggestions, Jefferson knew that ship construction was "subject to the further will of the Legislature," and he well knew Congress would make its own decision.[6]

Republican Samuel Smith believed that Congress would "authorize the President to commence building ships-of-the-line." Captains Edward Preble, William Bainbridge, and Samuel Barron hoped Smith was correct and urged Congress to consider the president's suggestion. Preble and Bainbridge even traveled to the capital city during the summer of 1805 and returned in December to voice their support. Even though Bainbridge expressed hope that seagoing vessels would be built, other officers, including Barron, thought that "there is little for naval men to expect." One officer even asserted that some congressmen preferred "to let [the ships] rot," especially because the proposal for "six seventy-fours would ruin the country." Thomas Tingey, commandant of the Washington Navy Yard, believed that "a majority of Congress [wanted to] wipe off even the little respectability that is considered ... to be attached to" the navy. In reality, the attitude of these officers was immaterial.[7]

Henry Adams asserted that the Ninth Congress was, at most, a lackluster assemblage. Despite the group's shortage of brilliance, it did produce one of Jefferson's most memorable and troubling legislative sessions. Problems began immediately because of Republican factionalism created by Nathaniel Macon's reelection as Speaker of the House. But it was Macon's reappointment of majority leader John Randolph as chairman of the powerful Ways and Means Committee that provided the catalyst for further agitation.[8]

Randolph was a vain and arrogant man, sure of his intellectual superiority. Despite his self-absorption, he possessed the ability to be of great assistance or annoyance to the Republican party. His stature and rhetorical skills could sway uncertain legislators. On the other hand, a sarcastic quip from his caustic tongue could be as deadly as a bullet for his political enemies. The upcoming legislative session did not bode well because Randolph was, as he claimed, "in a restless state of mind" and "ready for a plentiful harvest of bickering and blunders."[9]

The annual message provided fuel for Randolph's fire. The fellow Virginian felt that Jefferson's boldness was aimed at enhancing Madison's drive for the presidency, and Randolph completely despised the secretary of state. At the heart of the matter was the president's failure to request money in the annual message for the purchase of Florida, and Randolph vividly remembered the Louisiana precedent. Although this had little to do with naval appropriations, it created "great dissension and general dissatisfaction among the Democrats ... which forbode nothing good for the defense of the nation." It also created reverberations that permeated other issues during the session, including Jefferson's proposal for the nation's defense.[10]

The remarks in Jefferson's annual message relating to national defense were immediately sent to a select congressional committee chaired by John Dawson of Virginia. The committee responded on 23 December 1805 by proposing three basic resolutions to be considered by the House. The first proposal requested $150,000 for the protection of ports and harbors; the second $250,000 for the construction of fifty gunboats; and the third $660,000 for building six ships-of-the-line. Although the three resolutions were represented in different proposals, there was little possibility of separating the issues once debate began. Of the three resolutions, the gunboat proposal passed with little opposition, but antinavalists viciously assaulted the other two.[11]

Discussion of the first proposal began when Dawson introduced the issue to the House on 23 January 1806. George Clinton, Jr., of New York seized the opportunity to express his concern. Clinton and others believed that $150,000 would not even begin to fortify the country's harbors. To this Dawson agreed and responded that a larger sum could be allocated, but that "this appropriation is only in aid of another ... of $250,000 for gunboats." Peter Early of Georgia, recognizing that the three resolutions, although separate, constituted parts of an overall program, hesitated to make a decision until the House had more information other than "estimates" from the cabinet members. John Cotton Smith of Connecticut repeated Early's concern by proposing that the House gain further information from the president. The following day, Smith's proposal passed with little opposition.[12]

The House requested that the secretaries of the navy and war provide information concerning the nation's defense. Henry Dearborn, of the war department, provided a detailed report about existing fortifications, the predicted expense for their completion, and the advantages of using land batteries to defend ports and harbors. Completed by mid-February, weeks earlier than expected, the document was drafted so hastily that it provided a poor evaluation of harbor defenses using land batteries. Dearborn had realized that it was impossible to provide thoughtful analysis on such short notice, so he presented, as Jefferson suggested, the administration's view of a multifaceted defense.[13]

Smith's task was more arduous because he was to provide information about the overall "condition of the navy." This included the amount of money disbursed by the department since its establishment in 1799, the costs for all armed vessels either built or bought by the government, and an estimate of the annual expense of supporting the entire naval force in actual service. By mid-February, both his and Dearborn's reports were transmitted via Jefferson to the Speaker for perusal by House members until the issue once again reemerged before Congress.[14]

Some argued that any future debate was irrelevant, believing the country would not go to war "nor ... adopt any efficient measure of defense." But the upcoming debate was important because it determined the course of naval and defense policy in the years prior to the War of 1812. The question was no longer a response to the president's message nor about defense preparations but rather a debate over the formulation of naval ideology. Jefferson's multifaceted defense, with gunboats serving as one part of the program, fell by the wayside as antinaval Republicans carried the day and laid the foundation for an ideological and sectionally based, gunboat-oriented defense system.[15]

Sectionalism was partially responsible for emphasizing the gunboat program, but only inasmuch as it was created by ideology. The ideological attributes that created a successful Republican party in the South and West also produced opposition to a seagoing navy. Navies by their inherent nature constituted a permanent military establishment. Furthermore, they were extremely expensive, thereby draining resources from more important concerns. Republicans viewed these characteristics as distasteful. Josiah Quincy of Massachusetts summarized the situation later, when he remarked that "to gentlemen from the South and West, the very name of a navy is odious.... It is a power which, from their local position, they can never wield ... [and] of such a power, it is natural for men to be jealous." Despite the rationale for opposition to a seagoing navy, the antinaval position held sway as long as Republican ideology remained dominant in the South and West.[16]

When the resolution came again before the House on Friday, 28 February 1806, it encountered positions rigidly fixed for and against. Clinton opened discussion with an assertion that "something must be

done." Pennsylvanian John Smilie agreed but argued that more information was needed on the subject of commercial restrictions and nonintercourse before action could be taken. Dawson retorted, "If we intend to
support the American name and character something should be done"
and pushed the measure forward. Orchard Cook of Massachusetts moved
that the $150,000 of the first resolution be doubled. Fellow
Massachusetts Congressman Barnabas Bidwell disagreed, insisting that
the money was not intended for beginning new projects but rather for
repairs. [17]

At this point, lifelong antinavalist Nathaniel Macon of North Carolina
stepped from the Speaker's chair and carried the argument to a new
plateau. Macon believed the three resolutions embraced a contradictory
system of defense. "No nation can support both" a navy and fortifications, he argued, not even Great Britain. The English, he asserted, relied
solely on their navy. The United States, Macon believed, could not
support the construction of a large seagoing fleet because its building
facilities and funding appropriations were inadequate. Therefore, choices
had to be made. Macon then inquired rhetorically: If we agree to the
resolution and build ships-of-the-line, would they not be forced to remain
"docked here in the Eastern Branch" rather than on the seas during times
of war? With that, he concluded, it would be wiser to "lend our navy to
another nation also at war with [our enemy, for] ... such nation would
manage it more to our advantage than ourselves." This statement
reflected the antinaval attitude rather than the "American spirit" and
epitomized the argument of ideology over defense. [18]

Although Macon vehemently opposed the navy, he and other
congressmen felt that gunboats were "better adapted to the defence of our
harbors than any other" means. Matthew Walton of Kentucky agreed,
arguing that the turbulent events in Europe made defense preparations a
necessity, and that gunboats were "the most cheap and effectual defence
for our coasts, which is in our power to adopt." Virginian Abram Trigg
called the gunboats not only the most inexpensive but also the most
"certain defence of our ports and harbors." William Dickson of
Tennessee summarized the Republican position most accurately when he
proclaimed that defense measures should "wait for events, and be
governed by circumstances arising thereupon ... and in the mean time
[we should] prepare for internal defence, by fortifying our ports and
harbors." This statement by Dickson reinforced antinaval Republican
ideology. [19]

Orchard Cook struck to the heart of the matter when he stated that
merchants and mariners had as much right to "protection in their pur-

suits" as did farmers. Furthermore, "they must be protected ... in all places." The true argument had finally come to light. It was not a question of gunboats versus larger vessels to protect the country from the actions of other nations but rather a sectional struggle permeating virtually every issue coming before Congress during Jefferson's second term. [20]

During most of March 1806, Congress was busy with the commercial policy of "non-importation" from Great Britain. Trade policy ultimately played an important role in the nation's defense requirements. Should Congress lean towards trade and commerce, then a large seagoing fleet was necessary to protect those ventures. If an isolationist attitude prevailed and commercial restrictions levied, then the country did not need numerous capital ships and could concentrate on a passive coastal defense. Though Jefferson has been blamed for implementing the gunboat program, Congress's fateful decision was equally responsible. The resolution approved on 18 April 1806 prohibited the importation of "certain goods" from Great Britain and all but killed Dawson's third resolution for ships-of-the-line. Thereafter, gunboats were the only viable defense alternative supported by antinaval congressmen. [21]

Debate on Dawson's three original resolutions resumed on 25 March. The question over money for repairing fortifications passed without debate by a narrow margin of three votes. The second resolution, calling for $250,000 for fifty gunboats, passed by a more comfortable margin. The third resolution, however, provoked hostilities. Whereas fortifications and gunboats were obviously defensive weapons, seventy-fours were perceived as defensive only inasmuch as they defended trade on the open seas.

Surprisingly, Republican Matthew Lyon, the congressman who represented Vermont and Kentucky and ran for office in Arkansas during his career, deviated from his normal position and supported ships-of-the-line even though he had personally received several contracts to build gunboats in Kentucky, which he had represented during the Ninth Congress. Lyon's reasoning for supporting capital ships was puzzling. He said that he "neither wished nor expected to have seventy-four-gun ships built on the western waters" but instead wanted them for the protection of commerce. Perhaps he understood the marketability of using Kentucky hemp in either case, or even thought his support would convince his brethren to follow his lead. Another motive perhaps was his Irish heritage, believing that American ships-of-the-line could become a thorn in the British side. [22]

Debate on Dawson's third resolution crystallized the opposing sides. Most understood that the South was an agricultural region whereas the

Ninth Congress
April 1806
Legislation

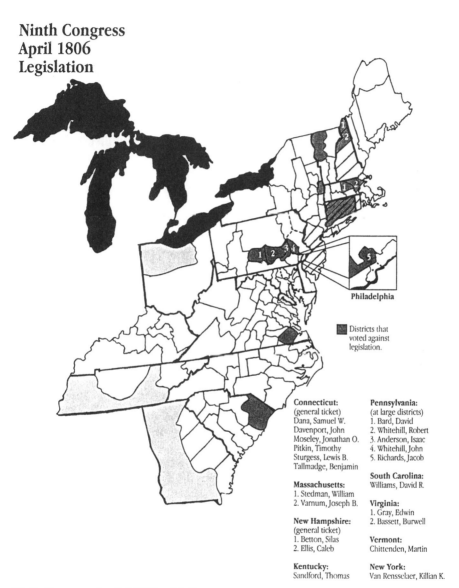

Philadelphia

Districts that voted against legislation.

Connecticut:
(general ticket)
Dana, Samuel W.
Davenport, John
Moseley, Jonathan O.
Pitkin, Timothy
Sturgess, Lewis B.
Tallmadge, Benjamin

Massachusetts:
1. Stedman, William
2. Varnum, Joseph B.

New Hampshire:
(general ticket)
1. Betton, Silas
2. Ellis, Caleb

Kentucky:
Sandford, Thomas

Pennsylvania:
(at large districts)
1. Bard, David
2. Whitehill, Robert
3. Anderson, Isaac
4. Whitehill, John
5. Richards, Jacob

South Carolina:
Williams, David R.

Virginia:
1. Gray, Edwin
2. Bassett, Burwell

Vermont:
Chittenden, Martin

New York:
Van Rensselaer, Killian K.

Ninth Congress April 1806 Legislation

Northeast's livelihood depended on commerce. Thomas Truxtun, one of the first six captains assigned to the navy after its organization in 1798, summarized the differences between the two regions. He exclaimed "that there were landsmen before there were any seamen and that it was a landsman who first invented a ship," but even that should not prohibit naval improvements to benefit the whole country. In 1796 he had suggested to President Washington that the country needed gunboat-type vessels for the conflict then taking place in the Mediterranean, but now he thought capital ships were needed. Political economist Tench Coxe summed up the opposition by writing that "*we cannot at present* and ought not to establish a naval force ... on account of the monstrous expence, [and] the danger to our civil institutions." In the end, the antinaval Republican attitude, as espoused by Coxe, held sway in the final vote.[23]

Dawson's resolution to build six ships-of-the-line met defeat by a margin of more than two to one. Pronavy congressmen tried to salvage part of the resolution by proposing the construction of two seventy-fours, and later three new frigates, but their efforts were to no avail. Even a proposal to build two frigates to replace those that had been lost or damaged failed to pass. Congress did, however, approve a provision allowing the president to sell any vessel believed to be beyond repair and to keep as many ships in service as was deemed necessary. Thereafter, the only restriction the president had to observe was a limit of 925 seamen for the entire service. In the end, Congress responded to Dawson's resolutions by passing appropriations for harbor repairs and gunboats, but it refused to consider any attempt to increase the navy. The Naval Peace Establishment Act of 1801, which required six frigates to be kept in constant service, was replaced by the gunboat system, which Congress preferred even though Jefferson had wanted it to be part of a naval program rather than the system itself.[24]

As the congressional session drew to a close, news arrived in the capital city of Napoleon's brilliant victories at Pressburg and Austerlitz as well as the formation of a new English government with Charles James Fox as foreign minister. There was finally a possibility that relations between the United States and Britain could once again become normalized. As the congressmen began their return journey to their districts on 22 April, most realized the energy that had been expended as well as the chasms created. Federalists had fought Federalists, Republicans had fought Republicans, and both parties had fought each other. But the session had ended on a reasonably good note.

Anglo-American relations appeared to be improving even though a Non-Intercourse Act had been passed. Secretary of State Madison assured the British government that good relations were possible. Yet there were still problems that needed to be overcome, including impressment and the "hovering" of British warships in American coastal waters. The former was a constant problem until the outbreak of the War of 1812. The latter became increasingly important after the *Leander* incident of April 1806.[25]

Jefferson breathed a sigh of relief as the legislative session came to an end, but events were soon to worsen as news arrived from New York of the atrocity committed by H.M.S. *Leander*. The British warship, which joined *Cambrian* and *Driver* near New York harbor, committed numerous aggressions against American commerce. The vessel and her sister ships inspected outbound merchantmen to determine if their cargoes were bound for France or any of her allies. Basil Hall, a midshipman aboard *Leander*, reported that the fleet stopped numerous vessels each morning, "making many lose tide, fair wind, and their markets." This angered Americans and remained a constant source of irritation, but it did not produce as much enmity as when an American citizen was killed by a British cannonball.[26]

A common practice for British warships was to fire across the bow of a vessel to force it to heave to and submit to a search. Captain Henry Whitby, while commanding *Leander* off Sandy Hook on 25 April, ordered such a warning shot fired. It struck the sloop *Delaware*, resulting in the death of an American citizen, helmsman John Pierce. The victim's brother then carried the "mangled body" back to New York, where public outrage seized the moment. Federalists and Republicans alike agreed that all intercourse with the British should be immediately stopped. Vigilante groups were formed to confiscate supplies destined for the enemy squadron and to hunt down British officers. A grand jury responded by indicting Whitby for murder and dispatching the appropriate affidavits to Washington. The responses made it clear that Whitby should not set foot on American soil again and that the British squadron should leave American waters. Before the incident was forgotten, another British warship, H.M.S. *Melampus*, destroyed a French warship within the Virginia Capes. Americans were now infuriated and wanted a suitable response.[27]

When Jefferson heard of the *Leander* incident he immediately called a cabinet meeting to determine the appropriate course of action. The consensus of his four department heads was that a redress of honor was necessary. But, without frigates ready for sea, that proved to be a problem. One frigate was decommissioned and would take a month to repair while the other two were still in the Mediterranean guarding commerce.

They could not be in home waters for at least five months. Furthermore, the gunboats assigned to New York had not yet arrived. Limited by his military possibilities, the president was left with few options. He believed, however, that peaceful coercion could be used "to obtain better provisions for the future," and this was always the basis of his diplomacy. In this instance it was his only alternative, and it proved fruitful. [28]

Jefferson was well aware that the country was militarily unprepared. He had suggested in his fifth annual message, however, that Congress consider building ships-of-the-line. Dawson's resolution for capital ships attempted to satisfy the president's request, but Congress was adamant in its decision not to build additional ships. Congress's failure to prepare for the inevitable placed the burden again on the president. Jefferson wrote to Jacob Crowninshield during the height of the *Leander* crisis that "building some ships of the line ... is not to be lost sight of." Furthermore, the country needed "a squadron properly composed to prevent the blockading" of our ports. James Monroe confirmed Jefferson's suspicions when he wrote from London that a navy was necessary to "form some balance against the ordinary detachments of these powers, in our seas in time of war." The chance for such a navy had been lost among the ideological and sectional prejudices of Congress. The time had come again for the comprehensive defensive system Jefferson envisioned. [29]

The second session of the Ninth Congress and the *Leander* incident provided the opportunity to reunite the splintered Republican party. Congress had weathered a turbulent session and Jefferson hoped all could be brought back into the fold. His next annual message provided the tone of forgiveness. The message, presented to Congress on 2 December 1806, virtually overlooked the question that was the catalyst for trouble during the first session. Instead of dwelling on foreign affairs, Jefferson unveiled his desire for a domestic program aimed at enhancing the nation's material progress. Because the debt was being liquidated at a faster rate than expected, other items could be pursued. Jefferson recommended that the attention of Congress be focused on founding a national university, implementing a system of roads and canals, abolishing the slave trade, organizing a national militia, and providing for the protection of ports and harbors. Although these measures would benefit the country, defense was obviously most important in a world still at war. [30]

Jefferson realized the country remained pitifully unprepared. He admitted that the nation's first concern should be to place her ports and harbors "in a situation to maintain peace and order within them." This concern had been expressed to Governor Morgan Lewis of New York during the *Leander* incident, and it had been repeated during the following summer. Jefferson rationalized, "Although our prospect is peace, our policy is to provide for defense by all those means to which our resources are competent." Thus far, however, Congress deemed gunboats the only resource.[31]

Jefferson's message expressed his desire to build additional gunboats while also suggesting that other means of defense be considered. Fortifications, he argued, should be repaired and "other such works as may have real effect in obstructing the approach of an enemy to our seaport towns" be "erected." He insinuated that floating batteries or perhaps even seagoing vessels should be constructed to prohibit an enemy from entering American harbors. Although Jefferson did not expressly state that he wanted to construct capital ships, he did understand that the "Atlantic frontier" needed to be protected against blockade, just as the western frontier needed protection from the Indians. He also realized that the seacoast's "exposure to potent enemies" afforded it "a proportionate right to be defended." The plan he unveiled during the ensuing session manifested this awareness.[32]

On the following day, 3 December, parts of Jefferson's message relating to "protection of our ports, towns, and rivers" were referred to a select House committee consisting of six northern and one southern congressmen. The Senate established a similar committee on 4 December. When the House committee's report was presented on 23 January, two nondescript resolutions emerged. One called for an unspecified amount of money for fortifications while the other asked for an unspecified number of gunboats. Federalist Fisher Ames predicted what the session would bring even before the resolutions were reported. "Mr. Jefferson's system," he asserted, "is now fixed. The sea is to have no defense but gunboats." Ames perceived the direction that Congress was leading the country even though it did not accurately represent what Jefferson wanted.[33]

On 5 February, the House requested that the president explain the administration's dependence on gunboats as the principal item for the defense of the nation. This call for information came after a month-long struggle over the question of coastal fortifications. The heated debate between navalists and antinavalists during January 1807, however, did not concern the question of fortifications or defense per se but instead concentrated on personnel. In any case, appropriations for $500,000 were defeated by a vote of 38 to 65. Subsequent appropriations suffered the same fate. Eventually, Congress approved a paltry $150,000 for improving the nation's coastal fortifications.[34]

Part of the reason for this legislative failure was that the request for major expenditures for harbor fortifications smacked of a large standing army, something that did not appeal to Republicans. On the other hand, gunboats obviously did, and a $250,000 appropriation passed by a comfortable 53 to 32 margin. Federalists in the Senate, however, were able to render the House's decision null by striking out the gunboat clause altogether. The commentary of one congressman epitomized the entire question of gunboats versus fortifications. The argument over these two resolutions, he remarked, appeared "as if those on one side had got into fortifications while those on the other were coming in gunboats to attack them."[35]

The result of the legislative debate during the second session was interesting. After two months of heated debate, the Naval Act of 3 March 1807 appropriated a trifling sum for fortifying ports and harbors and made no reference to either gunboats or capital ships. Viewing this legislation in retrospect, it should be remembered why the issue originally came before Congress. The *Leander* incident aroused popular indignation and forced Jefferson to take action. But by March 1807 the event was almost a year in the past and neither the country nor the people were at present threatened. Domestic issues precluded any immediate concern over national security. Isolationism bred a perceived confidence in the country's ability to prepare for war at a moment's notice and negated the necessity for expensive defense preparations.[36]

Without voting to build additional gunboats, the congressional session still produced Jefferson's most important blueprint concerning the craft and their role in national security. His response to the House's request for information provided not only the long-awaited rationale for his infatuation with the diminutive vessels but also a brief exposition of his overall defense theory.

Jefferson was apparently prepared for Congress's demand for information, because he submitted his report on 10 February 1807, only five days after the request. The report provided a study of his idea of defense, the gunboats' role within the system, the number of vessels needed, and their suggested stations. Included with his account were supporting letters from Generals Gates and Wilkinson, Commodore Samuel Barron, and Captain Thomas Tingey. The president had promptly responded to the House's demand, but his alacrity failed to secure passage of any defense appropriation during the session.[37]

Jefferson's defense ideology presented in this message was important, but equally significant was the number of gunboats he suggested the nation should possess. He had agonized over the number of craft necessary and had consulted the cabinet for their opinions. In mid-December 1806, he wrote to Robert Smith that "250 gunboats would be as compleat defence for all our seaports as should be provided in that line." He added that because seventy-five had already been built or were under construction, only 175 additional vessels were needed. To expedite their construction, he suggested that sixty be appropriated for the present and last two sessions of his presidency. This would, he believed, fulfill his "desire of leaving this branch of defense ... compleat on ... retirement from office."[38]

Jefferson's economy-minded treasury secretary, Albert Gallatin, thought otherwise, suggesting that only 200 rather than 250 be built. This number, he believed, was adequate for the defense of the nation. Additionally, the 127 gunboats needed to fulfill the quota of 200 could be built after war began, thus saving money on maintenance costs. Jefferson agreed that 200 gunboats would be an acceptable number, but he strongly argued that they should be built as soon as possible because they could not "be built in 1, 2 or even 6 months," as Gallatin thought. Another reason for immediately constructing gunboats was that if war ensued, building facilities would be assaulted and the vessels "destroyed by the enemy on the stocks." After further consideration, Jefferson rejected Gallatin's proposal and suggested that Congress build half the vessels during 1807 and the other half during the following year.[39]

Of the documents accompanying Jefferson's report, Thomas Tingey's letter was most reflective of the gunboat ideology and its relation to the proposed defensive system. Gates, Wilkinson, Barron, and Tingey agreed that the vessels' design made them suitable for shallow-draft service and a difficult target for the enemy. Those were generally accepted arguments. Tingey, however, was the only one who espoused that gunboats were to be a part of the overall system. He wrote that the vessels were not to be the only defense but rather to "assist in the defence of all the principal ports in our country." Perhaps Tingey was merely repeating the administration's policy, but it was more probable that he believed gunboats were only a part of the system and that frigates or ships-of-the-line would be built in the future as additional components to the program. Much to the navalists' dismay, the future did not arrive until after the war with England had begun, well after Jefferson's administration ended.[40]

The subject of defense became a moot point during the spring of 1807. Attempts to enlarge the gunboat flotilla or to appropriate enough funds for repairing fortifications had been stifled. But the subject once again attracted the undivided attention of the country "under circumstances emphatically demanding immediate attention to it." The circumstances surround the oft-told story of the *Chesapeake* incident.[41]

The frigate *Chesapeake*, under the command of James Barron, departed from Hampton Roads, Virginia, for the Mediterranean on a shakedown cruise on 22 June 1807. Captain S. P. Humphreys of the 50-gun H.M.S. *Leopard* hailed Barron's frigate before she was ten miles offshore. Humphreys stopped *Chesapeake* to retake men who had deserted from British vessels. When Barron refused to muster his men so identification could take place, Humphreys ordered *Leopard* to fire into the unprepared vessel. Afterwards, a British officer boarded *Chesapeake* and seized four men accused of desertion. Barron dramatically responded to the outrage by proclaiming his ship a prize of war, but Humphreys refused the offer. *Leopard* then rejoined the British squadron at anchor in Lynnhaven Bay while *Chesapeake*, which had twenty-two holes in the hull, limped back to Hampton Roads with three dead and eighteen wounded.[42]

Most Americans responded to the incident with demands for war. Federalists and Republicans alike publicly deplored the British atrocity and believed justice should be served. Town meetings across the country condemned the act of aggression and drew up petitions urging retaliation. Samuel Smith of Maryland wrote, "I have never seen so large an assemblage ... [and] there appeared but one opinion — War." Charlestonians even went as far as to wear black crepe bands to honor those killed in action. Although the majority of Americans believed drastic action should be taken, not all were willing to risk war. Federalist Congressman Josiah Quincy of Massachusetts, whose dislike of Jefferson stemmed from his belief that the president was an "intellectual fraud," felt that the incident should be downplayed so that it could be quickly forgotten and the administration not profit. Federalist Senator Timothy Pickering, also from Massachusetts, believed that despite the outrage the country should not take measures that might "inconvenience" the British. Both sides vociferously proclaimed their positions, hoping the president would adopt their arguments.[43]

As soon as Jefferson heard of the incident, he realized that a cabinet meeting needed to be called to determine what course the country should follow. Once again, the president was in a quandary, but this time any indecision on his part would have serious consequences in such a charged atmosphere. He knew, however, that the nation was ill-prepared for war. Only after serious deliberation did the administration determine what action should be taken. On 2 July, the cabinet unanimously agreed to accept a proclamation drafted by Jefferson and Madison ordering all British warships out of American waters. Additionally, the schooner *Revenge* was sent to Europe with instructions for James Monroe to demand satisfaction for the incident.[44]

At other meetings in early July, Jefferson and the cabinet agreed that Congress should be called into session on 26 October, weeks earlier than normal. This opening date gave the appearance of mollifying those demanding war. Yet Jefferson believed the three-month delay would allow hostile tempers to cool and prevent the country from going to the point of no return. The delay also provided the president with time to receive Britain's response to Monroe's demands. Moreover, Jefferson respected the power of Congress to declare war, and perhaps by October attitudes would change; thus he would not tie the nation's hands to a prescribed course of action. As Jefferson cautiously calculated each move, preparations were being made for the worst-case scenario. He hoped war could be avoided; but if not, defensive as well as offensive plans, including a winter invasion of Canada, were being prepared.[45]

During the summer of 1807, the defense of American ports and harbors was much more important than a proposed winter offensive against the Canadian frontier. As long as British warships remained off the American coast, no seaport was safe. Recognizing this, Jefferson instructed Governor William H. Cabell of Virginia to make preparations for the defense of the state, but under no circumstances should he strike the first blow. Likewise, other governors were instructed to muster their quota of militia and to stockpile ammunition, arms, and equipment in case of war. Other military preparations carried out secretly included increasing the army, navy, and marines; training militia; repairing fortifications; procuring materials for future gunboat construction; and recalling all American warships from the Mediterranean. The groundwork for war was being laid as Jefferson subordinated his pacifism to military preparedness. "Our greatest praise shall be," he wrote, "that we *appear* to be doing nothing." But that was not the case.[46]

The immediate danger subsided after about two and a half weeks, even though a British squadron remained in the Chesapeake Bay until October. Should relations not improve, Jefferson believed Congress might have to be called into session sooner than expected, a dreadful thought for one who did not want to spend summer along the Potomac River. Fortunately, by mid-July the situation had stabilized, thus making it unnecessary to schedule a legislative session earlier than October. Despite the improving international situation, defense preparations continued.[47]

Jefferson believed that the "English [were as] equally tyrannical at sea as [Napoleon was] on land" and that preparations needed to be taken to prevent invasion. Gunboats ideally served that function, and they were doubly attractive because they did not tie the legislature's hands to an offensive war by challenging Britain's supremacy on the seas. Jefferson therefore boldly suggested that Congress authorize building additional gunboats, even though a similar request had failed the previous session.[48]

As the congressional session drew near, Jefferson became increasingly convinced of the necessity of gunboats for the country's defense. Many agreed with his assertions. One constituent even wrote that the vessels were the only thing that could "save our harbors and cities from destruction," while another wrote that gunboats "would save the United States from ruin ... [and] strike a Terror in everyones heart, who would dare to invade this happy country." Jefferson obviously agreed because he had tried for almost two terms to express that same notion. In a message to Thomas Paine, the statement that navalists and anti-Jeffersonians use to justify their claim that he was hostile to the navy, Jefferson demonstrated his comprehension of the subject. "Gun-boats," he wrote, are the only *water* defence which can be useful to us, and protect us from the ruinous folly of a navy." Jefferson was not categorically opposed to a navy, and during his administration he accepted an important role for the country's sea forces, as illustrated by his ideas concerning gunboats and their function within the country's defense system. At the time of that statement, the United States was not a country that did not need or should not have a navy, but rather one in which circumstances prescribed gunboats as the most practical defense the nation could possess, especially in light of British naval victories at Copenhagen and Trafalgar. Congress, however, made the ultimate decision to rely solely on the gunboat program. It too agreed with the president's philosophy, although for different reasons.[49]

When Congress convened in October, virtually everyone felt that the country should make preparations for war, but not all concurred on what type of precautions should be taken. Navalists once again saw an opportunity to build capital ships to protect trade and national honor. Antinavalists felt otherwise, seeing the *Chesapeake* insult as having occurred because the country was inadequately defended. In the ensuing debate, both sides eloquently presented their arguments.[50]

When Jefferson presented his seventh annual message, he demonstrated an understanding of both the navalist and antinavalist positions as well as the country's defense needs. British outrages, he asserted, had backed the United States into a corner where the only alternatives were never to admit armed vessels into our ports or to place our harbors in a state of defense to "protect the lives and property of our citizens." Jefferson preferred the latter, even though its expense made it economically impractical. Therefore, armed vessels that defy the law "must be," he exclaimed, "viewed as rebels or public enemies." The only realistic solution was to order gunboats to New York, New Orleans, and into the Chesapeake Bay, which Jefferson did. But the country needed to do more, as the president well knew. "Whether our moveable force on the water, so material in aid of the defensive works on land, should be augmented in this or any other form is left to the wisdom of the Legislature." The wisdom of Congress, nonetheless, resulted only in further gunboat appropriations, which were not exactly what Jefferson wanted but just as he expected.[51]

Dawson once again initiated congressional discussion on 29 October when he moved that the president's remarks be assigned to a select committee, later known as the Committee on Aggressions. The group's duty was to investigate possible means for defending ports and harbors against future violations. It soon became obvious that the topic of capital vessels would get little, if any, attention. Josiah Quincy pleaded for the House to establish another committee whose purpose would be to examine aggressions on the high seas and to take appropriate measures. His plea, however, failed by an overwhelming 93-24 vote.[52]

Thomas Blount of North Carolina presented the committee's report to the full House for discussion on 24 November. Its conclusion was that "protection ... can best and most expeditiously be afforded by means of land batteries and gunboats." No provisions were made for capital ships, even though navalists vociferously tried to persuade their fellow congressmen of the value of such vessels. The resultant debate continued for seventeen days, until 11 December 1807, when Blount's measure for 188 gunboats (making 257 total vessels appropriated for during Jefferson's presidency) passed by a giant 111-19 majority. Congress had made its final allocation for gunboats — $852,500 — but not until navalists and anti-Jeffersonians had exhausted all means of persuasion against the diminutive vessels.[53]

During the debate, the gunboats' primary advocate was George Washington Campbell of Tennessee, the first westerner elected chairman of the Ways and Means Committee. Outspoken John Randolph, James Elliot of Vermont, Josiah Quincy, and to a lesser degree former Speaker Nathaniel Macon directed the opposition. It was a small but vocal group, and it possessed considerable legislative talent to play havoc with Campbell and the gunboats' supporters. Randolph, who wanted to "keep *our own ships and seamen* at home," declared that due to the humiliation of *Chesapeake* he could not in good faith vote money for "our degraded and disgraced navy." But it was Elliot's argument on the first day of debate that summarized the antinavalist position. Gunboats, he argued, "have never been of use but as auxiliaries to more extensive and substantial establishments." Ironically, his argument against the vessels was exactly why Jefferson favored their use.[54]

The gunboat legislation's overwhelming victory may be attributed to the belief that war was imminent and that few congressmen wanted to be portrayed as unpatriotic or not supportive of defense. John Davenport of Connecticut assumed war was impending, stating that "our political horizon ... [was] not only clouded but ... darkness visible." He did not, however, believe that the "philosopher's plan" for gunboats was the solution for the country's problems. Campbell, who carried the torch for the appropriation, disagreed. Gunboats, he believed, were the only thing that could save the country from a large naval establishment, or from what he called "the tomb of American Liberty." Fellow westerner Joseph Desha of Kentucky repeated Campbell's concern and argued that the nation was following a wise course by building gunboats rather than "ruinous" ships-of-the-line. Others disregarded both attitudes and warned that the country needed unity, especially with the nation on the eve of a war. This point of view struck home because "war for honour," as John Taylor of Caroline remarked, could result "in the destruction of the last experiment in favour of free government." Jefferson's gunboat system had been finally implemented regardless of the motives.[55]

The gunboat appropriation, according to Jefferson, was critical for improving Anglo-American relations. He hoped the timely decision of Congress would apprise Great Britain of the strained relations between the two countries and prevent procrastination in settling the *Chesapeake* affair. Accurately reading the country's pulse, Jefferson realized that he could not allow the British the luxury of time. Although Timothy Pickering did not agree, he understood the president's motives. When the new British minister arrived, Pickering wrote, "and sees the *dangers* of preparations for war," as expressed by the decision to build additional gunboats, his reports to London will be much different than if he found the country "on the hope of a continuance of peace." Thus, Jefferson was using the *Chesapeake* outrage, Congress's decision for defense preparations, and the embargo legislation approved by the president on 9 January 1808 to attempt to influence future British policy towards the United States.[56]

When viewing Jefferson's gunboat policy from the vantage point of historical perspective, many believe that the program was, as Charles Oscar Paullin claims, "a misdirection of the national resources." That is not necessarily true. The program as envisioned appealed to the president because of its place in a coordinated system of defense and to Congress

Tenth Congress
December 1807
Legislation

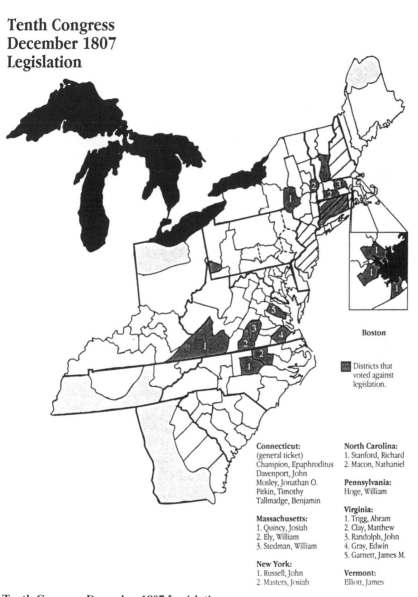

Boston

Districts that
voted against
legislation.

Connecticut:
(general ticket)
Champion, Epaphroditus
Davenport, John
Mosley, Jonathan O.
Pitkin, Timothy
Tallmadge, Benjamin

Massachusetts:
1. Quincy, Josiah
2. Ely, William
3. Stedman, William

New York:
1. Russell, John
2. Masters, Josiah

North Carolina:
1. Stanford, Richard
2. Macon, Nathaniel

Pennsylvania:
Hoge, William

Virginia:
1. Trigg, Abram
2. Clay, Matthew
3. Randolph, John
4. Gray, Edwin
5. Garnett, James M.

Vermont:
Elliott, James

Tenth Congress December 1807 Legislation

because of its supposed economy and antiestablishment characteristics. One can argue that defense at a cheaper price is not a misdirection of resources but rather a wise policy decision in fulfillment of a political objective.[57]

The political objective behind the gunboat program was unquestionably national defense, and as such the vessels should be discussed in the context of political-military questions rather than strictly in that of naval policy. True, gunboats were administered by the navy department, and they did sail on the seas, but Congress believed their primary function was to prevent an enemy invasion. Historian Dumas Malone, who has made one of the most complete analysis of Jefferson's policy thus far, holds their role was "to maintain the *status quo*." Malone is correct, but his assertion should be taken one step farther. Gunboats upheld Jefferson's policies, but because he was a realistic politician, his most important policy concerned national security. The other roles the gunboats fulfilled, whether suppressing the slave trade, curtailing piratical activities and privateers, or upholding the embargo law, strengthen the argument that they were part of an overall political-military policy.[58]

Even the conditions under which gunboat legislation passed lends credence to the arguments that the vessels were political and aimed at preserving the country's freedom. Whether the gunboats were a response to the Spanish closing of the Mississippi River or to the British outrage committed on the *Chesapeake,* they were discussed in the context of national defense and diplomacy. Furthermore, the gunboats' construction was a conscious political decision resulting from the actions of other countries, and the rationale was sensible in a world rocked by the ongoing European wars. Gunboats were not perceived as threatening or challenging but merely as defensive weapons that protected the country from foreign aggression in American waters. In this respect they accomplished exactly what Jefferson desired: an arms buildup enhancing national defense while not threatening British supremacy of the seas. The decision to promote the program was a logical choice for a president who wanted to maintain independence by a passive coastal defence.

Another argument, according to one author, was that the gunboat system, "obstinately maintained despite its failures, came close to undoing [Jefferson's] country." The gunboat program, as it resulted from congressional debate, did not truly represent the defensive system Jefferson preferred. He wanted a multifaceted defense system with gunboats as one part of the program rather than as the program itself. Antinavalists who controlled Congress wanted something else completely, and the end product after Jefferson's two terms was the gunboat system bearing his name. Congress had implemented the system, and those who blame Jefferson for coming close to undoing his country misplace the responsibility. True, Jefferson supported the system, and he did have a fascination with the diminutive craft, but Congress was equally, if not more, responsible for the final product.[59]

Perhaps the gunboats did provide the country with a false sense of security, but the ridicule that is placed on them is unjustified. They did not "undo" the country. Instead, the debate over gunboats and national defense served as a classic example of American democracy at its finest, ultimately strengthening the young republic's cherished principles. When Jefferson tolerated gunboats as an "end," or as the system Congress desired, rather than a means, he was demonstrating more practical wisdom than has been given to the "phylosophic" president.

5
Gunboat-Related Legislation:
"Visionary Schemes" of the President

A review of the gunboat program bearing Jefferson's name makes it obvious that the policy decision was a result of various pieces of related and nonrelated legislation and that sectional and ideological issues played major roles. Even some proposals not directly pertaining to gunboats had a significant impact on the direction of the policy. In this respect, the gunboat program was much like a jigsaw puzzle, since it was made up of various pieces of legislation that fit together to form the final product. Yet, when assembling a puzzle, one makes numerous choices before the final picture is revealed. Jefferson's dry-dock proposal and naval militia plan were recommendations that forced Congress to make choices ultimately affecting the direction taken by the gunboat program.

One point generally overlooked to those who claim to understand Jefferson's naval policy is that he wanted a small navy whose primary concern was national defense.[1] In his *Notes*, Jefferson explained that "a small naval force ... is sufficient [and] necessary" and "it should by no means be as great as we are able to make it." But when evaluating his naval policy, one becomes overwhelmed with small gunboats rather than with a small, balanced naval force. The resultant argument is that Jefferson wanted to replace the fleet rather than augment it. The story of how the country came to rely on small ships rather than a small navy rests in Jefferson's attempt during his first term to maintain economically the Federalists' reduced fleet by planning what became known as Mr. Jefferson's Dry Docks.[2]

Jefferson's main concern about the navy was its expense, particularly the major cost incurred not so much in original construction but in upkeep. In his *Notes*, Jefferson had said that the British government annually spent a sizable portion of its revenues for maintaining its navy. He realized that for the United States "to aim at such a navy as the greater nations of Europe possess, would be a foolish and wicked waste of the energies of our countrymen." Furthermore, he contended, "it would be to pull on our heads that load of military expence, which makes the European labourer go supperless to bed, and moisten his bread with the sweat of his brow." As such, Jefferson had to strike a balance between his desire for economy and the need for defense.[3]

Since Jefferson was a product of the Enlightenment, he had great appreciation for architecture and mechanical inventions, especially those that were labor-saving or brought improvements. He hoped his plan, in the fall of 1802, for a dry dock or stationary structure at Washington, D.C., from which water could be removed for the cleaning, repairing, and storing of ships would satisfy the questions of both defense and economy. He believed it could prevent exorbitant costs inherent in maintaining a seagoing navy while keeping the nation's small fleet of warships in a constant state of readiness.[4]

Jefferson first assigned Captain Thomas Tingey, commandant of the Washington Navy Yard, the task of finding water for implementing the proposal. That summer's war scare with Morocco in the Mediterranean only increased the president's urgency. In early November, Jefferson contacted Benjamin Henry Latrobe, requesting him to calculate the expense and supervise the construction of a dry dock for "the placing of a navy in a state of perfect preservation, so that at the beginning of a subsequent war it shall be as sound as at the end of the preceding one when laid up."[5]

Recognized as a remarkable architect and engineer, Latrobe was an excellent choice for the project. Before arriving in the United States in 1796, he had gained considerable experience in England in the construction of waterways. During his six years in America, Latrobe had gained a reputation for his improvement of the Susquehanna River, his work in Virginia with the Appomattox Company, his design of Philadelphia's Bank of Pennsylvania, and his construction of the same city's massive water works.[6]

Latrobe went to work immediately and within a month had prepared a report, complete with sketches of the proposed structure. He recommended a system incorporating two locks. At high tide, the first lock was to be filled to lift a ship twelve feet to the second, which in turn would carry the vessel another twelve feet to a turning area and the dry dock from which the water was drained and the hull deposited on a supporting frame beneath a protective roof. The design permitted docking for twelve frigates, in four rows three abreast, and covered an area approximately 175 feet wide by 800 feet long with an entrance 55 feet across. The plan called for what would have been the largest structure in America, encompassing more than three acres under a single roof.[7]

The naval arsenal housing the docked vessels, designed to admit the free passage of air from all sides, would be constructed of solid masonry faced with Aquia sandstone and topped by a roof modeled, as Jefferson himself suggested, "in the manner of that of the Halle au blé [eighteenth-century corn market] at Paris, which needing no underworks to support it, will permit the basin to be entirely open & free for the movement of the vessels." The roof would be covered with painted or varnished sheet iron, making it virtually incombustible. Supporting it were tremendous arched girders of laminated timber ribs, eliminating the need to procure solid wooden beams long enough to span the dry dock. The arch in turn was to rest on masonry piers at its springline, minimal support for so wide an arch but possible because of lightweight wood.[8]

Latrobe estimated that the project needed about 3,315,200 cubic feet of water. In their report of 22 October, Tingey and surveyor Nicholas King had recommended several alternative sources that would produce the required water. After carefully studying all options, Latrobe chose to employ the water of Tiber Creek, which by using canals in addition to several reservoirs with dams, weirs, and sluices, could fill the project's water needs in a minimum of three days.[9]

Final considerations for Jefferson's dry dock included the time and labor needed to complete the project. Latrobe estimated that, with favorable weather, the first frigate could be docked before the end of 1803 and the naval arsenal completed before the end of 1804. He believed this schedule was feasible because experienced craftsmen, trained by work on the Pennsylvania Bank and the Philadelphia Water Works, were numerous and available. The first priority was to acquire labor before the first of January because all quality workmen were by then usually engaged in contracts for the season. If workmen were not contracted for by at least March, the project would have to be delayed a year or have to be completed by day laborers at twice the expense.[10]

Latrobe's visionary design far exceeded Jefferson's comparatively economical and utilitarian expectations. The architect had instead combined utility with an aesthetic quality, creating not only a naval storage facility but also a piece of art. Yet Latrobe was modest about his accomplishment, evidenced by his signing the final product as engineer, not architect. Despite Jefferson's frugal nature, he approved the plan, estimated to cost $417,276.[11]

Treasury secretary Gallatin opposed the dry dock on political and fiscal grounds. He summed up his feelings about the proposal by telling Jefferson he was "*in toto* against this recommendation." With no "money to spare for the navy," he strongly suggested the president sidestep the plan and instead make "a general recommendation," thereby "leaving the Legislature free either to designate the place or entrust the Executive with the selection." In short, according to Gallatin, the dry-dock proposal was uneconomical and perhaps even beyond presidential prerogatives. Jefferson persisted though, and argued in a note to Gallatin in October 1802 that the project was well within his presidential power to support a navy. Once Jefferson settled the question of legality in his own mind, he was ready to make his plan public.[12]

On Wednesday, 15 December 1802, Meriwether Lewis, secretary to the president, presented the plans to the Senate and House in the form of Jefferson's annual message. "Presuming it will be deemed expedient to expend annually a sum towards providing the naval defense which our situation may require," Jefferson recommended "that the first appropriations for that purpose may go to the saving [of] what we already possess." Specifically because "no cares, no attentions, can preserve vessels from rapid decay which lie in water and exposed to the sun" except by "great and constant repairs" that "consume, if continued, a great portion of the money destined to our naval purposes," the president proposed adding "to our navy-yard here a dock, within which our vessels may be laid up dry and under cover from the sun." Jefferson concluded by asserting that "scarcely more than has been the cost of one vessel is necessary to save the whole." With this statement, the political battle lines were drawn.[13]

On 19 January 1803, physician Samuel L. Mitchill of New York, on behalf of a special committee, brought the proposal to the floor of the House. His committee approved authorizing the dry dock, and as customary, recommended "that for carrying the same into effect" a sum of money be appropriated. The proposal quickly became mired in the House's partisan and sectional debates, no doubt exacerbated by Mitchill's observation that the phrase "half a million dollars" should be added to the resolution and his proposal that "the Committee rise," thus halting any discussion on the matter. Not surprisingly, Federalist John Rutledge, Jr., of South Carolina disagreed. Discussion should continue, he insisted, so "that informed gentlemen, who were prepared might offer their sentiments."[14]

Even though he claimed his committee had voted unanimously in favor of the project, Mitchill at this point began expressing his own doubts. Perhaps, as he had already admitted, half a million dollars was too much to spend when the country was trying to reduce its national debt. He added, too, that maybe smaller dry docks capable of holding one ship apiece were more practical; Jefferson's plan, after all, was experimental. Mitchill did acknowledge that there were similar facilities in Venice, Sweden, and Russia, but he still questioned whether a covered dry dock would protect ships which had already "grown foul and water soaked in the ocean," whether the dampness acquired over the years would ever dry sufficiently to prevent rotting, and whether there was enough ventilation to disperse "septic vapors" with their "disorganizing powers." Furthermore, atmospheric conditions in summer and winter were bound to accelerate rotting and loosen the ships' copper-covered bottoms.[15]

William Eustis, from Massachusetts, brought up the sectional issue by questioning the facility's location in Washington. If preservation and protection of the navy was most important to the Atlantic states, why were the arsenal and dock some "300 miles" from the ocean? Navy yards near the sea coast, he argued, lessened the costs of construction as well as labor and supplies. His only question over design was an objection to placing the ships on "blocks or props," which he believed might in time damage the vessels' frames. Eustis concluded by questioning public expectation: if the project failed, would the city's future growth and development be retarded? His questions made a vivid impression on many because a failure would be a testimonial to the government's inability to carry out its plans.[16]

The proposal's chief advocate in the House was Samuel Smith, who tried to salvage the recommendation by discussing the success of the projects in Venice and Sweden. The Venetian arsenal, which he had seen, was one of the world's greatest shipbuilding facilities, containing berths for twenty ships that could be ready to put to sea in less than a month's notice. Smith also mentioned a letter that reported a conversation between navy captain Richard Dale and a Swedish official (probably Richard Soderstrom, consul general in Philadelphia). The official informed Dale that the proposed Swedish structure would contain eight 74-gun ships-of-the-line. Furthermore, these "vessels were to be washed with fresh water, perfectly drained, and opened to a circulation of air," after which there was "no doubt of their remaining in perfect repair in the dock for a century."[17]

Smith then refuted his opponent's contention that the stored ships would never dry out. He argued that could be accomplished by removing planks from the sides to keep the air "sweet" within the ships. As for the dock's location, Smith responded that "it was contemplated to make the experiment under the eye of the government," and if successful extend it to other areas such as Boston. Besides, Smith argued, the Potomac was deeper than the Delaware River and as deep as the harbor at New York. Additionally, Washington's location made it immune from sudden enemy attack (although the War of 1812 proved differently). Smith also pointed out Washington's proximity to the supply of naval stores in North Carolina, iron ore deposits from the Potomac mines, and wood from Virginia. He then posed the question: which is cheaper, to bring the men to the materials or the materials to the men? In conclusion, he urged his fellow representatives to delay their decision until a later session when more information would be available and more money could be spared from "objects of less importance."[18]

The opposition's argument rested on the proposition that because "'the British have never erected [dry docks],' ... they cannot be worth erecting." But the attack cut much deeper; it criticized the president himself. Federalist Roger Griswold of Connecticut regarded the president's plan as a "visionary scheme such as might be expected from the philosophy of the administration." Republican John Bacon of Massachusetts added, "It might be the decided opinion of the President that it was best to erect a dry dock at the City of Washington, but the President's opinion is not to govern me." Not all were critical of the dry-dock plan. Federalist James A. Bayard of Delaware believed that despite the House's agreement to equip all ships in ordinary, the president's proposal would still be adopted. It quickly became apparent, however, that the "visionary ideas" of the Jefferson administration were not the ideas of the congressional majority.[19]

The Federalist press naturally joined the assault. The *Salem Gazette* reported James Callender's quip that Jefferson wished to squander a million dollars on a project that "every cabin boy could have told him was certain to destroy" the vessels. Another Massachusetts newspaper, the *Columbian Centinel*, ran a mock advertisement for Jefferson's "'Patent Navy Medicine' for the 'cure of most diseases to which a navy is subject.'" In another issue, the *Centinel* took advantage of a double opportunity for sarcasm by noting, "even Tom Paine ridicules the President's idea of a dry dock. Tom would like it a little wet; about chin high more or less."[20]

Even Robert Leslie, a Philadelphia watchmaker and Jefferson supporter, questioned the plan on technical grounds. He pointed out that for one ship to be moved, the entire area would have to be flooded and every ship prepared for flotation. To remedy this flaw, he designed a plan which had twelve individual miniature dry docks bordering a common reservoir. Jefferson apparently was unimpressed with Leslie's objections, but it made little difference, because no appropriations were ever made.[21]

Samuel Smith did his best to save the proposal. His request that further debate and action be delayed to a future session provided a chance of success, albeit slim. The House returned the bill to a committee consisting of Mitchill, Rutledge, and three others "to inquire into the usefulness and propriety of constructing dry docks." The proposal never again came before the full House, instead dying a silent death in committee. Jefferson truly believed that in six or eight years the entire fleet would "be rotten ... or cost millions to repair," and that the legislature would then "come into the proposition of the dry dock to rescue themselves." Perhaps the president was too optimistic because the need for dry-dock facilities did not again come before Congress until 1811; the War of 1812 forestalled any action on the matter.[22]

Jefferson's plan attempted to satisfy his need for economy while maintaining a small navy to preserve national security. The president actually had alienated both pro- and antinavy politicians. In stabilizing the navy's growth, he was challenging a strengthened pronavy faction, which feared the project would eliminate future appropriation for new ship construction. On the other hand, antinavalists, opposed to a large fleet, voted against the measure for various reasons; some opposed a fleet controlled solely by the central government, while others showed their ignorance by accusing the administration of wishing to have a shore-bound navy. In any case, it was a major political setback for the administration.[23]

Jefferson was the father of the dry-dock plan; he conceived it, he nurtured it, and he proposed it to Congress. Naturally, the proposal's defeat disappointed him. In a letter to Lewis M. Wiss more than twenty years later, he gave a near-perfect recollection of the dry-dock proposal. Yet near the letter's end, Jefferson commented, "I have thought of it no more since." Only three years earlier, however, Jefferson had discussed the idea of a dry dock with John Adams and stated, "My papers furnish me nothing; my memory generalities only." Despite his denials, the idea, its details, and its ultimate fate apparently lingered in his mind late into life.[24]

Although Jefferson's proposal never passed congressional scrutiny, an alternative one did. While many in Congress considered Jefferson's plan to enclose twelve frigates ridiculous, his plan to construct gunboats and small sheds to house them was acceptable. In February 1803, less than a month after the dry-dock proposal had been returned to committee,

Congress authorized construction of fifteen gunboats, that ultimately were housed in small sheds.[25]

Jefferson's dry dock fit nicely into his defensive scheme. With the proposed structure, American ships could be placed in ordinary during peacetime. During times of war, they could be brought out of storage and combined with the country's privateers to create a respectable cruising force. The "rapid mobilization of a navy in times of war only" was not only consistent with Jefferson's naval policy but also with his overall defense theory. Besides, ships in storage did not need permanent military establishments but could rely on a militia.[26]

Jefferson thought that the dry dock would guarantee naval preparedness, but he believed the most practical idea for keeping the country in a permanent state of readiness was through a militia. The citizen soldiers of the Revolution, which Jefferson and the Republicans revered, had sprung to arms to ready the country for the ensuing war. But their appeal was more deeply seated than their heroic legacy; they fulfilled a dual role. Republican ideology viewed the militia as a cheap, reliable method for preparing for national defense, while it was also a way to eliminate "that scourge of civilization, that curse of Liberty, a permanent Military Establishment, which have, and ever will ... annihilate every free government."[27]

In his first inaugural address, Jefferson repeated his belief in the citizen soldiers and maintained that their participation had made the American government the strongest in the world. Furthermore, "a well disciplined militia" was "our best reliance in peace and for the first moments of war." He followed up six months later in his annual message by reminding Congress that a militia was "the only force which can be ready at every point and competent to oppose" an enemy invasion. Even though there were many disadvantages to the militia system, such as local versus federal control, Jefferson still regarded the reserve as the best land defense Republicans and the nation could possess. What made his plan unique was that he devised a way to incorporate the citizen soldiers into a "naval militia" to supplement the gunboat program.[28]

For Jefferson, the naval militia was a natural extension of the gunboat program. Because the craft were to be housed in ordinary until times of emergency, why should they not be manned by a naval militia which also would heed the call to arms in times of trouble? During the fall of 1805, Jefferson presented Congress with a well-conceived plan to organize the country's able-bodied men into units to be distributed throughout the nation's seaports.

The general inefficiency of the country's militia provided the immediate rationale for Jefferson's plan. In February 1805, the president reported to Congress that the nation's militia was shockingly inadequate because they lacked training, organization, and in many cases even weapons. This prompted Fisher Ames to remark that the country's reserves would easily be defeated by a professional army, and induced Jefferson to begin the enormous task of reorganizing the country's militia.[29]

The origin of Jefferson's naval militia is unclear. He apparently knew of a French plan to establish a "marine militia" or coast guard as early as 1787. At that time, he suggested to John Jay that the proposed French system might "become interesting to us." In May 1798, his own government ordered construction of several galleys to be manned by a "naval militia organized by the army." Perhaps these proposals convinced Jefferson to consider a similar plan for his country, but the opportunity did not present itself until after the gunboat program had been initiated. Jefferson himself credited the general militia reclassification, of which the naval reserve was a part, to Napoleon Bonaparte. Napoleon, Jefferson said, had conscripted the services of the young, healthy, and enthusiastic to conquer the Old World, and should Congress not adopt a similar plan he would soon conquer the New World too. This was a real threat because news of the French and Spanish fleet's destruction in October at Trafalgar had not yet reached the United States.[30]

Jefferson contacted Secretary of the Navy Robert Smith and Secretary of War Henry Dearborn in late October to discuss his plan for "a regular naval militia to be comprised of all our seafaring citizens." This defense, he believed, would allow the country "to man a fleet speedily by supplying voluntary enlistments" rather than relying on permanent garrisons. Even though his plan appeared to be simple, it was complicated and smacked of government bureaucracy and organization, contrary to the Republican ideology of local control.[31]

The president believed that by implementing his plan, an estimated 50,000 eligible men could be mustered into the naval militia. He thought this number conservative because it was based on the 1803 tonnage returns for foreign and coastal trade, whale and cod fisheries, which totaled 917,054 tons. Jefferson's calculations figured that normally "we are supposed to employ ... six men to every 100 tons" of commerce. But he knew that not all men were of military age nor free white citizens. For that reason, "5 [men] to the 100 tons" was an accurate estimation. Even so, this provided fewer than 46,000 men for the naval militia. The additional number to fulfill the 50,000 projected quota would be composed of "the seamen then in our navy, and those employed on the tide-waters within the United States." By using these additional forces, Jefferson believed that "we may safely state" that the entire force would total 50,000 men.

This illustration shows the typical uniform of a sailor of the War of 1812 period. Photo courtesy of the Naval Historical Center.

The plan required that "every free, able-bodied, white male citizen" between the ages of 18 and 45 whose "principal occupation" was on the seas or tidewaters be subject to service in the naval militia. They were to report to nearby towns, ports, or harbors to be formed into companies under the command of a state-appointed authority who would train them with artillery and "gunboats or other armed vessels" at least once every two months.

The "naval militia" was a separate unit, and those who served in it were not subject to concurrent duty in the land reserve. They were still required, however, to abide by all the rules and regulations of the land reserve. If a militiaman disobeyed or failed to carry out his duties, he was "liable to the same pains, penalties, and coercions, and to trial by a court martial." Should a person refuse to serve or even "delay to enter on duty," he would be arrested as a deserter and punished as such or be "compelled to perform his tour of duty." As with the land militia someone could commute his service within the naval reserve by finding a suitable substitute.

The duty of the naval militia was to ensure that the government did not come under attack by either domestic or foreign enemies. "In cases of insurrection, [or] of opposition to the civil authority," they were to report to their stations "to do duty with artillery on board any armed vessels" to quell the uprising or to enforce the existing laws. Should there be a foreign invasion, all militiamen under age thirty-five were immediately to report to their stations, expecting to serve a one-year term aboard "any" warship within the vicinity.[32]

Robert Smith warned Jefferson that his plan had numerous flaws. The major problem with the naval militia, according to Smith, was that the force would ultimately be under federal rather than state authority because ships of the United States were commanded by officers appointed by the president. Jefferson's plan also stipulated that the militia be under the command of a lieutenant-commandant and a second lieutenant appointed by the state. Smith reminded the president that a naval militia officer was inadequately prepared because professional officers needed "five or six" years of training before they could assume command of a public armed vessel. Captain Thomas Truxtun supported Smith's assertion, remarking "that a seaman will make a soldier in the field immediately ... but a soldier or other ordinary citizen cannot make a seaman, but from long experience and actual service." Moreover, Smith argued that the naval militia, because of the nature of their service, would be required to perform duties "beyond the limits of the United States," contrary to "the laws of the Union." The secretary concluded his argument by informing the president that the bill, as stated, "provides for *training* the naval militia" rather than describing the training which should be "under the authority of the states." This, he accurately predicted, would cause the bill to be defeated.[33]

In contrast, Dearborn's report suggested changes in the way the system was to operate rather than dwelling on questions of legality. He believed that the militia should meet only four days a year instead of once every two months. He also contended should a person miss a muster, despite the reason, he would be subjected to a fine. Should a person fail to provide a suitable substitute, he would be subjected to a fine and be held in custody until it was paid. Furthermore, Dearborn suggested, because of the perpetual problem of logistics, the secretary of the navy should provide each unit with two or more artillery pieces complete with ammunition in case no gunboats or armed vessels were available. This would allow training to occur without the direct involvement of the federal government.[34]

The naval militia as part of Jefferson's overall reorganization was referred to a select committee headed by stalwart Republican Joseph B. Varnum of Massachusetts. Varnum, as well as other Republicans, opposed any changes in the existing militia system. The Massachusetts congressman demonstrated his displeasure with the president's bill by presenting the House with an unfavorable report on the proposal. The Senate also defeated a similar bill, introduced by Samuel Smith, by more than a two-to-one vote. Jefferson believed, throughout the episode, that the proposal, perhaps with minor changes, would pass. Should the proposal be adopted, the United States would "need never raise a regular [army] *in expectation of war.*"[35]

Republican congressmen were not willing to bring more organization and federal control to an entity that was supposedly state oriented. They were also not willing to pass certain provisions within an act just because it was a pet project of the president. A naval militia could have been a valuable asset to the country, especially after the congressional act of 21 April 1806, which stipulated that the "whole number of able seamen, ordinary seamen, and boys, shall not exceed nine hundred and twenty-five" for the entire fleet, including gunboats. Even though the act limited the number of seamen, it did authorize 13 captains, 9 master-commandants, 72 lieutenants, and 150 midshipmen, providing the secretary with much-needed officers but relatively few seamen. Nonetheless, Jefferson and Smith still found that the legislation placed severe limitations on their ability to run the department effectively.[36]

Smith reported to Jefferson in January 1807 that the country already had about 700 seamen in actual service, not including the 412 men needed to outfit the frigates *Chesapeake* and *Wasp*. The commander at New Orleans, John Shaw, had also enlisted 400 additional men for the defense of that city. Smith had a hard enough time running the department, but now he found it impossible to man the country's limited number of vessels without violating the letter of the law. Congress saw its shortcomings during the spring of 1807 and increased the number of seamen to 1,425, tacitly acknowledging Smith's difficulty. But by January 1808, the secretary was once again in the same predicament. He reported to Jefferson that, should all the country's gunboats be manned, each with twenty-four ordinary seamen, and the frigates *Constitution* and *Chesapeake* with full crews, the department would exceed the 1807 act by more than 1,100 men.[37]

Jefferson's next discussion of a naval militia came with his special gunboat message to Congress in February 1807. Although the subject of the message was the use of gunboats for harbor defense, it also referred to a naval militia for manning the vessels. The president explained that while gunboats were not in service, they would be placed in ordinary. In times of emergency, they could be brought into action by "relying on the seamen and militia of the port." Jefferson did not elaborate on the militia in this message, and since Congress did not vote to build additional gunboats, the subject was moot. It would not be brought under congressional consideration again until the spring of 1808.[38]

During the summer of 1807, Jefferson became extremely concerned about the country's defenses, and especially the need for a naval militia. The United States was unable to man its gunboats, even at Norfolk where anti-British feelings were widespread because of the *Chesapeake* incident. The president believed that the only remedy for the shortage of seamen was "to erect our sea-faring men into a naval militia and subject them to tours of duty in whatever port they may be." Not surprisingly, later that fall Gallatin estimated that the president's proposed naval militia would cost the country about $1.5 million, a hefty sum for Republicans who wanted to eliminate the national debt, yet only a trifling sum in terms of security.[39]

Jefferson brought the question of the naval militia before Congress with his seventh annual message in late October 1807. The gunboats, he said, had already been assigned, in light of the *Chesapeake* disaster, to New York, New Orleans, and the Chesapeake Bay. But the country still needed more, and "for manning these vessels in sudden attacks," the nation's seamen should be formed into a "special militia." This unit, Jefferson argued, would "be called on for tours of duty in defense of the harbors" and work in combination with the land militia to ensure the country's security.[40]

The proposal went to a committee headed by Matthew Clay of Virginia on 16 November 1807. Jefferson understood the reason for the failure of his proposal in 1806, and this time he was wise enough to suggest that the reserve be "confined for the present to *harbor* defense" rather than serve on board seagoing ships. Jefferson believed that this would make the "seamen feel less alarm if [they were] restrained for the present to harbor defense" and ultimately help the bill pass congressional scrutiny. Even though Jefferson gave the impression that he wanted the unit solely for harbor defense, he knew if an emergency occurred that an amended bill allowing seamen to serve aboard seagoing vessels would probably pass. As such, Jefferson optimistically surmised that because the militia reorganization was being proposed "on a better plan" it would have "more probable success."[41]

Poor relations with Great Britain had underscored the need for bolstering the nation's defenses as well as reorganizing the structure of the militia. Jefferson's militia reclassification introduced a simpler system that should have been acceptable to Congress. The bill's ultimate fate, however, was that no vote was ever taken, even though the proposal was debated extensively. Congress instead chose to enlarge the regular army rather than restructure a militia system that most felt was acceptable. Moreover, the general impression was, why fix what was not broken?[42]

Jefferson's proposal for a naval militia was lost along with his general reclassification plan. Congress, however, was not deaf to the need for defense, because it had agreed to increase the number of gunboats. The additional gunboats placed Jefferson and Smith in a predicament because the number of seamen allowed by the navy was limited by Congress to 1,425. Smith reported that 1,277 additional seamen would be needed just to put the remainder of the gunboats into service. Without the naval militia, the administration quickly found that it had to reduce the number of men aboard each gunboat and even discontinue building the craft. This was a sad state of affairs for a country whose professed Republican ideology supported militias and gunboats but whose concern over federal involvement and economics prohibited a proper defense.[43]

Both the dry dock and the naval militia aimed at bolstering the country's defense while at the same time lessening the national debt. But in each case Congress felt that the federal government was assuming too much power and spending too much money. The result was that neither piece of legislation was ever enacted into law, even though both could have been useful.[44]

By viewing these pieces of gunboat-related legislation in retrospect, one can understand the problems Jefferson faced while trying to implement a naval policy. Even though the president was willing to modify his Republican ideology, he found Congress unreceptive. Republicans wanted less government involvement rather than more, even at the expense of national defense. Both the dry dock and the naval militia proposals aimed at enhancing the security of the nation and ultimately reducing expenditures, but neither passed because of Republican as well as Federalist prejudices. Although both ideas were Jefferson's, their fate was the same as that of the gunboats: dependent on congressional action.

6

The Politics of Construction:
Realization of Republican Philosophy

Politics has always played an important role in the development and implementation of naval policy as well as in arms procurement. Jefferson's gunboats were no exception. While gunboats were admittedly intended to be defensive weapons, part of the reason for their popularity was that the policy decision in favor of their construction confirmed the Republican idea of spreading government responsibilities and rewards to those governed. Once Congress made the decision to implement the program, the president and administration defined what designs should be followed and decided the locations for their construction and deployment. Captain David Porter, who understood the ideology of the program, remarked, "I know it is the intention of the government that its benefits should be equally distributed and for this reason our gunboats have been built in different parts of the United States." Despite the congressional rationale for implementing the program, Republican politics and ideology played a decisive role in constructing the final product.[1]

Secretary of the Navy Robert Smith demonstrated the government's desire to become involved in the gunboat program even before the policy was initiated. He had written to Captain Richard Morris in the Mediterranean during the summer of 1802 that "a few gunboats" were essential and that "their practice ought to be a guide to us." Once Congress decided to initiate construction, on 28 February 1803, in the wake of the Spanish closing of the Mississippi River, Smith was ready to commence construction. The month prior to the legislation's passage, Smith had written to John Gavino, American consul at Gibraltar, asking him to procure a model to be forwarded to the navy department. Smith had even asked Captains Samuel Barron, William Bainbridge, and Edward Preble to supervise their construction.

Because the Spanish problem was on the Mississippi River, hundreds of miles away, logistics proved overwhelming. Smith was astute enough, however, to plan for all contingencies. On 24 February 1803, the same day he wrote the captains about building gunboats, he also wrote George Harrison, navy agent at Philadelphia, asking him to buy a map of the western territory, perhaps for surveying possible building locations on the Ohio River.[2]

Smith decided that building gunboats at Pittsburgh, on the headwaters of the Ohio River, would expedite congressional intentions. The location also assured the quickest and easiest delivery of the vessels to the Mississippi because everything necessary for building the craft, except copper sheeting and bolts, could be secured at that location. Because Pittsburgh was obviously the administration's choice, the only remaining question was who would build them.[3]

The secretary asked Harrison to inquire if Eliphalet Beebe would build the gunboats and, if so, under what conditions. Beebe had gained a reputation for skillful workmanship and had recently designed as well as constructed the 100-ton schooner *Amity* and the 270-ton ship-rigged *Pittsburgh* for Tarascon Brothers, James Berthoud and Company. While awaiting Beebe's reply, Smith decided to have advertisements for gunboat contracts placed in the *Pittsburgh Gazette* and other western papers. Before any contracts were extended, the solution to the Spanish problem on the Mississippi rendered an immediate execution of the law unnecessary.[4]

The need for gunboat-type vessels once again became apparent before the end of 1803 due to the *Philadelphia* disaster. Jefferson remarked in his third annual message that gunboats needed to be built "on models most proved by experience." By late December, Smith had written Captains John Rodgers and James Barron (brother of Samuel), directing them to build a gunboat "by way of experiment and as a model." Jefferson realized that even though these were models, supplying names for the vessels would become a problem, should the country launch a serious building program. To remedy the dilemma, he suggested that designating them by number would "be the best way of naming them."[5]

Rodgers's vessel, designated gunboat *No. 1*, was built by master carpenter Peter Gardner at the Washington Navy Yard from materials already present. Although nothing has been found concerning her design, *No. 1* was probably modeled after the gunboats used by Naples. If so, she was probably built of oak and elm, "bound round and sheath'd with pine," 58'6" on the keel, 18'0" beam, with a 4'6" depth. Armed with one 32-pounder and two 6-pound swivel guns, she went into commission in July 1804, but because of her poor sailing qualities she was relegated to harbor duty and ordered under the command of John Lovell to Charleston, South Carolina. Jefferson wanted to send the vessel to New Orleans to prevent smuggling and to counter an armed Spanish schooner on Lake Borgne. But misfortune struck *No. 1* in September 1804, when a "dreadful storm" tore the vessel from her moorings and left her in a cornfield on Whitemarsh Island, eight miles from Charleston. Even though she was refloated by the first of November, the incident of *No. 1* left the gunboat program open to ridicule by the opposition.[6]

"Stephen Decatur Boarding the Tripolitan Gunboat" during the U.S. Navy bombardment of Tripoli, 3 August 1804. Portrait by Dennis Malone Carter. Photo courtesy of the Naval Historical Center.

James Barron considered building gunboat *No. 2* in Virginia at either Gosport, Portsmouth, or Norfolk, but after surveying his choices he instead picked Hampton. *No. 2*, built under the direction of George Hope, was launched in August 1804 and ordered under the command of John B.

Cordis to the Charleston-Savannah area to enforce health and revenue laws as well as to suppress piracy. Armed with a 32-pounder and several swivel guns, she was probably 64'5" between the perpendiculars, had a 16'10" molded beam, and was about 6'6" deep in the hold. The vessel was originally rigged with a lateen sail, had a copper-sheathed hull, copper fasteners, and a bowsprit and jib. Because of the position of the cannon, the bowsprit had to be placed higher on the stem so that the gun could be raised for firing. Before *No. 2* crossed the Atlantic to join the Mediterranean squadron in 1805, she was rerigged as a yawl (a two-mast, fore-and-aft rig, with a large mainmast). After serving with the squadron, she returned home in 1806 and was placed in ordinary for a time before being lost in a storm in 1811 off the Georgia coast, killing all but one man.[7]

Because the first two vessels were to serve only as an illustration of what a gunboat actually was, Rodgers and Barron were directed not to "be fettered by particular instructions as to model, dimensions, or kind of timber." The only requirement was that the boat should carry one long 32-pound cannon. The navy department's lack of instructions resulted in various design inconsistencies in the early vessels, with each usually reflecting the supervisor's preferences. Jefferson and Smith did not interfere in the design of the first models because they wanted the vessels readied "as expeditiously as possible" and "to see them finished before we order any."[8]

The difficulties Preble encountered in the Mediterranean during the spring of 1804 required immediate action, and Jefferson authorized the captain, even before completion of the American models, to rent or borrow as many gunboats as he needed. But Preble had problems acquiring the craft. First he applied unsuccessfully to the French government for vessels at Marseilles and Toulon before finding out that the Neapolitan government was willing to lend gunboats "to serve against the Common Enemy Tripoli." Even after Preble discovered he could acquire the craft from Messina, he found out that he could not obtain artillery unless it was from Genoa or Venice. Despite the problems, six gunboats, numbered *1* to *6*, were finally equipped and readied, and the American flag hoisted on the craft at 10:00 A.M. on 30 May 1804. On 14 July, the craft sailed for Tripoli, becoming the first gunboats employed by the American navy. They served until October 1804, when they were returned to the Neapolitan government.[9]

The gunboats Preble acquired reflected the type of shallow-draft vessels deployed extensively throughout the Mediterranean. Each weighing about twenty-five tons, the gunboats' official dimensions were 58'6" on the keel, 18'0" on the beam, with 4'6" depth. They were flat bottomed and, according to Preble, did "not sail or row even tolerably well." They "were never intended to go to sea," as they were designed for shallow coastal waters. Furthermore, each of the single-masted craft was rigged with a lateen sail and a jib, armed with a French 24-pounder mounted in the bow, and manned by 40 Neapolitan sailors.[10]

The Messina gunboats performed admirably during their short tenure with the American navy. In early August 1804, the six craft participated in a successful raid on Tripoli in which the American vessels chased nine Tripolitan gunboats into the coastal shoals. In the bloody battle that followed, American seamen boarded and captured three Tripolitan gunboats (later, numbers 7, 8, and 9 in the American service) killed seventeen, wounded four, and captured three while losing only one marine. Less than a year earlier the American fleet had suffered a terrible setback because the country had no shallow-draft vessels.[11]

Jefferson and Smith decided, even before Preble's fleet demonstrated the importance of the shallow-draft vessels, to continue the gunboat program. During June and July, eight contracts were issued to build vessels at Philadelphia, Washington, Baltimore, New York, Boston, and Charleston. Although the contracts were to be spread throughout the country, the first gunboats were built on the Atlantic seaboard because of the presence of "navy agents, skilful superintendents and experienced naval constructors." But once a satisfactory model was approved, the administration planned to "have some built upon the Western Waters."[12]

Numbers 3 through 10 were designed by the newly appointed "Head Ship Carpenter and Navy Constructor," Josiah Fox. In May 1804, Fox, regarded by Robert Smith as "a scientific as well as practical man, [who] stands high among the first in his profession," replaced William Doughty as naval contractor at the Washington Navy Yard. The following month, he prepared the basic plans for the next eight gunboats. Fox's first set of drawings was for a shallow-draft vessel intended for the waters of the Mississippi River–Gulf of Mexico region.[13]

Fox's first design for a gunboat probably served as the model for No. 3, built by Nathaniel Hutton at Philadelphia. She was contracted to Messrs. Hutton on 20 July 1804 for $2,500, even though her final cost ($5,838) was more than double the original estimate. Fashioned as a double ender, her design allowed for moving the rudder from stern to bow, so she could be rowed, using 50 ash oars 25 to 27 feet in length, or sailed in either direction. Armed with a long cannon on each end, she measured 71'0" between the perpendiculars, had an 18'0" molded beam, $4'8\frac{1}{2}"$ depth in the hold, and was launched on 3 December 1804. No. 3 was obviously designed for coastal shoals, as she was fitted with bilge keels and rigged as a yawl similar to *No. 2*. Because of the design, she was probably better suited for rowing in shoal waters than for sailing, thus enforcing Jefferson's idea of coastal defense. [14]

Fox's second design probably governed the construction of *No. 4*, contracted for on 28 June 1804, at the Washington Navy Yard. The main difference between this vessel and *No. 3* was that Fox had added nine and one-half additional inches of depth to *No. 4*. The deeper draft made her more seaworthy and allowed her to carry two 32-pound guns. The new design also left the interior of the vessel to the preference of the supervisor, thus contributing to the various models. *No. 4* was launched on 5 March 1805, and it proceeded to the Mediterranean to join the American squadron. [15]

Gunboat *No. 5*, contracted for on 24 July 1804, was built by William Price at Baltimore. It was to be partially based on Fox's design, and the head ship carpenter even traveled to Baltimore to oversee the equipping and placement of guns. The vessel had a copper-sheathed hull and copper fittings — 2,600 pounds altogether. Originally rigged with a lateen sail on a single mast that "was fixed exactly in the center amidship," she was armed with two 32-pound guns before leaving Hampton Roads for the Mediterranean on 15 May 1805. [16]

Lieutenant J. T. Leonard and Naval Agent John Beekman were supervisors of gunboats *No. 6* and *No. 7*, contracted for at New York on 7 July 1804. They, too, were based on Fox's models and were estimated to cost $5,077 each. Robert Smith advised the supervisors that Fox's plans should be closely adhered to. The interiors, however, were left to the discretion of the supervisors with the exception "that the magazine should be placed about midship, as the safest and most convenient place." Moreover, they were to have two masts rigged with lateen sails, even though *No. 6* was probably the only one completed as such. Both were launched in early February 1805 with two 32-pound guns and dispatched to the Mediterranean in May to join the American squadron. [17]

The fates of gunboats *No. 6* and *No. 7* in the Mediterranean were most interesting. Both vessels initially had trouble filling their complements and ultimately were forced to use men from the ship *John Adams*. *No. 7*, launched on 6 February 1805, departed for the Mediterranean under the command of Lieutenant W. P. S. Ogilvie. Less than a week out, *No. 7* damaged her mast and was forced to return to New York for repairs. On 20 June, she renewed her voyage, only to be "never heard of again" — lost with all hands. According to the official records she was "supposed to have foundered." [18]

Gunboat *No. 6*, commanded by Lieutenant James Lawrence, was only a little more fortunate. She arrived at Gibraltar in early summer yet, while off the coast of Cadiz, Spain, was detained by the British ships *Tenedos* and *Dreadnought*. While Lawrence was below deck with British officers, three of his seamen declared themselves English subjects and jumped aboard the *Dreadnought* before they could be stopped. Lawrence protested and demanded their return, but to no avail. The unfortunate incident prompted Commodore Rodgers to issue an order directing his officers not to allow their vessels to be detained, nor men taken, unless the craft was surrendered. Even though her fate was not that of *No 7*, she had still suffered considerable humiliation.[19]

Gunboat *No. 8* was contracted for on 24 July 1804 at Boston for $308 per ton. Built under the superintendancy of Sam Brown, she was supposedly built on Fox's second plan: copper fastened and sheathed. Robert Smith sent a plan for the original rigging in December 1804, but the drawings were changed in spring 1805 so that all "the gunboats should be rigged as nearly alike as may be convenient" to sail across the Atlantic. Armed with two 32-pound cannons, she was launched on 24 April 1805.[20]

The most interesting of the early gunboats was *No. 9*, built at Charleston, South Carolina, by Paul Pritchard. The vessel was built on Fox's double-ender model but with slight modifications approved by the secretary of the navy. Supervisors Nathaniel Fanning and William Smith, Sr., had the vessel enlarged so that she measured 71'0" between the perpendiculars, 21'0" in extreme beam, and 6'2½" in the hold. The revisions, which added three feet to the beam and eighteen inches to the depth, made the vessel more seaworthy. She was rigged as a fore-and-aft ketch, square sterned with a rudder at both ends, armed with one 32-pound gun, coppered, with a false keel later added. This vessel, launched on 4 March 1805, was distinctly different than the previous eight gunboats, leading Fanning to remark "that she [was] the most faithful built ... [gun]boat of any one [he had] yet seen." Furthermore, he believed this vessel would "be more *formidable*, strike more *dread* upon the enemy," and be "an acquisition to our squadron highly invaluable ... against the Tripolitans."[21]

The last gunboat contracted for in 1804 was built at the Washington Navy Yard by Fox. *No. 10*, ordered the same day as *No. 4*, was probably based on the builder's second model. Armed with a 32-pound cannon, it was launched on 30 April 1805 and proceeded, with *Nos. 5, 6, 7, 8*, and *9*, to the Mediterranean. Before they sailed, they were modified with false keels, a rudder that extended two feet below the keel, and a yawl rig to improve their sailing qualities. The changes were obviously for practical reasons, as the innovations were made so the vessels could sail across the Atlantic and fulfill a political role for which they had not originally been designed. None of these vessels saw combat in the Mediterranean because they arrived after the conflict had ended.[22]

Although the vessels were proposed for defense, Robert Smith wrote that "the result of the experiment cannot but give pleasure to every honest American." The secretary knew that "the Great desideratum ... [was] to prepare them well for fighting" because they were for defense, and sailing qualities were secondary. Their lack of sailing qualities was demonstrated by their having to stow their guns below deck during the transatlantic crossing. But the vessels' arrival at Gibraltar before the ship *John Adams*, despite severe weather, prompted Smith to remark that the vessels had "proven themselves ... [as] good sailers."[23]

On 2 March 1805, Congress passed a bill appropriating $60,000 for the construction of twenty-five additional gunboats "for the better protection of the ports and harbors of the United States." Jefferson signed this act even though the ten vessels already contracted for had not proved themselves: seven had been launched, three were still under construction, and none had seen action. The twenty-five provided by the March 1805 act, combined with ten of the fifteen built under auspices of the February 1803 act, would provide the United States with a respectable gunboat force, which in the spring of 1805 was especially needed at New York and New Orleans.[24]

The president wrote to DeWitt Clinton, mayor of New York City, in January 1805, expressing concern over the city's lack of defense. "Of the ... gunboats now built or building," Jefferson wrote, "we have always destined a full proportion to New York." Knowing full well that Clinton preferred harbor fortifications, the president tried to placate the mayor's fears by claiming that "nothing beyond [sending gunboats] is in the power of the executive," as building fortifications was left to the discretion of the state. The navy department, however, did grant two contracts on 15 March 1805 to build two vessels in the Northeast, one at Portland, Massachusetts, (later to be in the state of Maine) and the other at Newburyport, Massachusetts. Once completed, both could join the other vessels assigned to defend New York or other seaport towns.[25]

The contract for gunboat *No. 11* was granted to Nathaniel Dyer at Portland by Republican naval Captain Edward Preble. Preble had, with the help of Jacob Coffin during May and June 1805, drawn five gunboat designs for smaller, less costly, harbor or riverine boats. *No. 11*, based on Preble's second design, was 66'0" between the perpendiculars, had an

18'6" molded beam, and was 5'9" in the hold. Preble refused to copper the vessel's bottom, and instead sheathed it with half-inch spruce boards, which he considered cheaper, as easy to careen, and enough protection against worms. Rigged as a schooner, and armed with two 24-pound guns and two $5\frac{1}{2}$" brass howitzers, *No. 11* was ready to be launched by 24 October 1805. Preble instead allowed the vessel to remain on the stocks throughout the winter of 1805–6 so the timber would be seasoned before she went in the water on 1 May 1806.[26]

The second vessel Preble contracted for was *No. 12*, built at Newburyport, Massachusetts, by Jacob Coffin. Coffin, a master builder on the Merrimack River, had been recommended to Preble by Ebenezer Stocker, a Newburyport merchant who had directed the captain's financial affairs since the 1790s. Based on Fox's design for *No. 4*, she was 67'8" between the perpendiculars and had a 19'3" molded beam and a depth of 5'4". *No. 12*, a schooner rigged aft and armed with two 24-pound cannon and two 24-pound brass carronades, was launched on 24 May 1806 and sent to New Orleans. She served on the New Orleans station until she was condemned shortly before the War of 1812.[27]

One of Jefferson's major concerns was defending the gateway to the Mississippi. The president felt that because "the position of New Orleans destines it to be the greatest city the world has ever seen," the port should have an adequate gunboat defense. The navy department had, within two months of the March 1805 gunboat appropriation, awarded contracts to build twelve of the twenty-five vessels. Of those twelve, ten were to be built at Cincinnati and Marietta, Ohio, and at Louisville and Eddyville, Kentucky. All ten were meant for the defense of the Crescent City.[28]

Kentucky and Ohio were logical choices for building gunboats destined for New Orleans. Not only was the Ohio River a major tributary of the Mississippi, allowing quick delivery of the vessels, but the two states were also overwhelmingly Republican. Ohio's single representative and her two senators were all Republicans, and the state had cast all three of its electoral votes for Jefferson in 1804. Kentucky, a more populous state, with over 221,000 people, was represented by six legislators and two senators, all Republicans. Like Ohio, Kentucky's eight electoral votes had also been cast for Jefferson in 1804.[29]

The two states served as the locations for building gunboats *No. 13* through *No. 22*, which were ordered in April and May 1805. Robert Smith issued contracts for craft to be built under the supervision of General Henry Carberry, navy agent for the two states. Contracts went to Senator John Smith of Cincinnati, Ohio, for gunboats *Nos. 13, 14, 17,* and *18*; to Congressman Matthew Lyon of Eddyville, Kentucky, for *Nos.*

15 and *16*; to John Jordan of Lexington, Kentucky, for *Nos. 19* and *20* and to Edward Tupper of Marietta, Ohio, for *Nos. 21* and *22.* Although Smith issued the contracts, he expressed concern that the builders' lack of experience in constructing and equipping gunboats would result in the vessels being too expensive and not completed on time.[30]

The western gunboats generally followed Fox's standard design, even though there is reason to believe that Preble's plans were also consulted. The craft probably had a 60'0" keel, an 18'6" beam, and a 5'0" hold. Armed with two 24-pounders, they were sloop-rigged and equipped with two 700-pound anchors, a sixteen-foot boat, a spare set of masts and spars, and a 100-pound kedge used to pull the vessels off sandbars.[31]

Although Lyon's boats were sent to New Orleans by the beginning of 1806, Smith's fears about the excessive amount of time to complete their construction were well founded because the others did not arrive until late spring. Furthermore, when the vessels did arrive, John Shaw, commander of the New Orleans flotilla, found that they were extremely "rough" and built out of unseasoned poplar. Their poor construction prompted Shaw to remark that he would rather "build them [himself] from the keel, *if every material was at hand,*" than repair the western vessels.[32]

By January 1806, Congress had allocated funds for forty gunboats, even though only twenty-two had been constructed. The balance of money unexpended under the two acts was used to build four bomb vessels, the *Etna, Vesuvius, Spitfire*, and *Vengeance*. Jefferson knew that additional gunboats were needed to "secure our seaports from hostile attacks." His remedy, suggested in his annual message of 3 December 1805, was to build a "considerable" number of gunboats "to place our seaport towns out of the danger of insult." Congress responded to Jefferson's plea by authorizing fifty more vessels during April 1806. These vessels, the president believed, would "place our harbors in a situation to maintain peace and order within them."[33]

During the spring of 1806, Smith sent out a number of circular letters asking terms from those who had contacted the department and expressed interest in building large gunboats with a 60'0" keel, 16'6" beam, and 6'6" depth, as well as smaller models with a 55'0" keel, 17'0" beam, and 4- to 6-foot depth. Smith had also written to naval officers, asking for ideas "as to the construction and equipment of gunboats upon the most *economical* plan for *harbor service merely*." Smith did not intend these vessels to be used on the open seas but rather to protect the country's shore lines.[34]

"Every disposition exists with us," Jefferson wrote, "to distribute the advantages of public employment." Those benefits allowed by the fifty gunboat contracts, authorized during the spring of 1806, were distributed to eight states and the District of Columbia. The New England states, which were generally divided evenly among Republicans, neutrals, and Federalists during the Ninth Congress, were granted contracts for seventeen vessels, four in both Connecticut and Rhode Island, and nine in Portland, Massachusetts, and its environs. Thirteen contracts were granted to Jefferson's home state of Virginia, which was overwhelmingly Republican. The western Republican states of Ohio and Kentucky received contracts for another five vessels. Predominantly Republican New York obtained contracts to build twelve craft. One was built at the Washington Navy Yard, and Captain John Rodgers supervised one gunboat built at Havre d'Grace, Maryland, to replace the original *No. 7*, which had been lost at sea. Of the fifty allowed under the law, contracts for forty-eight were distributed throughout the country.[35]

Gunboats *Nos. 23* to *28*, built on Fox's design, were constructed on the western waters. John Connell and Peter Mills received a contract for one vessel, *No. 23*, to be built on the Kanawha River at Charleston, Virginia, (later West Virginia). Although this vessel was built in the West, it was a contract actually awarded to Jefferson's home state. Thomas Reagan built *No. 24* at Cincinnati, while Congressman Matthew Lyon received a contract for three additional vessels, *Nos. 25, 26,* and *27*, to be constructed at Eddyville, Kentucky. Lyon's vessels were probably built by someone other than the congressman, as the contracts were sublet to such builders as Thomas Vail of Marietta. All the western vessels seemed to have been completed during 1807–8, were armed with two 24-pounders, and were sent to New Orleans.[36]

Because of the poor construction of the western-built vessels, they were the last gunboats built on the Ohio. Smith informed General Carberry, in November 1806, that "the President has determined that he will build no more" gunboats in the West. The official reasoning was that it was impractical for one agent to supervise the building of so many vessels at so many different places. And even though Carberry had, as Smith charged, "done well," the vessels did not meet the standards that naval commanders in New Orleans wanted. It was ironic, but the predominantly Republican West, which was so supportive of the gunboat program, did not reap any more of its benefits, whereas New England did.[37]

Massachusetts benefited most from the 1806 appropriation. Perhaps this was because of Henry Dearborn, the secretary of war, or because of the influence Jacob Crowninshield exerted in Congress. More likely, since the state had more ports than all the other states together, it was a calculated plan to help the Republican party overcome entrenched Federalists in the state. In any case, Crowninshield had become a Jefferson stalwart, and the president had rewarded him for his service by offering him, which Crowninshield refused, the position of secretary of the navy when Smith was confirmed to fill the post of attorney general. The traditionally Federalist state had even awarded its 19 electoral votes to Jefferson in 1804.

Upon receiving the Massachusetts contracts from the navy department, Captain Preble contracted gunboats *Nos. 29* through *31* to William Moulton, Jr., and *Nos. 32, 33,* and *37* to Eleazer Higgins, both of Portland. Ephraim Hunt and Robert Giveen of Brunswick were given a contract to build *Nos. 34* through *36.* These vessels were completed to specifications (with hulls, masts, and spars) by November 1806, but due to the navy department's lack of money, they remained on the stocks under "awnings," and "in constant repair and fine order" until the following spring.[38]

Stephen Decatur, Jr., and Captain Isaac Hull served as the supervisors for gunboats *Nos. 38* through *45,* contracted for in August and September 1806. Decatur had initiated the process by soliciting proposals for builders in Connecticut and Rhode Island before he was replaced by Isaac Hull on 24 July. The resultant contracts were granted for eight vessels, of which four were to be built in each state. It was interesting that contracts were granted to these states because neither was overwhelmingly Republican. Rhode Island did, however, usually vote the Republican position, but the Connecticut vote was always uncertain because of the makeup of her delegation. On the one hand, she had such prominent Federalists as Samuel W. Dana, John Cotton Smith and Theodore Dwight, and such neutrals as Benjamin Tallmadge. Postmaster General Gideon Granger, a close friend of Jefferson's, hailed from the state. Yet Connecticut had cast her nine electoral votes for Charles C. Pinckney and the Federalist party in 1804. The rationale for the contracts is puzzling, but it was probably part of a calculated plan to enhance the Republican power within the region.[39]

Vessels *Nos. 38* through *41* were contracted to William Van Deursen at Middletown, Connecticut, on 1 September 1806. Van Deursen agreed to build hulls, 55'0" between the perpendiculars, 17'0" molded beam, and 4'6" depth, for $1,750 apiece. Contracts for gunboats *Nos. 42* through *45* were granted by Stephen Decatur to Benjamin Marble at Newport, and John Glacier at Greenwich, Rhode Island. These vessels, based on Preble's model, were to be 56'0" between the perpendiculars, 17'0" molded beam, and 4'6" in depth, and were contracted for on 15 August

1806. All of these vessels were completed and ordered to New York in July of the following year.[40]

A number of young shipbuilders in New York received contracts to build gunboats during the summer of 1806. Captain Charles Stewart issued contracts to Adam and Noah Brown for vessels *Nos. 46* through *49*, to Henry Eckford and Lester Beebe for *Nos. 50* through *53*, and to Christian Bergh for *Nos. 54* through *57*. Although New York had a contingent of Federalist and neutral congressmen, she was generally in the Republican fold, and her importance had been rewarded in 1804 when Jefferson chose New Yorker George Clinton as his vice-presidential candidate. Furthermore, New York's importance could not be ignored, as she was one of the most populous states, had the largest city in the country, and had cast all her 19 electoral votes for Jefferson in 1804.[41]

Captain Charles Stewart served as supervisor of gunboats *Nos. 46* through *57*. The vessels were designed by Christian Bergh and built in New York. Modeled for sailing rather than rowing, the vessels were 47'4" on the keel, had 18'0" molded beam, and were 5'6" in the hold. They were armed with either a 24- or a 32-pound cannon with 12-pound carronades on the sides, and were rigged as two-masted schooners without jibs. These gunboats were designed especially for New York's deepwater harbor and appear to be the only vessels built that took into account local operating conditions. Nevertheless, they upheld Jefferson's idea of harbor defense.[42]

The last twelve craft contracted for under the 1806 authorization were distributed throughout Virginia. George Hope of Hampton received a contract for vessels *Nos. 58* and *59*, while John Pool and Richard Servant, also from the same town, built *Nos. 60* and *61*. Contracts for *Nos. 62* through *65* were granted to John Patterson and Hunley Gayle of Matthews County, Virginia, on the Chesapeake Bay. Last, John and Joseph Forster of Portsmouth received the contract for vessels *Nos. 66* through *69*. Contracted for on 23 and 28 July 1806, all were built on Samuel Barron's plan of the same year, with a keel of 56'0", a molded beam of 16'6", and a depth of 6'6". The vessels' hulls, contracted for $1800, were to be completed by 1 May 1807.[43]

Jefferson knew that the forty-eight vessels being built were needed throughout the country, and in many respects the contracts had been planned accordingly. Those constructed in the West were destined for New Orleans to bring stability to the southern region, while those built on the Atlantic coast were ordered to Charleston, New York, and the Chesapeake Bay. Smith and Jefferson quickly found that even though the country had seventy craft completed or under construction, due to limited appropriations not all the vessels could be equipped and outfitted. But they could be placed under protective covering and brought out, manned, and equipped when needed, following the militia principle. [44]

The second session of the Ninth Congress did not produce legislation for additional gunboats. In fact, no more contracts were dispersed before December 1807. Although many within Congress had wanted further appropriations, none was forthcoming during the winter session of 1806–7. More importantly, the session did generate Jefferson's plan concerning distribution of the craft.

Jefferson responded to a House request of 5 February 1807 with a detailed exposition of the number of gunboats needed for the protection of the country. To afford the ports from New Orleans to Maine "a due measure of protection," Jefferson, after consulting his cabinet, believed that the country needed 200 gunboats assigned to stations throughout the country. Jefferson maintained that New Orleans and the Mississippi River needed 40, the Savannah and Charleston area 25, the Chesapeake Bay 20, the Delaware Bay and River 15, while both New York and the Boston and northward harbors needed 50 each. But Congress did not agree on the need, and the session produced no legislation for additional vessels. [45]

By the summer of 1807, only twenty-two of the country's vessels were ready for service. Jefferson's desire that the nation's ports and harbors be defended by sizable flotillas ready for action was not realized because no port had as many vessels as the president believed necessary, and even fewer vessels were ready for service. New Orleans, for example, had ten vessels, only four of which were ready for service; New York, fourteen, of which only two were ready for action. Even though most of the vessels could be outfitted and made ready for sea in ten to fifteen days, the country was still pitifully unprepared, as the *Chesapeake* incident of 22 June demonstrated. [46]

During June and July, Jefferson met with his cabinet to find a solution for the *Chesapeake* dilemma. The country demanded war and the president could have had it, but instead he called Congress into an early session in late October 1807. While preparing for the ensuing session, Jefferson and Smith began behind-the-scenes plans to provide for the nation's defense. Smith sent out letters to naval agents in New York, South Carolina, Maryland, Virginia, Pennsylvania, and North Carolina, informing them that because the president judged it expedient to construct more gunboats for harbor and port protection, they should be prepared to contract for additional vessels. [47]

Many concerns ran through Jefferson's mind as he prepared his seventh annual message. Jefferson, Dearborn, and Smith tried to make the country as safe as possible while remaining within the bounds of presidential prerogative. Gunboats in the Chesapeake Bay were put on alert, plans were drawn up detailing what the country would need to do in case of an offensive or defensive war, and the president entertained Thomas Paine's ideas of modifying gunboats by putting two cannons in their bows. But Jefferson well knew that building additional gunboats was "left to the wisdom of the Legislature."[48]

Congress, deciding during December that Jefferson's plea for more gunboats was reasonable, overwhelmingly passed an appropriation for an additional 188 vessels. By mid-January, Jefferson had encountered a serious obstacle. Congress may have been willing to appropriate money for construction, but it was unwilling to increase the number of sailors for manning such vessels. Because of this impasse, Jefferson and the administration had to limit the number of vessels being built during 1808 to 100, rather than the 188 as allowed by law.[49]

Records in the navy department indicate that 107 of the 188 vessels authorized by the December 1807 appropriation were actually constructed. The contracts for these craft were distributed to Massachusetts, Rhode Island, New York, Connecticut, Pennsylvania, Maryland, Virginia, North and South Carolina, as well as the District of Columbia. Although few contracts have survived, navy department letters indicate that the vessels were designed and constructed according to plans that emphasized political motivations. Robert Smith wrote to Captain Alexander Murray that the vessels were to be built for fighting, with sailing characteristics a secondary consideration. Furthermore, because they were for fighting, Smith contended that they should be sloop-rigged with a gun in the bow rather than schooner-rigged and a gun amidships. This gave the appearance that they were being designed to defend the home ports against future *Chesapeake*-like incidents.[50]

Gunboats *Nos. 70* through *78* were constructed at the Washington Navy Yard under the watchful eye of Thomas Tingey. Smith wanted to build the vessels there because he knew there was "small timber not fit for the repair of the frigates" which could be used for the gunboats. Work began in February and most were ready to be launched by the following November.[51]

The supervisor for vessels *Nos. 79* through *88* was Captain William Bainbridge, who preferred to have the craft schooner-rigged rather than sloop-rigged, as Smith had ordered. Contracted for on 30 December 1807, they were built by David Green at Portland and were armed with either a 24- or 32-pound cannon. Although most were ready to be launched by May 1808, they remained on the stocks due to a lack of money and men.[52]

Supervisor Isaac Hull issued contracts in Rhode Island and Connecticut for four vessels. *Nos. 89* and *90*, contracted for on 9 January 1808 for $4,000 dollars apiece, were built by Amos Cross on Pawcatuck River at Westerly, Rhode Island. They were sloop-rigged, as Smith had ordered, and armed with two guns. *Nos. 91* and *92*, also contracted on 9 January, were built by Elisha Tracy on the Thames River at Norwich, Connecticut, along the same lines and for the same price as the Rhode Island boats.[53]

Twenty-three gunboats were contracted for at New York by Commodore John Rodgers. The officer chose Henry Eckford and Lester Beebe to build five, Christian Bergh five, Charles Browne five, Adam and Noah Brown five, Robert Jenkins two, and Thomas Bell one. Rodgers contracted for the vessels' hulls at $2,600 each during the period mid-January to late April. *Nos. 93* through *115* were built at New York, at Hudson, and at Schanks, Long Island, and measured 45'0" keel, 16'0" molded beam, and either 4'6" or 4'9" depth. Armed with 32-pound cannons, most were completed within three months of the date of the contract but were allowed to remain on the stocks so that they should "be well done."[54]

Nos. 116 through *135* were built in Philadelphia, Pennsylvania, under the superintendency of Alexander Murray. Contracted in December 1807, all but seven of the twenty vessels were built at the Philadelphia Navy Yard. All adhered to the general specifications, even though some were built outside the navy yard. They apparently measured 50'4" between the perpendiculars, had 17'0" molded beams, and were 4'6" in the hold, sloop-rigged, armed with two 24- or 32-pounders, and intended to protect the Delaware Bay.[55]

Contracts for ten gunboats were issued to William Price and others at Baltimore, Maryland. *Nos. 136* through *145* were built according to Barron's plan, with a 60'0" deck, 16'6" beam, and 6'6" depth. It appears that *143* was built on smaller dimensions, as it had a 51'0" deck, 17'6" beam, and 4'2" draft. Contracted for in January 1808 under the superintendency of Master-Commandant Sam Evans, these vessels were probably sloop-rigged and armed with one or two 24- or 32-pound cannon.[56]

Nos. 146 to *155* were also contracted for in January 1808 but were built under the superintendency of Stephen Decatur. The craft were actually constructed by Theodore Armistead at Norfolk and were apparently ready to be launched by late spring 1808. Although no plans for these vessels have been located, it is presumed they followed either Barron's, Fox's, or Preble's designs. In any case, the vessels were to be protected on the stocks by awnings before they were launched.[57]

Navy Agent Nathaniel Ingraham and Son (consisting of James Marsh and Francis Saltus) was granted a contract on 13 February 1808 for gunboats *Nos. 155* through *165*. It was surprising that Robert Smith agreed to build vessels at Charleston, for in September 1806 he had refused because he felt the price for construction was too expensive. In 1808, however, the city did gain an opportunity to reap the benefits of a government contract. Marsh, originally from Philadelphia, had estab-lished a shipyard in South Carolina, gained a reputation as one of the region's leading builders, and was responsible for building five of the vessels. Saltus built the remaining five at Beaufort, South Carolina, according to Barron's plan. They measured 56'0" on the keel, 16'6" on the beam, 6'6" in the hold, and were sheathed with copper to "prevent the worm," which was prevalent in warmer waters. The state of South Carolina petitioned the government for additional ship contracts during 1813.[58]

In the aftermath of the *Chesapeake* disaster, pleas from the citizens of Wilmington persuaded Smith that the port needed protection. It was surprising that petitions from the people were able to achieve what a congressman could not. In January 1808, Smith informed North Carolina Republican Congressman William Blackledge that a vessel the legislator had suggested for the navy was too large and expensive for the gunboat service. While Smith rejected the congressman's suggestion in March 1808, he issued a contract to Amos Perry for gunboats *Nos. 166* (renamed *Alligator* during the War of 1812), *167*, and *168*, to be constructed at Smithville on the Cape Fear River, near Wilmington. The vessels, built under the superintendency of Navy Agent General Benjamin Smith, were supposedly assembled with a 60'0" deck, 16'6" beam, and 6'6" depth. Perry took the liberty to provide the craft with two 6-pound guns and a schooner rig, rather than the sloop rig the secretary of the navy had ordered. As the craft were nearing completion, Thomas Gautier wrote to the secretary of the navy that the gunboats "constructed here ... [are] superior to the rest of their class," with a probable duration of twenty to twenty-five years.[59]

Although the North Carolina gunboats were contracted for in March 1808, they were not completed until the summer of 1809, and they were not launched until 1811. The reasons for the delays were numerous, including lack of money and the necessity that the materials for the vessels be supplied by Commandant Tingey from the Washington Navy Yard. The setbacks delayed the launch of gunboat *166* until 1 April 1809, and then she was placed in ordinary by 30 May, less than two months later. Gunboat *167*, completed in October 1809, and *168* also suffered the same fate, as they too were placed in ordinary shortly after their completion.[60]

During the summer of 1808, contracts were issued to build four vessels on Lakes Champlain and Ontario. Two small gunboats for Champlain were contracted for on 22 July by John Winaus for $2,450 each, while Eckford and Bergh agreed, on 26 July 1808, to build two large 220-ton gunboats to be delivered to the government before 1 April 1809. The numbers of these craft and whether they were completed is unknown.[61]

No contracts can be found for the four remaining vessels, yet government records indicate that 177 of the 257 gunboats appropriated for were eventually built. That total is misleading although accurate. In the summer of 1809, the navy department recorded that 176 vessels had been constructed. But if one includes the original gunboat *No. 7,* which was lost at sea, then the total was 177.

Perhaps even the administration was confused about how many gunboats the country possessed. Robert Smith wrote to the president before leaving office in 1809 that the country had only 171 vessels. Paul Hamilton, Smith's successor at the navy department, stated in May 1809 that the nation had 170 gunboats. Two weeks later he reported that the country had built 176 vessels. The navy department's records indicate that soon thereafter the number of gunboats began to dwindle. Hamilton reported in December 1810 that the country had only 142 vessels and by February 1814 the number had been reduced to 125.[62]

What becomes apparent in the gunboat program is that the construction and design of the vessels was based upon political choices. The original vessels built for harbor protection were modified so they could fulfill policy objectives in the Mediterranean. Later vessels were built along the Atlantic coast or in the interior, depending upon where the government felt the threat lay. Those built on the Ohio River could easily make the voyage down the Mississippi to New Orleans. Those built along the seaboard could easily move to points of trouble when needed, and their designs generally reflected their prospective duties.

Another point supporting the conclusion that the vessels were part of a political policy rather than solely a naval program was that the construction of these vessels was distributed throughout the country. Moreover, they provided obvious advantages in the form of political patronage that ultimately benefited most of the country. In the end, contracts were issued to eleven of the seventeen states and the District of Columbia, and distributed throughout New England, as well as the middle, southern, and western states.

Distribution of
Gunboat Contracts

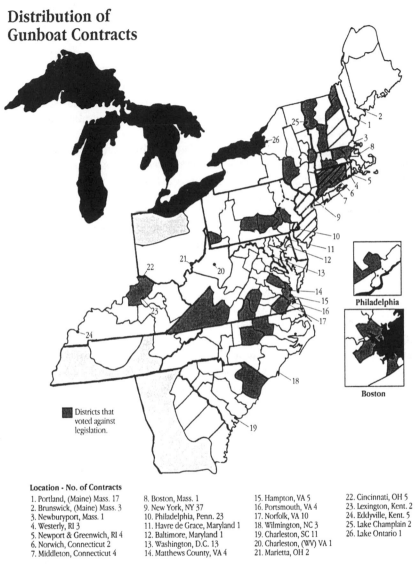

Philadelphia

Boston

Districts that voted against legislation.

Location - No. of Contracts

1. Portland, (Maine) Mass. 17
2. Brunswick, (Maine) Mass. 3
3. Newburyport, Mass. 1
4. Westerly, RI 3
5. Newport & Greenwich, RI 4
6. Norwich, Connecticut 2
7. Middleton, Connecticut 4

8. Boston, Mass. 1
9. New York, NY 37
10. Philadelphia, Penn. 23
11. Havre de Grace, Maryland 1
12. Baltimore, Maryland 1
13. Washington, D.C. 13
14. Matthews County, VA 4

15. Hampton, VA 5
16. Portsmouth, VA 4
17. Norfolk, VA 10
18. Wilmington, NC 3
19. Charleston, SC 11
20. Charleston, (WV) VA 1
21. Marietta, OH 2

22. Cincinnati, OH 5
23. Lexington, Kent. 2
24. Eddyville, Kent. 5
25. Lake Champlain 2
26. Lake Ontario 1

Distribution of Gunboat Contracts

The only states that apparently did not receive contracts were Vermont, New Hampshire, New Jersey, Delaware, Georgia, and Tennessee. There is a possibility that because some of the contracts are unaccounted for, some of these states did in fact receive contracts. The boats built on Lake Champlain, for example, could have been constructed in Vermont. That possibility is strengthened if one considers that of Vermont's six congressmen, five were faithful Republicans and one, James Fisk, was a friendly neutral. Furthermore, the state had cast all six electoral votes for Jefferson in 1804.

New Hampshire, on the other hand, was a different story. It is possible, but highly improbable, that the state received gunboat contracts. Although her seven electoral votes were cast for Jefferson in 1804, they went to the Federalist party in 1808. Moreover, her congressional delegation was unfriendly at best. Adding to the improbability was that her primary shipbuilding location (Portsmouth) was only some twenty miles from Newburyport, Massachusetts, and about fifty miles from Portland, both of which received numerous gunboat contracts.[63]

Of the middle states, only New Jersey and Delaware did not reap the benefits of contracts. New Jersey may have benefited from contracts issued to Pennsylvania because some of the vessels were built outside the navy yard at Philadelphia. While the state was generally neutral with only one stalwart Republican, she had cast all eight of her electoral votes for Jefferson in 1804 and would do the same for Madison in 1808. Delaware was another story. Of her three congressmen, her two senators were both staunch Federalists while her single representative was neutral at best. Her three electoral votes had also been cast for the Federalist party in 1800, as well as in 1804 and 1808.[64]

The only southern states not to receive contracts to build gunboats were Georgia and Tennessee. This is surprising because both states were strongly Republican. The explanation for Tennessee may be that she did not have any river ports with shipbuilding facilities, or perhaps no one bid for a contract. That Georgia did not receive a contract is more puzzling. She was generally Republican, but the coastal region was Federalist during the Ninth Congress. Another reason may have been that Savannah was only about forty miles from Beaufort, South Carolina, where a portion of the boats from that state were built; the city was only about ninety miles from Charleston. Since Savannah was not the major port of the region, it would seem futile to spread contracts for so few vessels throughout such a concentrated area and to a secondary port.[65]

The rationale for distributing contracts to other states is varied. Predominantly Republican states were rewarded for their loyalty, while those that were borderline could be brought into the Republican camp by using political patronage. In some instances, even those states that were Federalist were given a piece of the government pie. This helps to explain Jefferson's and the Republicans' attraction to the gunboat program that resulted in overwhelming congressional approval. At all times in American politics, congressmen scratch one another's backs as well as vote for programs that in theory they loathe but that will benefit their districts. Jefferson and Smith were wise enough to distribute contracts throughout the country, ultimately enhancing the idea of government for the people rather than government for the elite.

7

Prewar Operations:
Defense, and Other Diverse Duties

Alfred Thayer Mahan, the prophet of American naval supremacy, asserted that the "history of Sea Power is largely ... a narrative of contests between nations ... culminating in war." Mahan also admitted that the duties of a navy are guided by more than military considerations alone. He was convinced that a nation's naval strategy should encompass various elements, including political, economic, and military objectives. Others have agreed, defining naval strategy as "the comprehensive direction of power to control situations and areas to obtain broad objectives." Viewing the role of the navy in this light, it is obvious that its strategic operational function is concerned with political and economic as well as military objectives. [1]

A study of Jeffersonian gunboat operations is more than an analysis of the tactical employment of the vessels during the War of 1812 because the gunboats also enforced political and economic policy prior to the conflict. Those who have chronicled the gunboats' operational record, however, focus almost exclusively on the tactical failures of the craft in defense of the nation's coasts, ports, and harbors during the war. They minimize or overlook the experience and service of the gunboat flotilla that came not in the war itself but in carrying out political policy in the critical prewar period. An examination of gunboat operations before 1812 demonstrates that they were part of a political-military policy rather than the country's sole naval program.

Once completed, gunboats *No. 1* and *No. 2* were sent south to perform duties usually associated with the coast guard rather than a naval squadron. They received orders to cruise the Savannah-Charleston region, uphold revenue laws, check smuggling, suppress piracy, and enforce health and quarantine laws by checking all ships for contagious diseases before allowing them to dock. These duties suited the gunboats because of their small size and shallow-draft design. *No. 1*, however, soon became a victim of her diminutive size. In September 1804, a hurricane that leveled houses and forests, and even blew a 2-ton cannon at Fort Green nearly forty feet from its mountings, left the craft high and dry in a cornfield. Although the vessel was refloated by the first of November, she remained on the stocks, laid up out of commission until 20 December 1805, when Isaac Chauncey arrived at Charleston to assume command of the station. Six days later, Chauncey relaunched the craft and sent her on a cruise to Savannah to "bring to punishment any *unauthorized pirate*" violating commerce in American waters.[2]

While *No. 1* was protecting "all vessels whatever ... against the aggressions of the armed vessels publick or private of any nation," the vessels contracted for during summer 1804 were being readied for service. During May 1805, *Nos. 2* through *10*, inclusive, sailed to the Mediterranean to fulfill Jefferson's desire for an "honorable peace" with the Tripolitans. Of the nine vessels, eight safely reached Gibraltar in mid-June and proceeded on to Syracuse, where they arrived within forty-eight hours of one another.

Three of the gunboats had eventful journeys. *No. 8*, commanded by Nathaniel Haraden, had a turbulent voyage because of inclement weather. The 2-gun *No. 3*, commanded by Joseph Maxwell, arrived at Gibraltar, only to be seized by Spanish gunboats and detained for a short time before continuing on to Syracuse. A British squadron stopped *No. 6*, James Lawrence's boat, off Cadiz, Spain, and impressed three of her crew. Aside from these inconveniences, the flotilla arrived unscathed, only to find that a peace treaty providing for no future tribute and $60,000 ransom for American prisoners had been signed on 3 June 1805. The gunboats would have to wait for another opportunity to demonstrate their utility.[3]

During the gunboats' service in the Mediterranean, *No. 8* was the first gunboat, and the second American vessel, to make a friendly visit to the port of Tripoli. Commodore John Rodgers, commanding the American squadron, reported that the vessel aroused much interest and even received a twenty-one-gun salute from the Tripolitans, which she returned "in so handsome a manner ... that it would have done no discredit to a ship of the line." The pasha was apparently intrigued with the vessel's design because it was so different from his own. He even asked Lieutenant Haraden for permission to make a draft of the vessel; although Haraden refused, the lieutenant did allow the pasha to examine the craft. This helped soothe diplomatic relations with the Barbary state.[4]

Sending the gunboats to the Mediterranean was a political decision. The administration wanted to reduce naval expenditures and bring a speedy conclusion to the Barbary war. Moreover, Jefferson remembered the fate of the *Philadelphia* and understood the value of small, shallow-draft gunboats for close inshore operations. This was especially true because the Barbary pirates used similar craft extensively and avoided confrontation with more powerful vessels that could not navigate the coastal shoals. In fact, gunboats had become the principal weapon of the Barbary states; Tunis had more than twenty at the port of Farino alone; Algiers had about fifty of the craft; and the Tripolitans possessed a sizable gunboat flotilla. Although the decision to send the American gunboats to the Mediterranean was initially based on military necessity, since they were to serve in an offensive capacity for which they were not originally designed, the decision also reflected political reality.[5]

Gunboats *Nos. 2* through *10*, minus *No. 7*, remained with Rodgers's squadron in the Mediterranean until the summer of 1806, at which time they returned to the United States to join twelve vessels built under the auspices of the 2 March 1805 law. The administration began constructing additional vessels during the spring and summer of 1805 to ensure the protection of the nation's ports and harbors. Jefferson believed extra gunboats were essential for the nation's security because of the renewal of the European war and the increased activity of privateers threatening American interests. Moreover, those gunboats in the Mediterranean were needed at home to protect New York, Norfolk, Charleston, and New Orleans.[6]

The gunboats returned across the Atlantic without incident and went on to their respective stations. By December 1806, Robert Smith reported that gunboats *Nos. 1, 4, 5,* and *10* were at Norfolk; *Nos. 6* and *8* at New York; *Nos. 2, 3,* and *9* at Charleston; and four of the western-built craft, *Nos. 11, 12, 13,* and *14,* at New Orleans. Smith also expected as many as fourteen additional vessels on the New Orleans station by the following spring, providing the region with a respectable naval force — one that was badly needed in this vulnerable area.[7]

Increasing the naval force at New Orleans was necessary in light of the events of the summer and fall of 1806. During the spring and summer of the previous year, former vice-president Aaron Burr made a tour of the western territory, giving rise to numerous rumors. They ranged from the belief that Burr intended to form a separate independent government in the West to the idea that he planned to seize lands belonging to the Spanish Mexican empire. The speculation was substantiated when Spanish troops from Havana arrived in Pensacola, Florida, increasing the likelihood of armed conflict over disputed lands in the Gulf region.[8]

Master-Commandant John Shaw, commander of the New Orleans station, encountered problems trying to deal with the Spanish presence during the summer and fall of 1806. In the early morning hours of 18 September, misfortune struck as a hurricane swept in, beaching *No. 14* and damaging his other vessels. The gunboats' diminutive size made them extremely vulnerable to violent weather, but their size was also an advantage because the craft could also be easily repaired and relaunched. Shaw refloated his craft after only eight days, but he was unable, because of a shortage of military stores, to deploy his fleet until 10 October.[9]

Shaw ordered his gunboat commanders "to act entirely on the defensive" when encountering foreign troops because the United States and Spain were not officially at war. But the commander also reminded his officers that, above all, they were to "defend [themselves] in the best possible manner" and not to allow "an indignity to their flag." Shaw understood the dilemma his tiny flotilla faced, because Spanish forces numbered at least 900 armed men in the region and were supported by two small cruisers. He skeptically reported to Secretary Smith that, although his forces were proceeding to Natchitoches on the Sabine River to join army units commanded by General James Wilkinson, he expected that "*one action was to deside*" the fate of the country. Should the Spanish be victorious, he predicted "there was nothing preventing their marching to New Orleans," where they would find "numerous ... followers of a victorious flag."[10]

Jefferson and his cabinet reviewed the situation and responded by ordering two gunboats from New York, three of the four at Norfolk, and two of the three from Charleston to bolster the New Orleans flotilla. They were not needed, however, because between 27 October and 5 November Wilkinson and Colonel Simon de Herrera, stationed at Bayou Pierre, hammered out a peaceful arrangement by which Spanish troops withdrew west of the Sabine River and Americans remained east of the Arroyo Hondo. The officers agreed that the land between the two rivers would remain neutral territory until a boundary commission settled the matter diplomatically. Wilkinson used the "small and feeble" gunboat force to supplement his own troops, demonstrating American interest and removing the immediate threat of armed conflict in the region. Herrera, in reality, did not have the stomach for committing his "lazy, half-mutinous, barefooted soldiers" to a conflict that could be settled diplomatically. Yet, for Americans, it was more than a question of diplomatic relations; it was a matter of national security. If war erupted in the future, the United States would be prepared because additional gunboats, destined for New Orleans, were being built in Kentucky and Ohio.[11]

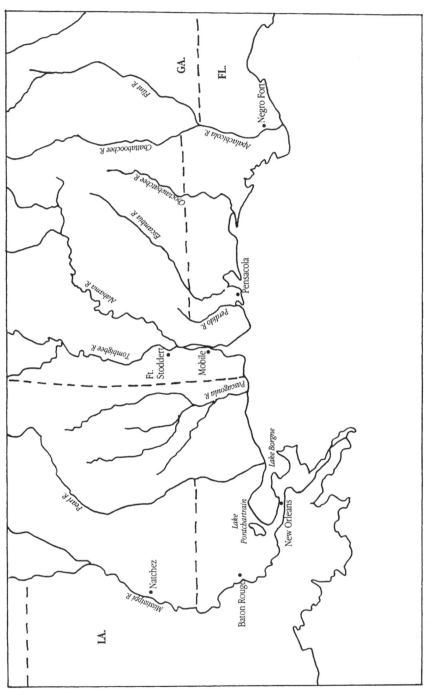

The Gulf Coast

On 20 November 1806, Shaw reported that "tranquillity again appears ... but for how long ... is very uncertain." Shaw recognized the uncertainty in the region, but he did not know that Louisiana was about to become embroiled in the conspiratorial schemes of Aaron Burr during the months preceding the confrontation with Spain. Louisiana and the West became involved in events that almost destroyed the young nation and brought the region to the brink of open hostility. [12]

During the winter of 1805–6, Burr had approached the Spanish and British ministers in Washington as well as influential friends in the East and West proposing a plan for a western empire. When talking with the British or Spanish, Burr's plans were to seize western lands from the United States. When discussing his intentions with Americans, he professed that Spanish lands were the object of his plans. No one really knew Burr's intentions. But most believed that Burr was raising a force of adventurers either to seize lands from Spain or to initiate a western revolution, making himself "Emperor of the west." The latter scheme gained much publicity as rumors emerged that the British were ready to join his volunteers at the mouth of the Mississippi River. Other stories even claimed that the "United States Navy stood ready to join" Burr's forces. This rumor gained more credence when John Shaw reported that Lieutenant Robert P. Spence, who had delivered dispatches from Eric Bollman to Aaron Burr in late October, was involved in the conspiracy. [13]

Throughout October and November, Burr's plans were "the exclusive subject of every conversation" in New Orleans. According to General Wilkinson, who was suspected as a coconspirator, Burr intended to gather a group of eight to ten thousand "associates" from the northern and western states, descend the Mississippi River, and be joined by men from Tennessee and the southern territories. They planned to rendezvous on 1 December in New Orleans and proceed with naval support against the Mexican port city of Vera Cruz by 1 February 1807. Burr had even gained the support of the Catholic bishop of New Orleans, three Jesuit priests, and Madame Xavier Taycon, mother superior of the New Orleans convent of Ursuline nuns. The clergy were supposed to infiltrate Mexican lands and win the masses to Burr's cause before the invasion began. [14]

For months, Jefferson listened to reports of Burr's proposed activities and refused to act on unsubstantiated rumors. Captain Thomas Truxtun, who had become privy to Burr's plans, reported his conversations with the former vice-president and suggested that the president use the gunboat flotilla to keep the "eggs of insurrection" from hatching. Truxtun believed that by using these craft the government could blockade New Orleans, control commerce, and prevent the arrival of foreign aid, all which were necessary for the success of Burr's expedition.[15]

Jefferson, however, took no action until he heard that "gunboats or strong vessels resembling them" were being built for Burr on the Muskingum River in Ohio. After receiving this information, Jefferson and Smith decided to dispatch Captains Edward Preble and Stephen Decatur to New Orleans. Furthermore, *Argus* and the nine gunboats from Atlantic ports were to proceed to the city to protect it from Burr as well as from the Spanish menace. On the following day, 25 October 1806, Jefferson rescinded the previous orders due to a lack of funds and other complications. The government would have to remain quiet until either Burr or popular indignation forced action.[16]

On 25 November, Jefferson received a second message from General Wilkinson claiming that Burr's plans also included an insurrection in the West once Mexico was subdued. Two days later, the president issued a proclamation urging civil and military officials to beware of suspicious movements in the West. Moreover, the army was ordered to be on guard, the militia was to be prepared, and the boats being built in Ohio were to be seized by federal authorities. Although Jefferson was concerned about taking such action, he thought it necessary because there was "a deep dark and widespread conspiracy, embracing the young and the old, the democrat and the federalist, the native and the foreigner, the patriot of '76 and the exotic of yesterday, the opulent and the needy, the ins and the outs."[17]

The gunboats on the New Orleans station were readied for Burr's anticipated assault. Shaw ordered *Nos. 13* and *14* to ascend the Mississippi to oppose any unauthorized body of men, while *Nos. 11* and *12* descended the river to prevent an attack from the south. Furthermore, Shaw ordered his flotilla to cooperate with General Wilkinson's forces to ensure no revolt succeeded. In late December, Jefferson once again suggested to Smith that the gunboats on the Atlantic be sent to New Orleans so that "we [could] ... see the value of *strong* vessels of little draught for the shoaly coasts of the Gulf of Mexico."[18]

In mid-January, after hearing that Burr had seized Matthew Lyon's gunboats in Kentucky, Shaw reported that his vessels were north of the city, waiting for the invasion. Even though his fleet consisted of only four vessels, sixteen guns, and one hundred thirty-four seamen, they stood ready for the assault. Shaw also exclaimed that the "country [was] on the Eve of destruction and that there [was] less exertion made *by those who guide its laws* than is reconcilable with our present state of danger." Governor William Charles Cole Claiborne did not feel the threat because, as he saw it, the naval force was "respectable" and "could discomfit, any Enemy, however numerous, who should be unprotected by Vessels of war."[19]

Through the cold of December and January, the Crescent City was warmed by the rumors of Burr's impending assault. Events, however, did not peak until mid-February, when Shaw's force, by this time including four gunboats and the bomb-ketches *Vesuvius* and *Aetna*, discovered not the thousands of "associates" they expected but only a handful of men and women. Their leader, under indictment and running from the law, was apprehended on 19 February 1807 by army Lieutenant Edmund Pendleton Gaines near Fort Stoddert (present-day Alabama, near the confluence of the Tombigbee and Alabama rivers) in the Mississippi territory. The Burr conspiracy in the West had been squelched. Thereafter, there would be other rumors of Burr and his forces seizing the West, but they would remain just that. After Burr's capture, his fate was in the hands of a jury, and that body would determine his intentions as well as his guilt or innocence.[20]

During the fall and early winter months of 1806–7, the gunboats demonstrated their value on the western frontier. They successfully participated in squelching a half-hearted attempt at territorial expansion that many believed could have resulted in the United States losing control of all lands west of the Mississippi. They had also been responsible for bolstering confidence in the government's ability to maintain stability and an American presence in a turbulent region. Furthermore, their part in quelling the insurrection demonstrated the government's determination to maintain civil obedience in the region by military force. Even though the gunboats were built for the defense of ports and harbors, it was obvious they could fulfill other functions.

The legislative session following Burr's capture produced a heated debate concerning gunboats but resulted in no additional appropriations. Before the session, Congress had authorized ninety vessels, but only seventy contracts had been awarded. Moreover, only eighteen vessels had been delivered to the navy, and eight of those were on the New Orleans station. Only three months after the Burr uprising had been silenced and the Spanish threat had subsided, Robert Smith ordered the gunboats to be placed in storage because of a lack of funds. John Shaw reported on 28 May 1807 that his flotilla was secured and in ordinary.[21]

During June 1807, the *Chesapeake* incident alerted the country to the pitiful state of its defense; the navy department responded by assembling the gunboats into two flotillas for immediate action. Captain Stephen Decatur, ordered to replace James Barron as commander of the damaged *Chesapeake*, assumed responsibility for the Norfolk flotilla while John Rodgers, who had been supervising the construction of the new *No. 7* building at Havre de Grace, Maryland, gained command of the New York flotilla.[22]

When Decatur arrived on the Norfolk station after the *Chesapeake* insult, he found a state of disarray and shamefully low morale. He immediately organized a response to the outrage and by 11 July had assembled four gunboats ready for action, with seamen eager to go to war against Britain if necessary. The captain also began repairing the *Chesapeake* because, as he well knew, gunboats could provide resistance should the British attempt a landing, but they could not successfully operate far at sea.

As the threat of a British invasion declined through the summer, Smith continued mobilizing the navy's forces. In late August, Decatur reported that the *Chesapeake* was ready for action and that he had assembled fourteen operable gunboats. With the growth of his flotilla, he admitted that he could man only eight gunboats because of a shortage of seamen. Had Smith not sent a reinforcement of sixty-five men from Baltimore, forty from Philadelphia, and thirty marines from Washington, Decatur would not have been able to relaunch the *Chesapeake* nor provide the gunboats with their full complements of crew.[23]

Commodore Rodgers arrived in New York from Maryland in mid-July to take command of a squadron that consisted of the bomb-ketch *Vengeance* and fourteen gunboats. By September, Rodgers had procured the bomb-ketches *Aetna* and *Vesuvius* from New Orleans and seventeen newly built gunboats from New England. The commodore, despite the state of emergency, found service at New York trivial and monotonous because the station was not directly affected by the *Chesapeake* crisis. But in early September the British frigate *Jason* and the brig *Columbine* entered New York harbor and threatened Rodgers's boredom. The captain responded by assembling five gunboats to enforce Jefferson's proclamation forbidding British ships in American waters. But because Rodgers did not completely understand the extent to which he should act, he traveled to nearby Governor's Island to confer with Gallatin over the meaning of Jefferson's message. The secretary informed Rodgers that the fleet was to be only a deterrent and that it was not the president's intention to use force should the British refuse to leave. Rodgers returned to his station to await further orders from the navy department, but before any news arrived, the British ships sailed, alleviating the necessity for action.[24]

In the case of the *Chesapeake* incident, the two gunboat flotillas served their original mission of protecting the ports and harbors from foreign enemies. There were no hostilities, but the vessels' presence

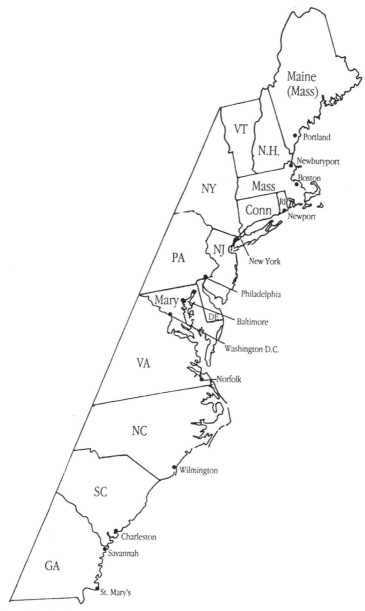

The Atlantic Coast

provided stability. While Jefferson was doing all he could to prepare the country for war, many chastised him for not doing more. Jefferson's administration appeared to be doing nothing, but in reality, when Congress gathered in October, preparations had been made for the worst scenario.[25]

The Ninth Congress, convening in October 1807, had a tremendous effect on gunboat operations. In addition to authorizing 188 more vessels, Congress also eliminated the importation of slaves from Africa and passed legislation supporting an embargo prohibiting American vessels from trading with foreign ports. Enforcement of these laws became the primary duties of the gunboats in the years before the war.

Upholding the ban on the international slave trade was pertinent primarily to the southern states. Master-Commandant David Porter, who arrived in New Orleans on 17 June 1808 to replace Shaw as commander of the station, found what he believed to be a conspiracy to break the slave trade act. Shortly after appraising his situation, he divided the station into four divisions to curtail all illegal activities, including the slave trade. He reported that foreign merchantmen, slavers, and disloyal elements in New Orleans were trying to subvert the slave importation laws. His fears were confirmed when he learned that the French privateer *L'Epine* was off the Louisiana coast with a load of slaves. Moreover, a Spanish ship, also believed to be carrying human cargo, was nearby. Before the end of 1808, Porter's squadron, scouring the numerous inlets, bays, and estuaries of the Gulf region, had captured three slavers violating the country's law.[26]

The risk-to-profit ratio was extremely low for those involved in the slave trade, and this provided the incentive for increased illegal activity. Porter wrote the secretary of the navy in January 1810 that the British brig *Alexandrina* from Jamaica had been captured with 127 slaves, and in May a Portuguese vessel with 104 slaves was seized for violating the law. Before Porter's departure from the station in July, he expressed fears that the profitability of the slave trade was going to suggest increased violations. His fears were confirmed when he learned that the French privateer *L'Epine* was off the Louisiana coast with a load of slaves, and a Spanish ship, also believed to be carrying human cargo, was nearby.[27]

During the summer of 1810, Captain Shaw, who returned to replace Porter as commander, found the increased activity his predecessor had predicted. Shaw noted that the Portuguese brig *Moreveto*, the French privateer *Le Guillamne*, and the Spanish ship *Alerto*, carrying 170 slaves, had all violated the law and smuggled the illegal cargo into Barataria (the area west of New Orleans to Bayou Lafourche and south to the Gulf of Mexico).

The following September, *No. 25* captured a British brig; in November, *No. 16* seized the brig *Adherbal*; and in December, *No. 22* apprehended the brig *Neptune*, all carrying slaves. Due to the conditions they faced, all Porter or Shaw could hope to do was station their vessels in such a manner as to frustrate as much of the illegal activity as they could.[28]

The proximity of New Orleans and other stations to Spanish-controlled lands made it virtually impossible to stop the slave trade. Even if the ships were forced to unload in Spanish-held lands, the illegal cargo could still reach its destination by moving slaves overland to avoid patrols. Captain Hugh Campbell's gunboats on the St. Marys, Georgia, station faced similar problems, especially during 1811 while his vessels were on a cruise. At that time, it was noted that illegal slave importations increased considerably. Within a two-week period during 1812 alone, his vessels captured the schooners *Camilla*, *Adventure*, and *Trimer*, all carrying slaves.[29]

While the gunboats were not successful in eliminating the slave trade, they did hinder such illegal ventures. But as with any illicit activity, it became more dangerous and profitable for those involved after it became illegal, thus providing an additional stimulus for increased activity. Whereas the gunboats were not successful in their endeavors, their operations along the Gulf coast contributed to a general shortage of slaves throughout the Louisiana territory, resulting in higher prices for labor needed in the southern plantation economy. True, the gunboats did not eradicate the African slave trade, but their participation in curtailing the illegal act set a precedent ultimately resulting in an American squadron being stationed along the coast of Africa.[30]

In contrast to the slave trade laws, which pertained primarily to the southern stations, the country's changing and ill-defined navigation laws affected all squadrons from Maine to New Orleans. Enforcing the Embargo Act of 1807 and the subsequent Non-Intercourse law was not only the most onerous duty for the gunboat commanders but also proved to be the most difficult. The first problem was the numerous strategic locations for smuggling, including the St. Lawrence River, Lake Champlain, Passamaquoddy Bay on the Maine-New Brunswick border, St. Marys, and New Orleans. The president also learned that smugglers did not necessarily need the presence of foreign territory to violate the embargo successfully. In February 1808, Jefferson noted that a British ship sailed into the Delaware Bay, loaded flour, and set sail for Jamaica, in direct violation of the law.[31]

Overt flaunting of the embargo law prompted Jefferson to use the gunboats to aid in its enforcement. He wrote to Gallatin and Smith in mid-February that the country "must employ some of [its] gunboats to aid in the execution of the embargo law." The decision to use the diminutive craft to uphold federal law, one historian wrote, "rocked the foundations of republicanism." It has also been claimed that Jefferson, by ordering the gunboats to administer the law, used his presidential author-ity without specific guidelines and without constitutional restraints. Some have argued that forcing adherence to the law with either the point of a bayonet or with a cannon primed and ready to fire threatened individual liberties and gave further impetus to the charges against large standing military forces.[32]

Whether Jefferson was violating civil liberties or simply enforcing a congressional act, he nevertheless used the gunboats as a primary instru-ment. He wrote Smith that "I think it will be advisable that during this summer all the gun-boats ... should be distributed ... to enforce the embargo." Jefferson even informed Smith that Secretary of War Dear-born had been instructed to "be on the alert, and fly to the spot where any open and forcible opposition shall be commenced, and crush it in embryo." In any case, Jefferson was adamant about enforcing the embargo law.[33]

It was much easier for the president to make eloquent statements about the intentions of the government to suppress violations of the law than it was to carry out those intentions. The gunboat commanders found their adversaries included not only those legally flying foreign flags but also armed marauders and pirates as well as American citizens trying to avoid bankruptcy by breaking the law. And if a vessel was captured for violat-ing the embargo, there were several obstacles to overcome before the cargo could be legally condemned. While all stations faced these difficul-ties during the fifteen months the embargo law was in effect, New Orleans, St. Marys, and Passamaquoddy Bay probably had the most exacting task carrying out Jefferson's design.

Shortly after the embargo had passed, Smith sent additional gunboats to St. Mary's to aid the revenue cutters, to strengthen the squadron, and to prevent smuggling of cotton into Spanish Florida. Yet, even with extra vessels "judiciously stationed," Lieutenant P. C. Wederstrandt found that he could not prevent smuggling. The major problem for the southern station, it was believed, was the numerous inlets that provided more possibilities for infractions "than all the other ports of the Union together." Not even the ten gunboats ultimately stationed in the region could ensure success. Despite the hardships, violations were curbed and *No. 2*, in April 1808, captured two American vessels. They were ulti-mately released because no infractions could be proved against them, but the government had demonstrated the intention to enforce its proclamations.[34]

The New Orleans station also had several obstacles to overcome to carry out the spirit of Jefferson's law successfully. Porter, acting with determination, divided his gunboats into four divisions and virtually declared war on the pirates and smugglers of Barataria. In August 1808, *No. 12* captured the British schooner *Union* from Jamaica, loaded with military stores, and less than a month later *Nos. 18* and *15* apprehended a schooner with 400 barrels of flour and window glass, plus a barge with twenty-eight additional barrels of flour. In the face of manpower shortages and deteriorating vessels, Porter's squadron continued its assault on illegal commerce.

Early in 1809, Porter's *No. 18* seized the schooner *Rover* carrying beef, oil, candles, and brine. The following March, the commander notified the navy department of a consignment of 6,000 bales of cotton ready for shipment through Pensacola. Although Porter claimed he would "endeavor to catch the cotton in our waters" he would not shirk from making "some encroachments on [the] National jurisdiction" of Spain. Fortunately, no international incident occurred, as Porter discontinued enforcing the embargo by 1 April 1809. Before the end of March, however, the Spanish schooner *Catalina,* commanded by Francisco Suarez, was detained and fifty-six barrels of flour seized.[35]

Porter learned the truth about enforcing the embargo law after *No. 15* captured the Spanish schooner *Precious Ridicule* — loaded with seventy-five barrels of flour, clothing for troops, wine, oil, and cheese — bound from Spanish Baton Rouge to Pensacola. The problem he faced was determining what portion of the cargo was American and what part was contraband, liable to seizure. After careful consideration, he surmised that the flour was obviously produced from American wheat, and impounded it. The other items, however, could possibly have been foreign, so his only recourse was to release them. This incident led Porter to conclude that the embargo would "be ineffectual as long as the *disputed Territory* [was] in the hands of Spain."[36]

Passamaquoddy Bay and the northern stations also had problems enforcing the embargo law. The president foresaw the difficulty facing Commodore Rodgers and decided that because "the danger [was] much greater from New York northwardly, principally from Massachusetts," all details concerning number and distribution of gunboats should be left to the discretion of Gallatin and Rodgers.[37]

The commodore analyzed his predicament and spread his squadron between Passamaquoddy and Delaware bays, where Jefferson believed naval stores were passing into Canada. Although most of Rodgers' force was stationed along the coast of Long Island and in New York harbor, two gunboats were at Passamaquoddy, two were at Barnstable, one was at New Bedford, one was at Newburyport, and one was at Newport. Rodgers's squadron captured a number of prizes, such as the schooner *Liberty* (apprehended by *No. 103*) loaded with fish that had been stolen from Plymouth, and a sloop (by *No. 6*) loaded with tobacco, flour, salted meats, and other items bound for the West India markets. Many, however, also escaped. In the case of *No. 6*, the captain and crew of the smuggler escaped the scene, allowing the gunboat an uncontested prize. In another instance, a large, armed mob at Newburyport kept government officials from fulfilling the law.[38]

Lieutenant Sam Evans of Baltimore, part of Commodore Stephen Decatur's squadron covering the Chesapeake Bay, Virginia, and the Carolinas, did not find the blatant disregard for the embargo law that Porter or Rodgers encountered. This was because Evans was not stationed near foreign-held lands, and southerners were generally supportive of the Embargo. The lieutenant did have other problems that made his duties equally difficult. Maintaining, equipping, and manning his fleet proved time consuming and expensive, and limited his squadron's operations. In spite of the troubles, Evans's *No. 5* detained the sloop *John Upshaw*, and *No. 144* seized the flour-laden brig *William of Dumfences*.[39]

Although gunboats had been designed as defensive weapons aimed at protecting the country's ports and harbors, they did serve in a preventive, offensive capacity while enforcing the slave trade and embargo laws. The gunboats cruised their respective stations seeking violations, and when infractions were found, they seized the initiative to bring the culprits to justice. This was, in a limited sense, offensive action because the craft were taking the initiative to enforce government policies, and their success depended on the motivation of the individual commanders as well as the squadron's proximity to foreign lands.

Before Jefferson relinquished the presidency, he signed the Non-Intercourse Act, repealing the embargo as of 15 March 1809 and allowing commerce with all nations except France and England. Jefferson's embargo had been a failure, and the president was displeased with its lack of results, but he did admit that while the "Embargo did not bring justice to the European powers, ... [it] did save our seamen and property." Others believed it was "the most judicious step that could be taken," considering the tenor of the times. But whether Jefferson's motives for the embargo were respected as being the best action for the

Gunboats capture French privateers on the Mississippi River, 1808. Portrait by Captain William Bainbridge Hoff. Photo courtesy of the Naval Historical Center.

country or the folly of an idealistic president, the law provided training for seamen and experience for the gunboats.[40]

Jefferson's successor, James Madison, had different ideas about the usefulness of gunboats. In April 1809, Acting Secretary of the Navy Charles Goldsborough ordered all the country's gunboats except those at New Orleans laid up in ordinary. As the navy decommissioned twenty of the New York gunboats in September 1811, a new naval policy emerged — one that ignored the usefulness of the diminutive craft.[41]

Between 1809 and the beginning of hostilities in 1812, the New Orleans flotilla remained in active operation. David Porter, commander of the squadron until the summer of 1811, encountered numerous problems on the station that seriously handicapped his efficiency. At the beginning of 1809, Porter's squadron consisted of fifteen gunboats, of which four were in service, four were ready for service, and the others were in various states of disrepair.[42]

Porter also faced a shortage of seamen. In fact, the four vessels he had ready for service could not even leave port because they lacked full complements. Additionally, Porter believed those vessels already in service were inadequately manned, leaving the station vulnerable should war begin. His remedy was to recruit locals from New Orleans. Using Creoles as acting-midshipmen, he believed, not only would fill out the gunboats' crews but would bring into the service men who could act as interpreters, who were accustomed to the climate, and who were familiar with the region. Furthermore, it would bond the people of Louisiana closer to the country and provide them with an opportunity to prove their loyalty.[43]

Porter spent his remaining years as commander of the New Orleans squadron, enforcing the Non-Importation and slave trade laws, trying to keep his gunboats in sailing condition, and bickering with General James Wilkinson. Porter's forces patrolled the waters between the Sabine and Perdido rivers in response to British and French vessels' violating the country's commercial legislation.

Both France and England were guilty of violating federal law, but French vessels provided the most problems for Porter. Three privateers in particular, *Le Duc de Montebello*, *L'Intrepide*, and *La Petite Chance*, for months had sailed the waters of the Gulf, plundering every Spanish or American vessel they met. In March 1810, Porter received information that the three craft were in the Mississippi delta. Assembling his gunboats for action, Porter confronted the heavily armed ships and demanded their surrender. Fortunately, the French ships heeded the commander's demand and struck their flags. Afterwards, Porter once again had to fight his battle in the corrupt legal system of New Orleans rather than aboard his tiny gunboats. [44]

Another of Porter's problems was the deceitful General James Wilkinson. Wilkinson's actions were always suspect, but the general alienated Porter because of the question of rank. Although Porter was only a master-commandant, a rank much inferior to a general, he was commander in chief of all naval forces in New Orleans and expected to be treated as Wilkinson's equal. The general, however, was hesitant to afford such respect. [45]

Porter and others believed that Wilkinson was trying to foment revolution throughout Latin America, using New Orleans as a base of operations. The uncertainty of his actions led many to believe that even "the town of Mobile [would] shortly be attached to" the United States. In mid-May, Wilkinson substantiated the rumor when he requested vessels to transport additional men to Fort Stoddert. Throughout the summer and fall, Wilkinson made various requests of Porter's gunboats, confirming the commander's suspicions. Wilkinson's plot never hatched because his supposed cohort, the Spanish governor of West Florida, Vizente Folch, left for Pensacola. Porter also refused to provide unquestionable naval support for Wilkinson's nefarious schemes. Thus, a diplomatic crisis was averted by the savvy of a loyal gunboat commander refusing to allow his vessels to become the instruments of revolution. [46]

A constant problem for Porter and for his replacement, Master-Commandant John Shaw, whether they were enforcing the country's commercial restrictions or sorting out Wilkinson's intrigues, was keeping the gunboats in sailing order. Porter reported during the summer of 1809 that the station had twenty gunboats, but many were in a serious state of disrepair. Porter attributed the vessels' rapid decay to the climate and waters of the region, unseasoned timber, and poor construction. Conditions were so bad that by January 1810, five gunboats had been condemned, and by the end of the year most of the others had undergone extensive repairs. Despite the importance of the Crescent City, the navy department sent no additional gunboats to New Orleans. By December 1814 and the Battle of New Orleans, the flotilla had decayed to the point that it had only six operable vessels. [47]

Before Porter left New Orleans, he gave command of the station to Lieutenant P. C. Wederstrandt, who served until John Shaw returned to the Crescent City in 1811. Shaw spent his second tour on the station trying to carry out the government's commercial legislation and preparing his diminishing flotilla for all contingencies. Throughout 1811 and until the summer of 1812, Shaw experienced strained relations with the

Spanish over Florida. Furthermore, Anglo-American relations were worsening, sending ripples as far as the frontier of Louisiana.[48]

Shaw constantly pleaded for additional vessels to replace those he lost, but neither Secretary of the Navy Paul Hamilton (15 May 1809–31 December 1812) nor his replacement, William Jones (19 January 1813–1 December 1814), nor Congress heard his requests. On 30 March 1812, Congress even ordered all gunboats to be laid up except those in places most exposed to attacks. A year later, on 3 March 1813, Congress authorized the president to dispose of those gunboats no longer needed by the country. It appeared that the gunboat navy was slowly being dismantled even before it had been given a full opportunity to prove itself.[49]

An analysis of the gunboats' operations in the years before the War of 1812 demonstrates that they fulfilled a political role. Chronicling their service reads like a report on the coast guard or revenue service rather than a naval or military force. While the gunboat program began in February 1803 with the first appropriation for vessels to settle the Spanish Mississippi problem, the craft did not see considerable duty until the last years of Jefferson's presidency. Once Congress passed the slave trade and embargo laws, the gunboats' role increasingly was the enforcement of government policy. From the beginning of Madison's presidency until the war, they served likewise by enforcing the Non-Importation and slave trade laws.

From a strategic viewpoint, the gunboats upheld policy, but from a tactical perspective, their duties were numerous. On more than one occasion the gunboats provided stability in light of a possible revolt in the western country and in so doing preserved peaceful relations with the Spanish. In this respect they served a valuable diplomatic role.

The gunboats also helped frustrate the African slave trade. Although they were not completely successful, they did hinder such illegal but profitable ventures. In fact, Baratarian pirate Jean Laffite's most fruitful business was the slave trade, and the gunboats, he said, frustrated his designs. Even so, the slaves he stole from the West Indies saturated the parish of Saint John the Baptist, which coincidentally, in 1811 saw the bloodiest slave insurrection in the country's history. The gunboats themselves did not take an active role in suppressing the rebellion, but numbers of their officers and crew did.[50]

Enforcing the country's commercial legislation was the most difficult duty for the gunboats, and while they were not completely effective, they were, once again, probably more useful than larger vessels. The vessels' small size and shallow-draft design permitted them greater freedom while pursuing their adversaries. But in reality it did not matter how many or what kinds of vessels were enforcing these laws because the legislation did not have popular support, and people could find ways to avoid authorities.

The gunboat program was a logical response to the turmoil facing the United States, and it was a way to fulfill immediate political objectives. Without the gunboats, the embargo and other commercial restrictions would have been nothing but paper proclamations; the slave trade laws would have been nothing but rhetoric. The gunboats provided a mechanism for enforcing the federal government's laws, and although they did not eradicate illegal activities, they did force villains to proceed cautiously. In doing so, they gained experience and training that benefited them in the War of 1812.

8
The Legacy:
A Lesson Unlearned

Once the War of 1812 ended, "a new episode in American history began" — one in which Americans viewed themselves as a single people and nation, with a destiny they alone could fulfill. It was a fresh beginning for the country; it was a chance to learn from the mistakes that had almost yielded disaster, disunion, and even loss of freedom. But despite the political shortcomings that many believed had brought the country to the brink, the nation survived, and a new group of leaders emerged. These men, although molded by Jeffersonian policies, were a new breed who replaced the Republican old guard and the policies it stood for.[1]

The gunboat program was a policy that underwent change well before the Treaty of Ghent was signed and the new order emerged. In fact, the program began to change even before Jefferson left office in the early spring of 1809. In November 1808, in his eighth annual message, Jefferson reported that the nation's defenses were adequate and that the country had a "sufficient" number of gunboats. In early January 1809, he repeated this belief in another report in which he claimed that seaport cities were "safe against naval enterprise[s]." Jefferson was secure in the defense system his administration had created. The program had kept the country out of war, although many charged it had done so at the expense of national honor. (Honor was an issue which at times could be sacrificed, whereas national security was non-negotiable.) Jefferson had preserved security through eight turbulent years.[2]

As the Madison administration took the reins of government, many believed Anglo-American relations were improving. But events quickly demonstrated the opposite. The Tenth Congress responded to the deterioration by proposing to augment the nation's naval forces from 1,440 to

2,000 men, who were needed to put the gunboat flotilla in full operation. Navalists naturally agreed that additional men were needed and saw an opportunity for a legislative coup. Seizing the occasion, navalists successfully attached a provision to the manpower bill allowing four additional frigates to be fitted out, manned, and sent to sea. While it has been claimed that this "was *not* a rejection of the president's defensive policy," it certainly was a setback for the gunboat program because the craft were relegated to a lesser position even before they had the opportunity to prove or disprove themselves.[3]

The gunboats' future appeared equally dim in April 1810, when John Randolph proposed that the government sell all the diminutive craft. Randolph did not single out the gunboat program but rather called for the complete elimination of the navy. The proposal, an attempt to abolish something Randolph believed existed solely for the protection of commerce, was not considered serious, even though it should have fore-warned the country of the naval policy crisis emerging.[4]

In 1811, Madison's first secretary of the navy, Paul Hamilton, confirmed the crisis when he reported that the number of gunboats had been reduced to 169 because of decay and losses at sea, and most of these were in ordinary. Another factor affecting policy was the refusal of Congress to appropriate money for new ships, even with war looming on the horizon. Hamilton's belief that gunboats were generally unsatisfactory and that building new ships was the alternative did not find many friends in Congress. Furthermore, Congress passed an act on 30 March 1812 that appeared to seal the fate of the gunboat program and naval policy in general.[5]

On 30 March, Congress voted that "all gunboats then in commission should be laid up ... and distributed [to] the several harbors ... most exposed to attack." It was ironic that Congress voted to discontinue building the craft and to place those already completed in ordinary when, as Nathaniel Macon had predicted in January 1812, the nation would go to war with Great Britain before the legislative session ended. Hamilton also believed that war was imminent and requested Commodores John Rodgers and Stephen Decatur to submit a plan by which the navy could "annoy ... the trade of Great Britain without exposing itself to her immense naval force." The Madison administration's search for a naval policy ended once war was declared. Under the press of events, Hamilton breathed new life into the gunboat program by ordering the craft to be readied for service without regard to expense. They were finally going to be tested.[6]

The War of 1812 provided the gunboats with the opportunity to prove their value, warranting a detailed operational study in itself. But because of the number of gunboats and the overwhelming number of wartime incidents involving them, only the major operational uses will be mentioned here. Although there were several cases of gunboats succumbing to British vessels, some of the craft held their own against heavily overmatched enemies. In most cases, however, the gunboats faced superior opponents because their foe was a major sea power and the only munitions the people of this country had to take into the conflict was a small fleet and the American spirit.

In December 1812, the British squadron in American waters numbered ninety-seven vessels, of which thirty-nine were either frigates or ships-of-the-line. The entire British navy included more than a thousand warships, or more than "three fighting ships for every American gun." But the war was fought in American waters, and the gunboats had the opportunity to serve the purpose for which they had been originally designed — port and harbor defense.[7]

Considered by some to be lacking in general performance, the gunboats nevertheless offered valuable service. They were a "force in being" that had to be eliminated before the enemy could assault a target, and in many instances their participation provided great benefits. In March 1813, Joseph Tarbell stationed *Constellation* and his gunboat flotilla in a crescent formation near Craney Island to prevent a British invasion through the Chesapeake Bay. In June, however, his flotilla, tired of waiting for the inevitable, took the offensive and aggressively confronted the British frigates *Junon*, *Barrosa*, and the 24-gun ship *Lauresitnus*, all stationed to keep watch on *Constellation*. The gunboats fired on the enemy vessels for half an hour but because of choppy seas and poor powder, their volleys were ineffective, resulting in an American withdrawal. Lacking offensive capacity in this case, the gunboats' still helped prevent an immediate British landing and occupation.[8]

During the summer of 1814, Joshua Barney's flotilla encountered serious opposition while trying to defend Washington. Blockaded in the Patuxent River, Barney's gunboats advanced on 8 June against a rocket boat and numerous enemy barges, supported by *Loire* and *Narcissus* (each with thirty-eight guns) and the 18-gun schooner *Jasseur*. The gunboats performed admirably as they drove the smaller craft back to the cover of the larger ships. Later that evening, twenty additional barges joined the British to attack Barney's position again, but still to no avail. The following day, 9 June, British barges, supported by two schooners, tried another assault, which resulted in the British schooner *St. Lawrence* being abandoned, a barge cut in half, and a rocket boat hulled and left sinking. Barney's flotilla held its own.[9]

On 26 June, Barney's forces attacked the British vessels in an attempt to raise the blockade. After two hours of sustained fire, the American flotilla drove the British ships down the Patuxent into Chesapeake Bay. Although the American victory was not conclusive, it temporarily raised the blockade and forced the British to be more cautious when there was an American force present.[10]

Barney was not content with his victory because he knew time was expiring and the British would renew their offensive. He realized that Washington was the British objective, and he held out little hope that his flotilla could prevent its capture. On 8 July, Barney received news that *Albion*, flagship of Rear Admiral George Cockburn, was at the mouth of the Patuxent River. This was an obvious sign that a larger force was on its way, and by 26 July this force appeared at the mouth of the Potomac River. By 19 August, the British fleet had grown to two seventy-fours, a sixty-four, a razee, seven frigates, and twelve other assorted craft. On the following day, Cockburn personally led a British assault up the Patuxent to eliminate Barney's flotilla and remove the American threat. Barney, sacrificing his gunboats to prevent them from falling into British hands, received great satisfaction as his vessels exploded only moments before being captured by the enemy. Barney did not allow his vessels to be captured, but when he scuttled them, American naval resistance ended and Washington's destiny was in British hands.[11]

The capture and burning of Washington was the most humiliating incident for the country during the war. Barney's men, taking the guns from their vessels before setting them afire, joined army and militia forces trying to prevent the enemy onslaught. On 24 August 1814, British forces easily marched into the city, set fire to its public buildings, including the White House and Capitol, and departed two days later after losing only about 500 men. For two months, Barney's flotilla had kept the British from attacking, but once overwhelming superiority had been achieved, the British easily eliminated the threat of the American flotilla and captured the capital city.[12]

The gunboats on the northern lakes were more successful than those on the Atlantic coast. Shortly after war had been declared, Isaac Chauncey received the all-important command of Lakes Ontario and Erie. In mid-September 1812, William Jones, Madison's second navy secretary, demonstrated the importance of the lakes when he instructed Daniel Dobbins to contract for four gunboats to be built on Lake Erie. Later that same month, Lieutenant Thomas Macdonough was ordered to assume command on Lake Champlain. Realizing the importance of the lake campaigns, the navy department sent experienced officers to command each post.[13]

By the end of November 1812, Chauncey's forces appeared to have control of Lake Ontario, but it was only temporary. Although the opposing fleets met on several occasions throughout 1813-14, there was never a conclusive battle to determine control of the lake. The war on Lake Ontario raged, as C. S. Forester wrote, "in seesaw fashion, with each side building feverishly and securing or losing command of the lake alternately with each accession of strength." The events on Lake Ontario demonstrated the importance of the northern waters as well as the importance of shallow-draft gunboat-type vessels. [14]

In February 1813, Master-Commandant Oliver Hazard Perry received orders to proceed to Erie, in the northwest corner of Pennsylvania, supervise completion of the gunboats under construction there, and "gain reputation for [himself] ... and honor for [his] country." By 27 March, Perry had arrived at Lake Erie, and the pieces were in place for the climactic events that provided the United States with military control of that northern lake. [15]

The turning point in the struggle for Lake Erie came in the early fall of 1813. On 10 September, Perry's nine vessels, carrying fifty-four guns, confronted six British vessels, carrying sixty-three guns, and battled for control of the lake. Perry's decision to take the initiative and his "acceptance of necessary risk" by closing the enemy at the Battle of Lake Erie brought immediate success. Furthermore, his use of gunboats to capture *Chippeway* and *Little Belt* was, as Alfred Thayer Mahan maintained, "contributive" to a victory that destroyed the British threat in the Northwest. It, however, did even more. Perry's victory finalized the war in that region because nothing happened to reverse its results, and the gunboats contributed to the final outcome. [16]

During the winter of 1812–13, Thomas Macdonough laid up his two gunboats and three schooners on Lake Champlain and planned for the ensuing spring season. The following April, he put his forty-three guns afloat to prevent the enemy from gaining "ascendancy on Lake Champlain." But soon after putting out, Macdonough's fleet suffered a terrible setback. In June, while training green recruits from Maine, Macdonough's 16-gun *President* ran aground, seriously damaging the ship's hull. With *President* out of commission, Macdonough learned that the sloops *Growler* and *Eagle* had run aground and been captured by British gunboats. This temporarily gave command of the lake to the British, and they exploited their advantage. In late July and early August, British troops plundered Plattsburg and several other small settlements. All Macdonough could do was stand by, because the ships he was building, including six gunboats to replace those lost, were not completed

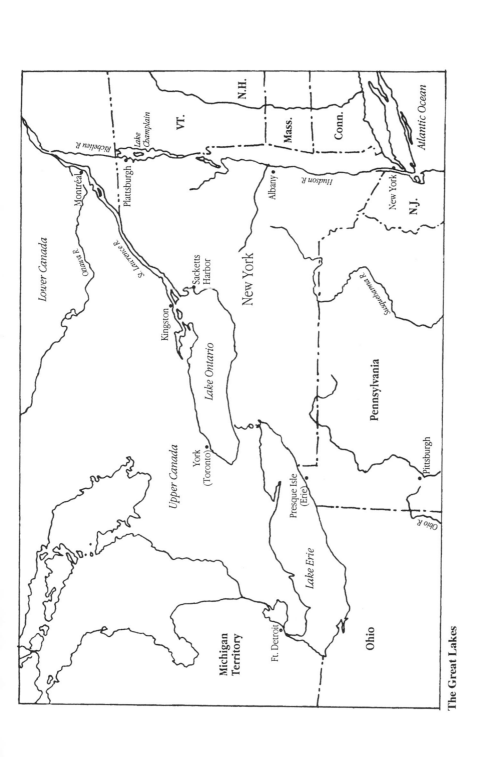

The Great Lakes

until 6 August. Once they were finished, the struggle for Lake Champlain remained at a standoff until the summer of 1814.[17]

During the winter of 1813–14, Macdonough augmented his fleet by building the 26-gun ship *Saratoga* and six large gunboats, and by converting the steamship *Vermont* into a two-masted schooner renamed *Ticonderoga*. He was preparing for the upcoming sailing season, one that would change the complexion of the struggle on Champlain. In early spring, Napoleon abdicated the French throne, ending the European war and leaving the Duke of Wellington's best troops bound for the New World, with at least twelve thousand headed for Canada. The Americans had to gain control of the Lake Champlain corridor to prevent a British invasion from the north.[18]

September 1814 saw the climactic battle for control of Lake Champlain. Macdonough's fourteen vessels, carrying eighty-six guns, were anchored in a defensive position outside Plattsburg Bay. On 11 September, sixteen British vessels carrying ninety-two guns approached the American flotilla and began their assault. In the face of a superior enemy, the American ships held fast and delivered continuous volleys into the approaching ships. When the smoke cleared, Macdonough's lake force had won an all-important victory for the United States. Afterwards, the northern frontier was safe for the remainder of the war. The gunboats did not prove to be the decisive factor in the battle. They did, however, guard the spaces between Macdonough's larger vessels and prevent the British from boarding.[19]

There were several other instances in which gunboats encountered larger ships, without conclusive results. In October 1813, twenty-six of the thirty gunboats on the New York station attacked the British frigate *Acasta* and the sloop *Atalante* in Long Island Sound. Commander Jacob Lewis and his gunboats approached courageously, but because of rough seas they were forced to withdraw to New York before any action occurred. The British were also forced to retire. In May 1814, eleven gunboats attacked the ship-of-the-line *Valiant* before being driven back by superior firepower. Later in May 1814, nine gunboats, accompanied by thirteen barges and the bomb-ketches *Spitfire* and *Vesuvius*, fought a sloop and the frigate *Maidstone* for three hours before nightfall. By daylight, seven additional heavy ships and several smaller craft had joined the British detachment, forcing the American flotilla to retreat. It was true that confrontations such as these did not change the complexion of the war, but they did prove that the gunboats were a force that could not be taken for granted.[20]

The southern stations did not have to counter the frequent British incursions the North experienced and did not have as many gunboat-

"The Battle of Lake Champlain, September 1814." The American force at left is firing at the advancing British ships. Engraving by J. F. Davis after J. O. Davidson. Photo courtesy of the Naval Historical Center.

capital ship confrontations. This was probably because the numerous sandbars and islands off the coast of Georgia and the Carolinas limited the approaches that could be navigated by deep-draft vessels. Furthermore, the coastal waters provided the gunboats with the tremendous advantage Jefferson had recognized. Shortly before war was declared, the gunboats had demonstrated their potential in landing operations. Hugh Campbell, commander of the St. Marys flotilla, used his gunboats as a force-in-being to help a group of insurgents capture Amelia island in March 1812. Before the war ended, American gunboats had captured thirty-one vessels off the coast of Charleston and St. Marys. None of the prizes was a capital ship, but the gunboats protected Charleston and Savannah from British attack.[21]

Many regard Perry's victory on Lake Erie as the most dramatic small-craft battle of the war. Others point to Thomas ap Catesby Jones's spirited defense of New Orleans on 14 December 1814. For two hours, Jones, with his five gunboats and the dispatch boat *Sea Horse* stationed in a defensive position on Lake Borgne, faced forty-five barges loaded with more than twelve hundred troops. Jones fought his gunboats valiantly and inflicted heavy casualties on the enemy, only to see his vessels fall, one by one, to superior British numbers; Jones himself became a prisoner.[22]

The British capture of Jones's gunboats at New Orleans has been proclaimed by some authors as "an American disaster," which could have brought defeat to a commander with less fortitude than Andrew Jackson. Others have charged that "Jones sacrificed his small flotilla to gain [much-needed] time for Jackson." Regardless, it was apparent that Jones's service at New Orleans cannot be overlooked, because his defense obviously demonstrated the gunboats' value in waters that larger ships could not navigate.

British Admiral Alexander Cochrane, commander of the assault, recognized the importance of gunboats in offensive as well as defensive operations. Believing gunboats would be especially useful in supporting troop landings, he manned the captured craft with British crews and used them to protect his troop transports before attacking Jackson. Jones's capture was certainly an American setback, but it also provided an unintentional benefit. Jones and his fellow American prisoners fed British intelligence faulty information about the locations and strength of Jackson's troops, providing Jackson with time.[23]

The gunboats did not win the engagement on Lake Borgne or prevent the Battle of New Orleans from being fought. But that was not the fault of the gunboats or their commander. Had twenty operable gunboats been stationed at New Orleans, as called for by the navy department, the British may have never been able to cross Lake Borgne. But because of hurricanes, tornadoes, and decay, the flotilla only had six vessels on the station, five of which were in service on Borgne when the British began their assault. Furthermore, had Jones's craft been equipped with oars, as had been ordered by the secretary of the navy, the British barges probably would not have caught the gunboats. But such was not the case. The capture of Jones's gunboats unfortunately provided further argument for those who despised the gunboat program. [24]

Theodore Roosevelt, in his *Naval War of 1812*, said that "the various gun-boat attacks accomplished little or nothing of importance. On the other hand, their loss amounted to nothing." Walter Millis, in *Arms and Men*, says that the gunboats "accomplished little or nothing towards hindering the British." Yet he also points out that "neither [did] the ocean-going frigates, the Army, nor the militia system." Gunboats did, however, serve a valuable function during the conflict. British ships had to consider gunboats a potential threat when planning an operation. They contributed to successful operations on Lakes Erie, Champlain, and even at New Orleans. Those victories and the ship-to-ship duels fought early in the war were the high points of the American war effort. [25]

In contrast, the gunboats' performance has not been viewed in such a positive light. Few have acknowledged their importance, even during the war. Congress certainly did not, for in March 1813 it authorized the president to sell or dispose of "so many of the gun boats ... as may no longer be necessary to be retained by the government." The act demonstrated that congressional attitudes concerning the vessels had changed. On 27 February 1815, shortly after the war had concluded, Congress, in its last act on the subject, gave the president the authority to sell the remaining gunboats. [26]

Once the war ended, the navy department complied with congressional mandate to sell the gunboats. Benjamin Crowninshield, who replaced Jones as Madison's third navy secretary, instructed several commanders to sell their craft. Vessels on the Savannah, Charleston, Baltimore, New York, Newport, New Bedford, Norfolk, and Wilmington, North Carolina, stations were laid up in ordinary and their armaments dismantled before being sold at public auction. [27]

The gunboats sold for only a fraction of their original cost. Charles Goldsborough recounted in his *Naval Chronicle* that "the sum they sold for was not one-tenth of their original cost." *Niles' National Register* reported that at one government auction on 17 May 1815, forty-four gunboats were sold for $18,840, with prices ranging from $220 to $690 each. The navy department reported in August 1825 that the government's combined naval force at Sacketts Harbor (Lake Ontario), Erie, and Whitehall had been sold for a mere $52,151.27. The government's condemnation was a paradoxical end to a program that had consumed $1,848,000 of the taxpayers' money.[28]

"The Gallant Attack and Capture of the American Flotilla near New Orleans, Dec. 1814, in Lake Borgne, by the Boats of the Squadron under the Command of Capt. N. Lockyer." Painting by Thomas L. Hornbrook. Courtesy of the United States Naval Academy Museum.

A few gunboats remained in active service after the war, with some even demonstrating offensive potential. *Nos. 149* and *154*, part of the New Orleans flotilla, participated in a joint army-navy expedition against Negro Fort in July 1816. Negro Fort, located on the east side of the Apalachicola River about twenty-five miles inland from the Gulf of Mexico, commanded transportation and communication routes into the southern regions of Alabama and Georgia.[29]

Once the war concluded, the British left the fort and its contents, including cannons, small arms, and ammunition, to their former Indian allies and runaway slaves. The result was that the fort became a sanctuary for runaways as well as a base of operations for depredations against American territory and citizens.[30]

The Spanish, in whose territory the fort was located, considered the stronghold an annoying obstacle to peace in the region. But there was little the Spanish government could do to exercise control of the situation, which prompted Major General Andrew Jackson, commanding the southern military forces, to authorize the fort's destruction. Gunboats *Nos. 149* and *154* were sent to cooperate in that mission.[31]

On the morning of 27 July 1816, Sailing Master Jarvis Loomis, commanding the gunboat force, decided, after consulting with army commanders, that his vessels would assault the fort without land support. While moving into position, Loomis's vessels were fired at by the fort's 32-pound cannon. *No. 154*, commanded by Sailing Master James Bassett, returned four volleys to determine the fort's range. The fifth discharge, a hot shot heated in the gunboat's galley, landed in the fort's largest powder magazine, resulting in an "awful" explosion that destroyed the fort and killed 207 of the 334 people within. After five shots and a certain degree of luck, the fort and the threat it represented were eliminated.[32]

By 1820, virtually all of the Jeffersonian gunboats had been removed from service. Those surviving the auction block were generally in various states of disrepair and destined to deteriorate further. During his tenure as secretary, William Jones had established the navy department's position concerning the vessels. The craft, he felt, were a "waste of money." Moreover, he claimed that since they were not useful on the open seas, the navy department need not be concerned with them "at all." The gunboat program still ran its course. In December 1822, gunboat *No. 158* was listed on the navy rolls as an active part of the West Indian squadron. As late as 1825, *Nos. 67* and *95* were serving as tenders at Washington and Boston, respectively. These apparently were the last of the vessels.[33]

The Jeffersonian gunboat program was a classic example of the functioning of early American democracy. In a narrow sense, the gunboats were a naval policy; but in a more comprehensive way, they were a political-military program upholding broader government decisions. The program initially enjoyed nearly overwhelming popular and congressional support. Nevertheless, there were still those who opposed the craft. Federalists and navalists alike ridiculed the "whirligigs of the sage of Monticello," "Jefferson boats," or "Jeffs," as the visionary ideas of an idealistic antinaval president. Many were quick to point out the debacle of *No. 1*, remarking that "if our gunboats are no use on the water, may they at least be the best on earth!" Others emphasized the "wasteful imbecility" of "money thrown away." Despite the opposition, Congress still implemented the program. This occurred because Congress, embroiled in the much larger naval-antinaval debate of the period, concluded that if the gunboats were unquestionably naval vessels, they at least placated the fears of some about a large, permanent flotilla.[34]

The opinions of naval officers generally mirrored societal attitudes. As with the populace at large, there were officers who supported the program as well as those who loathed the craft. Many navy men despised the gunboats because of their limited blue-water sailing ability, or because of their seemingly constant state of decay. Others felt the craft provided little nautical experience and produced derelict seamen. Some officers experienced difficulty recruiting seamen because the gunboats generally did not provide the opportunity for glory or prize money that bigger ships offered. But, despite these disadvantages, the service did appeal to some. Those seamen who wanted to remain close to home liked the ships because they did not go to sea often or venture to distant stations. Moreover, they also provided many people with simultaneous opportunities for training and practical experience.[35]

Thomas Gautier summed up the attitude concerning the little vessels when he wrote, "The gunboats have so many enemies that it allows all that the service [has] to keep up its dignity." Gautier was correct, but the navy department was unwilling to expend its energies to support the gunboat program. Once the War of 1812 was over, navalism triumphed and the Jeffersonian gunboats were viewed as a "necessary evil" which had strengthened American resolve for a seagoing fleet. Yet the transformation from the gunboat program to a "blue water" navy symbolized larger economic and political changes within the country itself. No longer was the United States a colony or a *de facto* part of the British Empire; it was independent, self-reliant, confident, and ready to take on new responsibilities.[36]

With the triumph of navalism a new policy emerged within the navy department. The policy cast aside the knowledge and experience that should have been gained from the gunboat program. Instead of realizing the abilities and importance of shallow-draft vessels, navalists concluded that bigger ships (frigates, ships-of-the-line) and distant stations were necessary. Alfred Thayer Mahan, some three-quarters of a century later, eloquently espoused that same idea. Mahan, a product of his time, concluded in his monumental work, *The Influence of Seapower upon History*, that control of the seas was essential to the survival of an empire. Gunboats obviously could not gain control of the seas.

As the ideas of Mahan gained in popularity, greatly supported by President Theodore Roosevelt, the lessons that should have been learned from the gunboats' performance were forgotten. Instead, history declared them to have been an aberration that provided no benefits. Yet, if one examines the performance of the navy in the Seminole War or the Mexican War, the importance of shallow-draft vessels becomes obvious. Gunboat-type vessels were the only craft that could infiltrate the shallow swamps of south Florida. During the Mexican War, shallow-draft craft were important in supporting Winfield Scott's landing at Vera Cruz. Even during the American Civil War, shallow-draft riverine vessels played an important role in determining the outcome of the conflict. In the twentieth century, shallow-draft vessels played a useful contributive part during World War II and the Vietnam War. In each case, however, their importance was downplayed in favor of "blue water" ships and control of the seas.[37]

Although neither the gunboats nor other shallow-draft vessels were responsible for winning a war, they amply demonstrated their importance as adjuncts to a seagoing navy. It was a lesson Jefferson reiterated when he introduced the gunboat program. As president, he sought to diversify the country's defenses. He wanted forts; seagoing ships; gunboats; floating, moving, and stationary batteries; and a trained militia, all working together for the country's security. But his program was ridiculed and never completely implemented. Instead, Congress saw the gunboats as substitutes for the president's more comprehensive strategic plan, and the policy thereafter became stereotyped as the "Jeffersonian gunboat program."

But what would have happened if the gunboat program had never been implemented? The country would probably have depended exclusively on seagoing vessels and may have incurred the wrath of the British even earlier than she did. And if that were not the case, once war began, the outcome might have been much different. Because the big American frigates were blockaded in port for most of the war, many of the country's best seamen and most of its resources were sent to the northern lakes. The result was a victorious campaign that wrested control of the lakes from the British and prevented Wellington's seasoned peninsular veterans from invading the United States. Had the lakes been lost because of the predominance of a totally seagoing naval policy, other major cities might have experienced the same humiliation that Washington endured. Although purely conjectural, it may be this scenario that suggests the hidden value of the gunboat program.

There are valid reasons to condemn Jefferson's gunboat program as it developed, and it can be viewed as a failure in light of the president's original conception of how the vessels were to be integrated into the nation's defense. On another level, the craft did not inspire confidence either from their commanders and crews or from the people. They were generally ridiculed, and few placed much emphasis on their capabilities. Thomas Gautier wrote in 1813, "I then shall sit down in a sullen retire-ment and view the boats in the mud and then reflect on the situation of my state not [acting with the] armed vessels allotted for her defense." This statement accurately described the gunboats' use as well as how they were perceived. Ironically, the program was never given a full opportunity to demonstrate its value or to function as it was originally conceived. If the program was a failure, it was due neither to Jefferson's ideas nor to the vessels themselves, but perhaps to the American political process, which is a lesson relevant in any age.[38]

Notes

Chapter 1
Introduction

1. Merill Peterson, *Thomas Jefferson and the New Nation* (New York: Oxford University Press, 1970), viii.
2. John T. Morse, *Thomas Jefferson* (Boston: Houghton, Mifflin and Company, 1898), 259.
3. B. L. Rayner, *Sketches of the Life, Writings, and Opinions of Thomas Jefferson* (New York: A. Francis and W. Boardman, 1832), 401.
4. Thomas Gautier to John Dent, 26 September 1812, Thomas Gautier Papers, Southern Historical Collection, Library of the University of North Carolina at Chapel Hill (hereafter cited as SHC-UNC).
5. Jefferson to John Adams, 27 May 1813, Andrew A. Lipscomb and Albert Ellery Bergh, *The Writings of Thomas Jefferson* (Washington, D.C.: The Thomas Jefferson Memorial Association, 1904), 13: 249; Julia H. Macleod, "Jefferson and the Navy: A Defense," *Huntington Library Quarterly* 8 (1944–45): 153.
6. Howard I. Chapelle, *History of the American Sailing Navy* (New York: Bonanza Books, 1949), 179–241.
7. Craig Symonds, *Navalists and Antinavalists; The Naval Policy Debate in the United States, 1785–1827* (Newark: University of Delaware Press, 1980), 105–30; Macleod, "Jefferson and the Navy," 153–84.
8. Harold and Margaret Sprout, *The Rise of American Naval Power* (Princeton, NJ: Princeton University Press, 1946), 60; Alfred Thayer Mahan, *Sea Power and Its Relation to the War of 1812* (1905; reprint, New York: Haskell House Publishers, Ltd., 1969) 1: 187–88, 296; Jefferson, "Special Message on Gun-Boats" to the Senate and House of Representatives, 10 February 1807, James D. Richardson, *A Compilation of the Messages and Papers of the Presidents* (New York: Bureau of National Literature, Inc., 1897), 1: 407–9; Mary P. Adams, "Jefferson's Military Policy with Special Reference to the Frontier: 1805–1809" (Ph.D. dissertation, University of Virginia, 1958), v-vi; Macleod, "Jefferson and the Navy," 176.

9. David S. Muzzey, "Abraham Alfonse Albert Gallatin," Allen Johnson, ed., *Dictionary of American Biography* (New York: Charles Scribner's Sons, 1928); Henry Adams, *History of the United States of America* (New York: Charles Scribner's Sons, 1891; reprint, New York: Literary Classics, 1986), 162.

10. Alexander S. Balinky, *Albert Gallatin* (New Brunswick, NJ: Rutgers University Press, 1958), viii; Alexander S. Balinky, "Albert Gallatin, Naval Foe," *Pennsylvania Magazine of History and Biography* 82 (1958): 296; Raymond Walters, Jr., *Albert Gallatin: Jeffersonian Financier and Diplomat* (New York: The Macmillan Company, 1957), 194.

11. Thom M. Armstrong, *Politics, Diplomacy and Intrigue in the Early Republic* (Dubuque, IA: Kendall/Hunt Publishing Company, 1991), 5–7; Charles Oscar Paullin, "Naval Administration Under Secretaries of the Navy Smith, Hamilton, and Jones, 1801–1814," *United States Naval Institute Proceedings* (December 1906): 1292.

12. Frank L. Owsley, Jr. "Robert Smith," Paolo Coletta, ed., *American Secretaries of the Navy* (Annapolis, MD: Naval Institute Press, 1980), 1: 77–88.

13. Walter Millis, *Arms and Men: A Study of American Military History* (New York: G. P. Putnam's Sons, 1956), 56.

Chapter 2
A Means to an End:
Gunboats and Jefferson's Theory of Defense

1. Alfred Thayer Mahan, *The Influence of Sea Power Upon History* (privately printed, 1890; reprint, New York: Sagamore Press Inc., 1957), 3 n . Hermocrates supported a policy of an offensive defense, by attacking the Athenian flank as it advanced on the city of Syracuse.

2. Mahan, *War of 1812*, 1: 295.

3. Joel Barlow to Jefferson, 11 February 1804, Jefferson Manuscripts, Library of Congress, Washington, D.C. All manuscript collections in the Library of Congress will henceforth be cited as MSS., LC. Barlow wrote that only Russia and the United States were "powerful in ... their physical means of defence" because neither country had anything to protect other than itself.

4. Jefferson, *Notes on the State of Virginia* (Philadelphia: Prichard and Hall, 1788), 187; Dumas Malone, *Jefferson the President: Second Term, 1805–1809* (Boston: Little, Brown and Company, 1974), 492.

5. Macleod, "Jefferson and the Navy," 161–63; Jefferson to Colonel James Monroe, 30 May 1813, Lipscomb and Bergh, *The Writings of Thomas Jefferson*, 13: 251.

6. Michael Palmer, *Stoddert's War: Naval Operations During the Quasi-War with France, 1798–1801* (Columbia: University of South Carolina Press, 1987), 238.

7. David M. Cooney, *A Chronology of the U.S. Navy: 1775–1965* (New York: Franklin Watts, Inc., 1965), 24; Charles Oscar Paullin, *Paullin's History of Naval Administrations, 1775–1911* (Annapolis, MD: United States Naval Institute Press, 1968), 128; *Public Statutes at Large of the United States* (Boston: Charles C. Little and James Brown, 1845), 2: 110–11.

8. Mahan, *War of 1812*, 1: 296.

9. J. C. A. Stagg, *Mr. Madison's War: Politics, Diplomacy, and Warfare in the Early Republic, 1783–1830* (Princeton, NJ: Princeton University Press, 1983), 134; Chapelle, *History of the American Sailing Navy*, 189.

10. Malone, *Jefferson the President: Second Term*, 502–3.

11. Charles Goldsborough, *The United States Naval Chronicle* (Washington, D.C.: James Wilson, 1824), 4.

12. Mary P. Adams, "Jefferson's Military Policy." This work expounds the thesis that Jefferson was extremely concerned with national defense and took measures to that end. She concurs that gunboats were only a part of his defense policy. Jefferson to the Senate and House, "Special Message on Gun-Boats," 10 February 1807, Richardson, *Messages of the Presidents*, 1: 407–9. Jefferson reveals, in this message, that his strategy for defense was a multifarious plan, consisting of more than just gunboats. Malone, *Jefferson the President: Second Term*, 496; Macleod, "Jefferson and the Navy," 153.

13. Mary P. Adams, "Jefferson's Military Policy," iii.

14. Jefferson to Mr. Bowdoin, 10 August 1806, Jefferson MSS., LC.

15. Jefferson to Albert Gallatin, 11 October 1809, Paul Leicester Ford, *The Writings of Jefferson* (New York: G. P. Putnam's Sons, 1899), 9: 264; Malone, *Jefferson the President: Second Term*, 494.

16. Jefferson to Albert Gallatin, 11 October 1809, Ford, *The Writings of Jefferson*, 9: 264; Walter Jones to William Brent, 18 January 1810, Walter Jones Papers, Virginia Historical Society, Richmond; Nathaniel Macon to Joseph H. Nicholson, 31 January 1806, Joseph H. Nicholson MSS., LC.

17. Malone, *Jefferson the President: Second Term*, 494; Sprout and Sprout, *The Rise of American Naval Power*, 45, 54; Balinky, "Albert Gallatin, Naval Foe," 300–301; Jefferson to the House of Representatives, 18 February 1806, Walter Lowrie and Walter S. Franklin, *The American State Papers; Naval Affairs, March 3, 1789–March 5, 1825* (Washington, D.C.: Gales and Seaton, 1834), 149 (hereafter cited as *ASP)*; Jefferson to Elbridge Gerry, 26 January 1799, Ford, *The Writings of Jefferson*, 7: 328.

18. Jefferson to the Senate and House of Representatives, "Special Message on Gun-Boats," 10 February, 1807, Richardson, *Messages of the Presidents*, 1: 407–9.

19. Dumas Malone (*Jefferson the President: Second Term*, xx, 496) claimed that "Jefferson's opinion, especially after Trafalgar, that a strong seagoing navy would have been an utter waste was not as silly as certain later enthusiasts for seapower were to claim." Marshall Smelser (*The Democratic Republic: 1801–1815* [New York: Harper and Row, 1968], 229) exclaimed that "after Trafalgar, a lonely, microscopic American fleet would have been gold cast into the sea." Jefferson realized that antinavalist Republicans would not approve the construction of a seagoing navy despite his pleas.

20. Symonds, *Navalists and Antinavalists*, 109–10. Before Trafalgar, Jefferson sincerely entertained the idea of using the American navy to balance power in Europe, but afterwards there was no hope, for, as Congressman Lemuel Sawyer proclaimed, "the time was now elapsed" (*Annals of the Congress of the United States* [Washington, D.C.: Gales and Seaton, 1834–56], 10th Congress, 1st session, 9 December 1807, 1089).

21. Emanuel Raymond Lewis, *Seacoast Fortifications of the United States*, 2nd ed. (Annapolis, MD: Leeward Publications, Inc. 1979), 21–25. Lewis provides a basic description of the three types of fortifications, giving their differences and similarities, on pages 25–31. Open batteries were small works in positions of

secondary importance or near forts as supporting adjuncts. Masonry-faced forts utilized a combination of earth and an exterior scarp reinforced with masonry. The all-masonry forts were granite-constructed, high-walled harbor defenses that implemented the casemated gun emplacement.

22. Jefferson to Tadeusz Kosciuszko, 26 February 1810, Agnieszka Glinczanka, and Jozef Paszkowski, eds., *Korespondencja; 1798–1817* (Panstwowy Instytut Wydawniczy, 1976), 80.

23. Arthur P. Wade, "Artillerists and Engineers: The Beginnings of American Seacoast Fortifications, 1794–1815," (Ph.D. dissertation, Kansas State University, 1977), 181–82.

24. Jefferson to Henry Dearborn, 27 January 1806, Jefferson MSS., LC, quoted in Richard Alton Erney, *The Public Life of Henry Dearborn* (Ph.D. dissertation, Columbia University, 1957; printed by Arno Press, New York, 1979), 155; Jefferson to Mr. Nicholson, 29 January 1805, Jefferson MSS., LC.

25. Jefferson to DeWitt Clinton, 29 January 1805, DeWitt Clinton Papers, Columbia University Library, New York; Jefferson to Mr. Nicholson, 29 January 1805, Jefferson to Governor Lewis, 2 May 1806, Jefferson MSS., LC; Jefferson to Senate and House of Representatives, "Special Message on Gun-Boats," 10 February 1807, Richardson, *Messages of the Presidents*, 1: 407–9.

26. John Shaw to General James Wilkinson, 9 May 1813, 4 June 1813, John Shaw Papers, Naval Historical Foundation Collection, Library of Congress, Washington, D.C. (hereafter cited as NHF-LC).

27. Jefferson to Mr. Nicholson, 29 January 1805, Jefferson to Henry Dearborn, 27 January 1806, Jefferson MSS., LC; Jefferson to Senate and House of Representatives, "Special Message on Gun-Boats," 10 February 1807, Richardson, *Messages of the Presidents*, 1: 407–9.

28. Jefferson to Mr. Nicholson, 29 January 1805, Jefferson MSS., LC; Jefferson to Senate and House of Representatives, "Special Message on Gun-Boats," 10 February 1807, Richardson, *Messages of the Presidents*, 1: 407–9; Jefferson to Governor Wilson C. Nicholas, 2 April 1816, Lipscomb and Bergh, *The Writings of Thomas Jefferson*, 14: 446–47.

29. Jefferson to Secretary of the Navy, 19 June 1805, Jefferson MSS., LC.

30. Jefferson to Robert Smith, 19 May 1806, Jefferson MSS., LC, quoted in Joseph G. Henrich, "The Triumph of Ideology: The Jeffersonians and the Navy, 1779–1807" (Ph.D. dissertation, Duke University, 1971), 360; Rayner, *Sketches*, 442.

31. Jefferson to Jacob Crowninshield, 13 May 1806, Jefferson MSS., LC. Dumas Malone, Marshall Smelsor, and Craig Symonds all agree that Jefferson considered building capital vessels until the British victory at Trafalgar. Malone and Julia Macleod even argue that Jefferson wanted ships-of-the-line. Frederick Leiner, however, concludes that if that were true, Jefferson was certainly sending mixed and confusing signals. Frederick C. Leiner, "The 'Whimsical Phylosophic President,' and His Gunboats" *American Neptune* 43 (Fall 1983): 250–51, 253.

32. *Annals*, 9th Congress, 1st Session, 23 December 1805, 302; 25 March 1806, 842–47.

33. Macleod, "Jefferson and the Navy," 176; Rayner, *Sketches*, 422.

34. Jefferson to John Jay, 23 August 1785, cited in James Truslow Adams, ed., *Jeffersonian Principles* (Boston: Little Brown and Company, 1928), 82–83.

35. Jefferson to James Monroe, 11 August 1786, Julian P. Boyd, ed., *Papers of Thomas Jefferson* (Princeton, NJ: Princeton University Press, 1954), 10: 225.

36. J. G. de Roulhac Hamilton, "The Pacifism of Thomas Jefferson," *Virginia Quarterly Review* 31 (1955): 615.

37. Symonds, *Navalists and Antinavalists*, 109.
38. L. Sprague De Camp, *The Ancient Engineers* (New York: Ballatine Books, 1963), 78.
39. Thomas Paine, "Of Gun-Boats," Philip S. Foner, *The Complete Writings of Thomas Paine* (New York: The Citadel Press, 1945), 1069.
40. Spencer C. Tucker, "Mr. Jefferson's Gunboat Navy" *American Neptune* 43 (Spring 1983): 135; Circular Letter of Robert G. Harper, 23 July 1798, Bayard Papers, MS. 109, Manuscripts Division, Maryland Historical Society Library, Baltimore.
41. Joseph Desha to his Constituents, 29 March 1807, Breckinridge Family MSS., LC.
42. Lieutenant-Governor Henry Ellis to William Pitt, 16 April 1760, Gertrude Selwyn Kimball, *Correspondence of William Pitt* (London: Macmillan Company, 1906, reprint, New York: Kraus Reprint Co, 1969), 2: 277–79; Jefferson to William Call, 12 April 1781, Boyd, *Papers of Thomas Jefferson*, 5: 413.
43. Albert Gallatin to Jefferson, "Notes–Message Respecting Gunboats," 8 February 1807, Henry Adams, ed., *Writings of Albert Gallatin* (1879; reprint, New York: Antiquarian Press, 1960), 329; Jefferson to the Senate and House of Representatives, "Special Message on Gun-Boats," 10 February 1807, Richardson, *Messages of the Presidents*, 1: 407–9.
44. Jefferson to the Senate and House of Representatives, "Special Message on Gun-Boats," 10 February 1807, Richardson, *Messages of the Presidents*, 1: 407–9; Chapelle, *History of the American Sailing Navy*, 189.
45. Secretary of the Navy to Alexander Murray, 29 January 1808, "Gunboat Letters," National Archives, Washington D.C., Record Group 45, Entry 173. Nonmicrofilmed materials from the National Archives will henceforth be cited by their record number and entry, for example, RG45: 173.
46. Thomas Paine, "Of the Comparative Powers and Expense of Ships of War, Gun-Boats, and Fortifications," Foner, *Writings of Thomas Paine*, 1075.
47. Jefferson to the Senate and House of Representatives, "Special Message on Gun-Boats," 10 February 1807, Richardson, *Messages of the Presidents*, 1: 407–9; Jefferson to James Madison, 21 May 1813, Lipscomb and Bergh, *The Writings of Thomas Jefferson*, 13: 233.
48. Samuel Barron to Jefferson, 8 February 1807, *ASP*, 164.
49. Jefferson to James Madison, 21 May 1813. Lipscomb and Bergh, *The Writings of Thomas Jefferson*, 13: 234; Jefferson to Mr. Bowdoin, 10 July 1806, Jefferson MSS., LC.
50. Balinky, "Albert Gallatin, Naval Foe," 293; "A Statistical Table for the United States of America, for a Succession of Years," October 1803, Jefferson MSS., LC. This table indicates that that country's expenditures rose from $8,740,329 in 1796 to $12,945,455 in 1801.
51. Memo from Robert Smith to Jefferson, 22 November 1804, Jefferson MSS., LC. Rough estimate for construction of gunboat was between five and six thousand dollars. Jefferson to the House of Representatives, 18 February 1806, *ASP*, 149; Robert Smith to Thomas Jefferson, 19 January 1803, Jefferson MSS., LC. Smith estimated that a 16-gun ship would cost twenty-four thousand dollars.
52. Paul Hamilton to Richard Cutts, 9 June 1809, *ASP*, 200.
53. Jefferson to John Adams, 1 November 1822, cited in Leonard D. White, *The Jeffersonians* (New York: Macmillan, 1951), 266.
54. Jefferson, *Notes*, 188.
55. Jefferson to Albert Gallatin, 9 February 1807, Albert Gallatin Papers, The New-York Historical Society, New York.

56. Robert Smith to Nathaniel Macon, 27 January 1806, *ASP*, 148.

57. Paul Hamilton to House of Representatives, 12 June 1809, *ASP*, 193; Jefferson's Fourth Annual Message, 8 November 1804, Richardson, *Messages of the Presidents*, 1: 357–61. Jefferson wrote that the economical aspect of gunboats was from their maintenance and preservation when not in actual service. Robert Smith to Jefferson, 13 December 1804, Jefferson MSS., LC.

58. Jefferson to the Senate and House of Representatives, "Special Message on Gun-Boats," 10 February 1807, Richardson, *Messages of the Presidents*, 1: 407–9. Jefferson estimated that in times of peace only six or eight gunboats needed to be in service. Eight gunboats in service at $11,039.46 per year is $88,315.68; an estimated 192 gunboats in ordinary at $2,147 per year is $412,224, totaling $500,539.68. The amount for the actual cruising force was less than the maintenance for one frigate, and those in storage increased the costs to less than five frigates.

59. Gene A. Smith, "'For the Purposes of Defense': Thomas Jefferson's Naval Militia," *American Neptune* 53 (Winter 1993): 30–38.

60. Secretary of the Navy to John Beekman, 8 January 1805, "Gunboat Letters," RG45: 173.

61. Jefferson to Mr. [Joseph] Nicholson, 29 January 1805, H. A. Washington, *The Writings of Thomas Jefferson* (Washington, D.C.: Taylor and Maury, 1854), 4: 568.

62. Robert Smith to Jefferson, 27 March 1805, Jefferson MSS., LC.

63. David Porter to Secretary of the Navy, 12 May 1808, *Letters Received by the Secretary of the Navy from Commanders, 1804–1886*, National Archives, Washington D.C., RG45, M147 (hereafter cited as *Commanders Letters*).

64. Ship's Contracts, National Archives, Washington, D.C., RG45: 235; "Register of Ships and Officers," National Archives, Washington, D.C., RG45: 171.

65. William Eustis's opposition was printed in the *National Intelligencer and Washington Advertiser,* 24 January 1803, *Annals*, 7th Congress, 2nd session, 19 January 1803, 406.

66. David Porter to Secretary of the Navy, 30 April 1808, *Commanders Letters*.

67. Jefferson to Robert Smith, 12 August 1808, Jefferson to James Madison 12 August 1808, Jefferson to Jacob Crowninshield, 21 July 1804, Jefferson MSS., LC; John Shaw to Paul Hamilton, 10 July 1812, John Shaw MSS., LC.

68. Jefferson to Robert Smith, 14 February 1808, Robert Smith to Jefferson, 16 December 1808, Jefferson MSS., LC; David Porter to Secretary of the Navy, 19 September 1808, Porter to Secretary of the Navy, 26 June 1808, *Commanders Letters*.

69. Jefferson to Joseph Nicholson, 20 November 1804, Joseph Nicholson MSS., LC.

70. "Notes for Consideration, and for Instructions to armed vessels which may be sent out to protect commerce on our coasts," Jefferson MSS., LC.

71. David Porter to Secretary of the Navy, 1 January 1810, 4 May 1810, *Commanders Letters*.

72. The rebellion mentioned was the Louisiana "River Road" Slave Insurrection of January 1811. Naval forces from the New Orleans squadron helped put down the revolt. Wade Hampton to William Eustis, 16 January 1811, Clarence Edwin Carter, ed., *The Territorial Papers of the United States; The Territory of Louisiana and Missouri, 1806–1814* (Washington, D.C.: Government Printing Office, 1949), 9: 917–19; John Shaw to Paul Hamilton, 18 January 1811, K. Jack Bauer, ed., *The New American State Papers* (Wilmington, DE: Scholarly Resources Inc., 1981), 1: 205–9; Paul Hamilton to John Shaw, 25 February 1811, *Letters Sent by Secretary of the Navy to Officers, 1798–1868*, National Archives, Washington, D.C., RG45, M149.

73. "1804 Estimate of Louisiana Indian Warriors," Jefferson MSS., LC. Jefferson actually believed the number to be about 30,000 if one added the Aliahtans, or Snake Indians.

74. Erik W. Austin and Jerome M. Clubb, *Political Facts of the United States Since 1789* (New York: Columbia University Press, 1986), table 5.1; Jefferson to Secretary of the Navy, 13 July 1804, Jefferson MSS., LC.

75. William Clark to Secretary of War, 24 February 1813, Carter, *Territorial Papers*, 14: 632; William Clark to Secretary of War, 12 September 1813, Carter, *Territorial Papers*, 14: 693.

76. Joseph Tarbell to Secretary of the Navy, 7 December 1810, Dent to Secretary of the Navy, 21 November 1810, Daniel Patterson to Secretary of the Navy, 31 January 1814, *Commanders Letters*.

77. David Porter to Secretary of the Navy, 29 March 1807, *Commanders Letters*.

78. Robert Smith to Jefferson, 28 June 1804, Jefferson MSS., LC.

79. Christopher McKee, *A Gentlemanly and Honorable Profession; The Creation of the U.S. Naval Officer Corps, 1794–1815* (Annapolis, MD: Naval Institute Press, 1991), 156–57.

80. Albert Gleaves, *James Lawrence: Captain, United States Navy, Commander of the "Chesapeake"* (New York: G. P. Putnam's Sons, 1904), 57.

81. Adams, *History of the United States*, 1036.

82. William S. Dudley, ed., *The Naval War of 1812: A Documentary History,* vol. 1: *1812* (Washington, D.C.: Naval Historical Center, 1985), 1: 12 n .

83. Leiner, "The 'Whimsical Phylosophic President' and His Gunboats," 252.

84. Albert Gallatin to Jefferson, "Remarks on Jefferson's Fourth Annual Message," 29 October 1804. Paul Leicester Ford, *The Writings of Jefferson* (New York: G. P. Putnam's Sons, 1897), 4: 327.

85. Forrest McDonald, *The Presidency of Thomas Jefferson* (Lawrence: University of Kansas Press, 1976), 44; William M. Fowler, Jr., *Jack Tars and Commodores* (Boston: Houghton Mifflin Company, 1984), 145; Sprout and Sprout, *The Rise of American Naval Power*, 58.

86. John Adams to Jefferson, 15 October 1822, cited in Rayner, *Sketches*, 442–43.

87. Jefferson to Samuel Harrison Smith, 2 March 1808, Samuel Harrison Smith MSS., LC.

Chapter 3
The Emergence of Policy: First Term, 1801–5

1.   Richard S. Westfall, *The Construction of Modern Science: Mechanisms and Mechanics* (New York: John Wiley and Sons, Inc., 1971), 151–52.

2.   Symonds, *Navalists and Antinavalists*, 109–10.

3.   Robert Middlekauf, *The Glorious Cause* (Oxford: Oxford University Press, 1982), 586–87; Samuel Flagg Bemis, *Jay's Treaty: A Study in Commerce and Diplomacy* (Knights of Columbus, 1923; reprint, New Haven: Yale University Press, 1962), 23–26.

4.   Smelser, *The Democratic Republic*, 85.

5.   Robert Ferrell, *American Diplomacy* (New York: W. W. Norton, 1975), 105–7; Dumas Malone, *Jefferson the President: First Term, 1801–1805* (Boston: Little,

Brown and Company, 1970), 264; Jefferson's Second Annual Message, 15 December 1802, Richardson, *Messages of the Presidents*, 1: 330–34.

6. Ferrell, *American Diplomacy*, 105–6; Adams, *History of the United States*, 289–90.

7. Adams, *History of the United States*, 288–91; Malone, *Jefferson the President: First Term*, 264–69; Ferrell, *American Diplomacy*, 105–6; Jefferson to the House of Representatives, 22 December 1802, Richardson, *Messages of the Presidents*, 1: 334–38.

8. Adams, *History of the United States*, 291–92; Jefferson to James Monroe, 13 January 1803, Jefferson MSS., LC.

9. John Smith to Jefferson, 15 January 1803, Jefferson MSS., LC.

10. *Annals*, 7th Congress, 2nd session, 14 February 1803, 88; John Randolph to William Branch Giles, 19 January 1803, John Randolph Letter, Manuscripts Division, Special Collections Department, University of Virginia Library, Charlottesville.

11. Adams, *History of the United States*, 292–94; Malone, *Jefferson the President: First Term*, 278–79; Robert Smith to DeWitt Clinton, 16 February 1803, cited in Leiner, "The 'Whimsical Phylosophic President' and His Gunboats," 248.

12. *Statutes at Large*, 28 February 1803, 2: 206; Robert Smith to DeWitt Clinton, 16 February 1803, cited in Henrich, "The Triumph of Ideology," 354–55.

13. Circular letter from William Dickson to Moses Fisk, 30 March 1803, Noble Cunningham, Jr., ed., *Circular Letters of Congressmen to their Constituents, 1789–1829* (Chapel Hill: University of North Carolina Press for the Institute of Early American History and Culture, Williamsburg, Virginia, 1978), 1: 350; Thomas Truxtun to George Libbald, 4 October 1803, Thomas Truxtun Papers, United States Naval Academy Museum, Annapolis, MD.

14. John Stanly, "Letter to his Constituents" (Washington, D.C. 1803), *Early American Imprints*, series II, no. 5097, 22.

15. Alfred Owen Aldridge, "Thomas Paine's Plan for a Descent on England," *William and Mary Quarterly* 14 (January 1957): 77–78. In Jefferson MSS., LC there is a 1 October 1800 document in Paine's hand that describes the plan presented to the directory. However, the date Jefferson received this letter is in question. Jefferson to William Call, 12 April 1781, Boyd, *Papers of Thomas Jefferson*, 5: 413.

16. Robert Smith to John Gavino, 24 January 1803, *Miscellaneous Letters Sent by the Secretary of the Navy, 1789–1886*, RG45, M209; Secretary of the Navy to Samuel Barron, 24 February 1803, Bauer, *The New American State Papers*, 46; Chapelle, *History of the American Sailing Navy*, 182; Robert Smith to George Harrison, 17 March 1803, 19 March 1803, *Misc. Letters Sent*.

17. Arthur Preston Whitaker, *The Mississippi Question; 1795–1803* (New York: D. Appleton-Century Company for the American Historical Association, 1934), 231–32; Jefferson to Sir John Sinclair, 30 June 1803, Jefferson MSS., LC.

18. Adams, *History of the United States*, 334–35; Adams chronicles the Mississippi question and the Louisiana purchase on pages 337–92. Malone, *Jefferson the President: First Term*, 284; Malone's coverage of the same topic is on pages 262–363.

19. Jefferson to Thomas Mann Randolph, 5 July 1803, Jefferson MSS., LC.

20. E. B. Potter and Chester W. Nimitz, *Sea Power: A Naval History* (Englewood Cliffs, NJ: Prentice-Hall, Inc., 1960), 195–96.

21. Benson J. Lossing, *The Story of the United States Navy* (New York: Harper and Brothers, 1880), 76–78; Smelser, *The Democratic Republic*, 58; Gardner W. Allen, *Our Navy and the Barbary Corsairs* (Boston: Houghton Mifflin, 1905; reprint, 1967), 77, cited in Potter and Nimitz, *Sea Power*, 196.

22. Jefferson to Secretary of the Navy, 20 September 1802, The Papers of Thomas Jefferson Papers, Manuscripts Division, Special Collections Department, University of Virginia Library, Charlottesville; Malone, *Jefferson the President: First Term*, 98–99; Potter and Nimitz, *Sea Power*, 196–97; Smelser, *The Democratic Republic*, 58.

23. Potter and Nimitz, *Sea Power*, 196–97; Felix Howland, "The Blockade of Tripoli, 1801–1802," *United States Naval Institute Proceedings* 43 (1937): 1702–4; Mary Lewis Cooke and Charles Lee Lewis, "An American Naval Officer in the Mediterranean, 1802–1807," *United States Naval Institute Proceedings* 47 (1941): 1535; Peterson, *Thomas Jefferson and the New Nation*, 798; Robert Smith to Richard V. Morris, 31 August 1802, Dudley W. Knox, ed., *Naval Documents Related to the United States Wars With the Barbary Powers; Naval Operations Including Diplomatic Background from 1785 through 1807* (Washington, D.C.: Government Printing Office, 6 vols., 1939–44), 2: 261. Hereafter cited as *Barbary Powers*.

24. Jefferson's Third Annual Message, 17 October 1803, Richardson, *Messages of the Presidents*, 1: 347–49; Symonds, *Navalists and Antinavalists*, 105; Dice Robins Anderson, *William Branch Giles: A Study in the Politics of Virginia and the Nation from 1790 to 1830* (Menasha, WI: George Banta Publishing Company, 1914; reprint, Gloucester, MA: Peter Smith, 1965), 87–88.

25. Christopher McKee, *Edward Preble: A Naval Biography, 1761–1807* (Annapolis, MD: Naval Institute Press, 1972), 179–82; Potter and Nimitz, *Sea Power*, 199–200; Peterson, *Thomas Jefferson and the New Nation*, 798–99; Allen, *Our Navy and the Barbary Corsairs*, 173.

26. Jefferson's Third Annual Message, 17 October 1803, Richardson, *Messages of the Presidents*, 1: 348; Secretary of the Navy to John Rodgers and James Barron, 21 December 1803, Knox, *Barbary Powers*, 3: 282–83;

27. James Leander Cathcart to Edward Preble, 18 November 1803, Knox, *Barbary Powers*, 3: 229; Preble to Cathcart, 31 January 1804, Knox, *Barbary Powers* 3: 379; Preble to Secretary of the Navy, 11 March 1804, Knox, *Barbary Powers* 3: 485–86; Degen Purviance to Preble, 30 January 1804, Edward Preble Papers, LC; Charles Moran, "Commodore Preble's Sicilian Auxiliaries," *United States Naval Institute Proceedings* 65 (Jan-June 1939): 80–82; Jefferson to the Senate and House of Representatives, 20 March 1804, Jefferson MSS., LC; Goldsborough, *Naval Chronicle*, 322; author unknown, pamphlet enclosed in Thomas Truxtun to Jefferson, 25 September 1804, Jefferson MSS., LC (pamphlet reflected Jefferson's views and may be the work of Truxtun himself); Jefferson to Larkin Smith, 7 September 1805, Jefferson Papers, Henry E. Huntington Library, San Marino, CA; Jefferson to James Madison, 15 April 1804, Jefferson Papers, Coolidge Collection, Massachusetts Historical Society, Boston.

28. Chapelle, *History of the American Sailing Navy*, 193; Leiner, "The 'Whimsical Phylosophic President' and His Gunboats," 248; Henrich, "Triumph of Ideology," 356–57.

29. Adams, *History of the United States*, 592–93; Barnabas Bidwell, "An Address to the People of Massachusetts" (Boston: Adams and Rhoades, 1804), 13, *Early American Imprints*, series II, no. 5871.

30. Bradford Perkins, *The First Rapprochement: England and the United States; 1795–1805* (London: Cambridge University Press, 1955), 182–86; Malone, *Jefferson the President: First Term*, 441; Lynton K. Caldwell, *The Administrative Theories of Hamilton and Jefferson* (New York: Russell and Russell, Inc., 1964), 177; Jefferson

to Horatio Gates, 11 July 1803, Thomas Jefferson Papers, Rare Books and Manuscripts Division, The New York Public Library, Astor, Lenox and Tilden Foundations.

31. "Private Memoirs while Secretary to President Thomas Jefferson and Congress, 1804–1818," William Burwell MSS., LC, 12–13; Jefferson to Jacob Crowninshield, 21 July 1804, Jefferson MSS., LC.; Horatio Gates to Jefferson, 19 October 1804, and James Wilkinson to Jefferson, 10 November 1804, both included in Jefferson to Senate and House of Representatives, 10 February 1807, *ASP*, 163–64.

32. Horatio Gates to Jefferson, 19 October 1804, James Wilkinson to Jefferson, 10 November 1804, Jefferson MSS., LC.

33. James Wilkinson to Horatio Gates, 5 March 1805, "Reflections on the Fortifications and Defence of the Sea Ports of the United States," cited in McKee, *Edward Preble*, 317–19.

34. Albert Gallatin to Jefferson, "Remarks on President's Message," October 1804, Adams, *Writings of Albert Gallatin*, 1: 214–15.

35. Henrich, "Triumph of Ideology," 340–41; Armstrong, *Politics, Diplomacy and Intrigue in the Early Republic*, 91–92; Owsley, "Robert Smith," Coletta, *American Secretaries of the Navy,* 1: 85. Owsley claims that Smith "opposed Jefferson's gunboat policy from the start." After a closer examination of original materials, it is revealed that Smith was a skillful politician, as Owsley later suggests, and that his support of the gunboat program varied over the years. During 1804 and 1805, Smith avidly supported the program, but by 1806 he felt that larger ships were also needed. This attitude reflected the president's ideas but was overshadowed by an antinaval Congress that refused to support measures for the development of a seagoing navy.

36. Jefferson's Fourth Annual Message, 8 November 1804, Richardson, *Messages of the Presidents*, 1: 357–61.

37. Jefferson's Fourth Annual Message, 8 November 1804, Richardson, *Messages of the Presidents*, 1: 357–61; Jefferson to Joseph H. Nicholson, 20 November 1804, Joseph Nicholson MSS., LC.

38. *Annals*, 8th Congress, 2nd session, 31 January 1805, 1061–62, 8 February 1805, 1188; Jefferson to Wilson Cary Nicholas, 6 December 1804, Jefferson Papers, Huntington Library.

39. William Plumer, *Memorandum of the Proceedings in the United States Senate, 1803–1807*, ed. Everett Somerville Brown (New York: Macmillan Company, 1923), 192; William A. Robinson, "William Plumer," *Dictionary of American Biography*; Peterson, *Thomas Jefferson and the New Nation*, 838–39.

40. *Annals*, 8th Congress, 2nd session, 8 February 1805, 53; ibid., 12 February 1805, 54; ibid., 28 February 1805, 67; *Statutes at Large*, 2 March 1805, 2: 330.

41. William O. Lynch, *Fifty Years of Party Warfare* (Bobbs-Merrill Company, 1931; reprint, Gloucester, MA: Peter Smith, 1967), 183.

Chapter 4
The Failure of Ideology: Second Term, 1805–1809

1. "Notes on Armed Vessels," 4 July 1805, Ford, *Writings of Jefferson*, 10: 152–53; Jefferson to Jacob Crowninshield, 12 September 1805, Jefferson MSS., LC.

2. Bernard C. Steiner, ed., "Some Papers of Robert Smith, Secretary of the Navy 1801–1809 and Secretary of State 1809–1811," *Maryland Historical Magazine* 20 (1925): 142–44; Robert Smith to Jefferson, 16 September 1805, Jefferson MSS., LC.

3. Henry Adams, *Life of Albert Gallatin*, reprint (New York: Peter Smith, 1943), 334–35; Leiner, "The 'Whimsical Phylosophic President' and His Gunboats," 250; Macleod, "Jefferson and the Navy," 177.

4. Symonds, *Navalists and Antinavalists*, 105; Leiner, "The 'Whimsical Phylosophic President' and His Gunboats," 250; Walters, *Albert Gallatin*, 189; Smelser, *The Democratic Republic*, 228–29; Thomas Paine reconfirmed Jefferson's ideas when he wrote that "Nelson's victory ... will have no influence" on the French decision to use gunboats (Thomas Paine to Jefferson, 30 January 1806, Jefferson MSS., LC).

5. Adams, *History of the United States*, 691; Jefferson's Fifth Annual Message, 3 December 1805, Richardson, *Messages of the Presidents*, 1: 370–76.

6. Jefferson's Fifth Annual Message, 3 December 1805, Richardson, *Messages of the Presidents*, 1: 370–76; Leiner, "The 'Whimsical Phylosophic President' and His Gunboats," 250.

7. Samuel Smith Letterbook, 7 December 1805, Samuel Smith Family Papers, LC; McKee, *Edward Preble*, 337–41; William Bainbridge to John Ridgely, 27 January 1806, Bainbridge MSS., NHF-LC; Thomas Tingey to John Rodgers, 7 March 1806, Rodgers Family Papers, series 3A, LC.

8. Adams, *History of the United States*, 690–91; Malone, *Jefferson the President: Second Term*, 67–70.

9. Adams, *History of the United States*, 690–91; Malone, *Jefferson the President: Second Term*, 66–67; John Randolph to Albert Gallatin, 25 October 1805, Adams, *Writings of Albert Gallatin*, 1: 331–33.

10. Hugh A. Garland, *The Life of John Randolph of Roanoke* (New York: D. Appleton and Company, 1851), 271–73; Adams, *History of the United States*, 693–95; Ralph Volney Harlow, *The History of Legislative Methods in the Period before 1825* (New Haven: Yale University Press, 1917), 172–73; James A. Bayard to Andrew Bayard, 31 January 1806, Bayard Family MSS., LC.

11. *Annals*, 9th Congress, 1st Session, 23 December 1805, 301–2.

12. *Annals*, 9th Congress, 1st Session, 23 January 1806, 377–90.

13. *Annals*, 9th Congress, 1st Session, 24 January 1806, 391–97; Erney, *The Public Life of Henry Dearborn*, 153–54.

14. *Annals*, 9th Congress, 1st Session, 24 January 1806, 391–97; Robert Smith to the House of Representatives, 28 January, 30 January, 18 February 1806, *ASP*, 147–50.

15. James A. Bayard to Andrew Bayard, 7 February 1806, Bayard Family MSS., LC.

16. Malone, *Jefferson the President: Second Term*, 493, 501; *Annals*, 10th Congress, 1st Session, 10 December 1807, 1140.

17. *Annals*, 9th Congress, 2nd Session, 28 February 1806, 523–24.

18. *Annals*, 9th Congress, 2nd Session, 28 February 1806, 524–25; William E. Dodd, *The Life of Nathaniel Macon* (New York: Burt Franklin, 1908; reprint, 1970), 210–12.

19. *Annals*, 9th Congress, 1st Session, 28 February 1806, 524–25; Matthew Walton to John Breckinridge, 27 March 1806, Abram Trigg to John Breckinridge, 13 April 1806, Breckinridge Family MSS., LC.; William Dickson to Moses Fisk, 6 April 1806, Cunningham, *Circular Letters*, 1: 414, 420, 448.

20. *Annals*, 9th Congress, 1st Session, 28 February 1806, 525–26.

21. *Annals*, 9th Congress, 1st Session, 17 March 1806, 823, 18 April 1806, 1259–62.

22. *Annals*, 9th Congress, 2nd Session, 17 March 1806, 846, 15 April 1806, 1048–51;

William A. Robinson, "Matthew Lyon," *Dictionary of American Biography*; Symonds, *Navalists and Antinavalists*, 113.

23. Thomas Truxtun to Timothy Pickering, 17 March 1806, Timothy Pickering Papers, Massachusetts Historical Society, Boston; clipping in Thomas Truxtun Papers, Naval Academy Museum, Annapolis, MD; Eugene S. Ferguson, *Truxtun of the "Constellation"* (Baltimore, MD: Johns Hopkins Press, 1956), 121; Tench Coxe, "Thoughts on the Subject of Naval Power in the United States of America and on Certain Means of Encouraging and Protecting their Commerce and Manufacturing" (Philadelphia: 1806), *Early American Imprints*, series II, no. 10223, 11.

24. *Annals*, 9th Congress, 1st Session, 18 April 1806, 1076, 15 April 1806, 1051, 21 April 1806, 1287; Robert G. Albion, *Makers of Naval Policy, 1798–1947* (Annapolis, MD: Naval Institute Press, 1980), 184; Leiner, "The 'Whimsical Phylosophic President' and His Gunboats," 251. Leiner claims that Jefferson did nothing "to help the high-seas fleet" during the session. Federalist Senator Timothy Pickering of Massachusetts supports Leiner's assertion. Pickering claimed that Jefferson "behind the curtain, directs the measure he wishes to have adopted" and as such measures for a seagoing fleet would have passed if Jefferson had wanted (Pickering to his wife, 31 January 1806, quoted in Noble E. Cunningham, Jr., *The Process of Government under Jefferson* [Princeton, NJ: Princeton University Press, 1978], 193). Leiner, however, does not take into account the struggle Jefferson encountered during the Ninth Congress.

25. Harrison Gray Otis to John Rutledge, 1 October 1807, John Rutledge Papers, SHC-UNC. Otis claimed that a nonintercourse act would be the first step to war rather than a peaceful measure. Peterson, *Thomas Jefferson and the New Nation*, 831; Adams, *History of the United States*, 739; Manley Discon to Captain Dickinson, 23 November 1814, H.M.S. *Penguin* "Orderbook," Nimitz Library, United States Naval Academy, Annapolis, MD. Discon wrote that British warships were to take every opportunity to employ men for the British squadron, but not to "take more than 2 men out of 10, 3 from 15, and 7 from 21. First mates and carpenters ... are not to be impressed."

26. Reginald Horsman, *The Causes of the War of 1812* (New York: A. S. Barnes and Company, 1962), 29–30.

27. Symonds, *Navalists and Antinavalists*, 110–11; Horsman, *The Causes of the War of 1812*, 84; Adams, *History of the United States*, 740–42; Malone, *Jefferson the President: Second Term*, 115; Smelser, *The Democratic Republic*, 157.

28. Jefferson, "Anas," 1 May 1806, Ford, *The Writings of Jefferson*, 1: 315–16; Jefferson to Jacob Crowninshield, 13 May 1806, Jefferson to Governor Lewis, 3 May 1806, Jefferson MSS., LC; Adams, *History of the United States*, 742.

29. Jefferson to Jacob Crowninshield, 13 May 1806, Jefferson MSS., LC; James Monroe to John Randolph, 16 June 1806, Stanislaus Murray Hamilton, ed., *The Writings of James Monroe* (New York: G. P. Putnam's Sons, 1900), 4: 463–64.

30. Jefferson's Sixth Annual Message, 2 December 1806, Richardson, *Messages of the Presidents*, 1: 393–98; Adams, *History of the United States*, 840–42.

31. Jefferson to Governor Lewis, 13 May 1806, Jefferson to Mr. Bowdoin, 10 July 1806, Jefferson MSS., LC.

32. Jefferson's Sixth Annual Message, 2 December 1806, Richardson, *Messages of the Presidents*, 1: 393–98; Jefferson to Jacob Crowninshield, 13 May 1806, Jefferson MSS., LC.

33. *Annals*, 9th Congress, 2nd Session, 3 December 1806, 113–14. The committee consisted of Roger Nelson of Massachusetts, Thomas Thompson of New Hampshire,

Benjamin Tallmadge of Connecticut, John Rea of Pennsylvania, David Thomas of New York, James Elliot of Vermont, and the lone southerner, Thomas Wynns of North Carolina (*Annals*, 4 December 1804, 17). The committee consisted of Samuel L. Mitchill of New York and Samuel Smith of Maryland as well as antinavalist William Branch Giles of Virginia (*Annals*, 384; Fisher Ames to Timothy Pickering, 22 December 1806, William B. Allen, ed., *Works of Fisher Ames* [Boston: Seth Ames, 1854; reprint, Indianapolis: Liberty Classics, 1983], 1539–40).

34. House of Representatives to Jefferson, 5 February 1807, Jefferson MSS., LC; *Annals*, 9th Congress, 2nd Session, 23 January 1807, 392–93, 400–401; Symonds, *Navalists and Antinavalists*, 116–17.
35. *Annals*, 9th Congress, 2nd Session, 23 January 1807, 400–401, 1286; Symonds, *Navalists and Antinavalists*, 116.
36. *Annals*, 9th Congress, 2nd Session, 3 March 1807, 1286.
37. Jefferson to Senate and House of Representatives, "Special Message on Gun-Boats," 10 February 1807, *ASP*, 163–64; Jefferson to Robert Smith, 6 February 1807, Washington, *The Writings of Thomas Jefferson*, 5: 41–42; Weymouth T. Jordan, *George Washington Campbell of Tennessee, Western Statesman* (Tallahassee: Florida State University, 1955), 56.
38. Jefferson to Robert Smith, 12 December 1806, Jefferson MSS., LC.
39. Albert Gallatin to Jefferson, 8 February 1807, "Notes-Message Respecting Gunboats," Adams, *Writings of Albert Gallatin*, 1: 328–31; Jefferson to Gallatin, 9 February 1807, Jefferson Papers, The New-York Historical Society, New York; Jefferson to Senate and House of Representatives, "Special Message on Gun-Boats," 10 February 1807, *ASP*, 163–64.
40. Horatio Gates to Jefferson, 19 October 1804, James Wilkinson to Jefferson, 10 November 1804, Samuel Barron to Jefferson, 8 February 1807, Thomas Tingey to Jefferson, 9 February 1807, *ASP*, 163–64; Symonds, *Navalists and Antinavalists*, 117.
41. Goldsborough, *Naval Chronicle*, 324.
42. Samuel W. Bryant, *The Sea and the States* (Samuel W. Bryant, 1947; reprint, New York: Thomas Y. Crowell Company, 1967), 148–50; Malone, *Jefferson the President: Second Term*, 419–22; Symonds, *Navalists and Antinavalists*, 120; Adams, *History of the United States*, 929–45.
43. E. Wilder Spaulding, *His Excellency George Clinton* (Port Washington, NY: Ira Friedman, Inc., 1964), 286; Samuel Smith to James Madison, 30 June 1807, Jefferson MSS., LC.; Frank A. Cassell, *Merchant Congressman in the Young Republic: Samuel Smith of Maryland* (Madison: University of Wisconsin Press, 1971), 136–37; Marvin R. Zahniser, *Charles Cotesworth Pinckney, Founding Father* (Chapel Hill: University of North Carolina Press for the Institute of Early American History and Culture at Williamsburg, Virginia, 1967), 248; Charles Henry Ambler, *Thomas Ritchie; A Study in Virginia Politics* (Richmond, VA: Bell Book and Stationery Company, 1913), 42–43; Samuel Eliot Morison, *Harrison Gray Otis, 1765–1848* (Boston: Houghton Mifflin Company, 1969), 280–81; Robert A. McCaughey, *Josiah Quincy: 1772–1864, The Last Federalist* (Cambridge: Harvard University Press, 1974), 42, 65; Henry Putnam Prentiss, *Timothy Pickering as the Leader of New England Federalism, 1801–1815* (reprint, New York: Da Capo Press, Inc., 1972), 38–39.
44. Jefferson to Henry Dearborn, 25 June 1807, Jefferson MSS., LC; Jefferson, "*Chesapeake* Proclamation," 2 July 1807, Richardson, *Messages of the Presidents*, 1: 410–12; Malone, *Jefferson the President: Second Term*, 426–27.

45. Jefferson to Governor Cabell, 29 June 1807, Jefferson to John Page, 9 July 1807, Jefferson MSS., LC; Adams, *Life of Albert Gallatin*, 358; Mary P. Adams, "Jefferson's Military Policy," 202–20; Peterson, *Thomas Jefferson and the New Nation*, 877; Burton Spivak, *Jefferson's English Crisis* (Charlottesville: University of Virginia Press, 1979), 78–79.

46. Jefferson to Governor Cabell, 8 July 1807, Jefferson MSS., LC; Peterson, *Thomas Jefferson and the New Nation*, 876–78; Mary P. Adams, "Jefferson's Military Policy," v–vi, 128–37; Albert Gallatin to Jefferson, 25 July 1807, Adams, *Writings of Albert Gallatin*, 1: 340–45; Malone, *Jefferson the President: Second Term*, 431–33; Jefferson, "Anas," 28 July 1807, Ford, *The Writings of Jefferson*, 1: 415.

47. Malone, *Jefferson the President: Second Term*, 431–32, 435; Peterson, *Thomas Jefferson and the New Nation*, 877.

48. Jefferson to Mr. Lieper, 21 August 1807, Jefferson to John Page, 9 July 1807, Jefferson to Samuel Smith, 30 July 1807, Jefferson MSS., LC.

49. John Keemle to Jefferson, 29 June 1807, William Essenbach to Jefferson, 9 January 1808, Jefferson to Thomas Paine, 6 September 1807, Jefferson MSS., LC.

50. Symonds, *Navalists and Antinavalists*, 121–22.

51. Jefferson's Seventh Annual Message, 27 October 1807, Richardson, *Messages of the Presidents*, 1: 413–18; Jefferson to Governor Cabell, 19 August 1807, 25 October 1807, 1 November 1807, Jefferson MSS., LC; Jefferson to TMR (Thomas Mann Randolph), 30 November 1808, Jefferson MSS., LC.

52. *Annals*, 10 Congress, 1st Session, 29 October 1807, 795, 5 November 1807, 805–16.

53. *Annals*, 10th Congress, 1st Session, 24 November 1807, 955–57, 11 December 1807, 1171–72.

54. Jordan, *George Washington Campbell*, 60–63; Dodd, *Nathaniel Macon*, 222; John Randolph to Edward Dillon, 12 February 1808, John Randolph Papers, Virginia Historical Society, Richmond; Henry Adams, *John Randolph* (Boston: Houghton, Mifflin & Co.), 1882), 226. The debate is chronicled in *Annals*, 1066–172, 10 December 1807, 1109.

55. John Davenport to John Cotton Smith, 15 December 1807, John Cotton Smith MSS., LC; George Washington Campbell to Moses Fisk, 22 January 1808, Cunningham, *Circular Letters*, 2: 522; Joseph Desha to Constituent, 29 March 1808, Breckinridge Family MSS., LC; J. Semple to Burwell Bassett, Burwell Bassett MSS., LC; John Taylor to James Mercer Garnett, 14 December 1807, John Taylor Papers, William R. Perkins Library, Duke University; Robert E. Shalhope, *John Taylor of Caroline: Pastoral Republican* (Columbia: University of South Carolina Press, 1980), 123.

56. Jefferson to John Minor, 7 November 1807, The Papers of Thomas Jefferson, Manuscripts Division, Special Collections Department, University of Virginia Library, Charlottesville; Timothy Pickering to Thomas Fitzsimons, 3 December 1807, Timothy Pickering Papers, Massachusetts Historical Society, Boston; "Copy of the Embargo Law," Jefferson Papers, William R. Perkins Library, Duke University.

57. Paullin, *Naval Administration*, 135.

58. Dumas Malone, *Jefferson the President: Second Term*, 502–3.

59. Leiner, "The 'Whimsical Phylosophic President' and His Gunboats," 266.

Chapter 5
Gunboat-Related Legislation:
"Visionary Schemes" of the President

1. Symonds, *Navalists and Antinavalists*, 87.
2. Jefferson, *Notes*, 187; Goldsborough, *Naval Chronicle*, 355; Gene A. Smith, "'A Perfect State of Preservation,' Thomas Jefferson's Dry Dock Proposal," *Virginia Cavalcade* 39 (Winter 1990): 118–28.
3. Jefferson, *Notes*, 187.
4. Talbot Hamlin, *Benjamin Henry Latrobe* (New York: Oxford University Press, 1968), 257; Nathan Schachner, *Thomas Jefferson: A Biography* (New York: Appleton-Century-Crofts, 1951), 2: 711.
5. Robert Smith to Thomas Tingey, 22 October 1802, *ASP*; Jefferson to Benjamin Henry Latrobe, 2 November 1802, John C. Van Horne and Lee W. Formwalt, eds. *The Correspondences and Miscellaneous Papers of Benjamin Henry Latrobe* (New Haven: Yale University Press, 1984), 1: 221.
6. Eugene Ferguson, "Mr. Jefferson's Dry Dock," *The American Neptune* 11 (1954): 110. Hamlin, *Latrobe*, 67–233, provides a detailed account of his various projects in the United States.
7. Benjamin Henry Latrobe to Robert Smith, 4 December 1802, *ASP*, 105; Darwin H. Stapleton, *The Engineering Drawings of Benjamin Henry Latrobe* (New Haven: Yale University Press, 1980), 116.
8. Jefferson to Benjamin Henry Latrobe, 2 November 1802, Van Horne and Formwalt, *Papers of Benjamin Henry Latrobe*, 221–22; Hamlin, *Latrobe*, 257 n .
9. Benjamin Henry Latrobe to Robert Smith, 4 December 1802, *ASP*, 105–6; Thomas Tingey to Robert Smith, 22 October 1802, *ASP*, 107–8.
10. Jefferson to Benjamin Henry Latrobe, 2 November 1802, Horne and Formwalt, *Papers of Benjamin Henry Latrobe*, 1: 222; Benjamin Henry Latrobe to Robert Smith, 8 December 1802, *ASP*, 106.
11. Paul F. Norton, "Jefferson's Plans for Mothballing the Frigates," *United States Naval Institute Proceedings* 82 (1956): 740; Benjamin Henry Latrobe to Robert Smith, 4 December 1802, *ASP*, 107.
12. Albert Gallatin to Jefferson, 21 November 1803; Gallatin to Jefferson, 18 January 1803, Jefferson MSS., LC; Adams, *Life of Albert Gallatin*, 306; Norton, "Jefferson's Plans for Mothballing the Frigates," 738; Jefferson to Albert Gallatin, 13 October 1802, Ford, *The Writings of Jefferson*, 8: 174.
13. Jefferson's Second Annual Message, 15 December 1802, Richardson, *Messages of the Presidents*, 1: 330–34; *Providence Gazette*, 25 December 1802.
14. *Annals*, 7th Congress, 2nd Session, 19 January 1803, 401–3; *Daily National Intelligencer and Washington Advertiser*, 24 January 1803.
15. *Annals*, 7th Congress, 2nd Session, 19 January 1803, 403–4.
16. Ibid., 405–7.
17. Ibid., 407–9; Benjamin Henry Latrobe to Jefferson, 15 December 1802, Horne and Formwalt, *Papers of Benjamin Henry Latrobe*, 1: 248–49.
18. *Intelligencer*, 24 January 1803; *Annals*, 7th Congress, 2nd Session, 19 January 1803, 409; Jefferson to Secretary of War, 23 November 1802, Jefferson MSS., LC.
19. Benjamin Henry Latrobe to Jefferson,'15 December 1802, Horne and Formwalt, *Papers of Benjamin Henry Latrobe*, 1: 248–49; *Annals*, 7th Congress, 2nd Session, 20 January 1803, 410–11; Malone, *Jefferson the President: First Term*, 263;

Ferguson, "Mr. Jefferson's Dry Dock," 114; James A. Bayard to Andrew Bayard, 19 January 1803, 1 February 1803, Elizabeth Donnan, ed., "The Papers of James A. Bayard, 1796–1815," *Annual Report of the American Historical Association for the Year 1913* (Washington, D.C.: 1915), 156, 194.

20. Macleod, "Jefferson and the Navy," 172.

21. Robert Leslie to Jefferson, 10 January 1803, Jefferson MSS., LC.

22. *Annals*, 7th Congress, 2nd Session, 20 January 1803, 411; Jefferson to Caesar Rodney, 31 December 1802, Jefferson MSS., LC; Jefferson to Benjamin Henry Latrobe, 6 March 1803, The Papers of Thomas Jefferson, Manuscripts Division, Special Collections Department, University of Virginia Library, original in Benjamin H. Latrobe Papers, MS. 2009, Manuscripts Division, Maryland Historical Society Library, Baltimore; Macleod, "Jefferson and the Navy," 173.

23. James Fenimore Cooper, *History of the Navy of the United States of America* (Cooperstown: H & E Phinney, 1848), 194.

24. Jefferson to Lewis M. Wiss, 27 November 1825, Lipscomb and Bergh, *The Writings of Thomas Jefferson*, 15: 400; Jefferson to John Adams, 1 November 1822, ibid., 16: 138.

25. *Annals*, 7th Congress, 2nd Session, 28 February 1803, 1565.

26. Symonds, *Navalists and Antinavalists*, 87–88.

27. Jefferson to Thomas Mann Randolph, 11 December 1791, The Papers of Thomas Jefferson, Manuscripts Division, Special Collections Department, University of Virginia Library; Peterson, *Thomas Jefferson and the New Nation*, 689, 833; Joseph Bartlett, "An Oration Delivered at Biddleford, 4 July 1805," *Early American Imprints* (Saco, ME: William Weeks, 1805), series II, no. 7956, 12–13.

28. Jefferson's First Inaugural Address, 4 March 1801, Richardson, *Messages of the Presidents*, 1: 309–12; Jefferson's First Annual Message, 8 December 1801, ibid., 1: 314–20; Arthur M. Schlesinger, Jr., ed., *History of American Presidential Elections, 1789–1968* (New York: Chelsea House Publishers and McGraw-Hill Book Company, 1971), 1: 172; Malone, *Jefferson the President: Second Term*, 512; Smith, "For the Purposes of Defense," 30–38.

29. Jefferson to the Senate and House of Representatives, 28 February 1805, Richardson, *Messages of the Presidents*, 1: 366; Peterson, *Thomas Jefferson and the New Nation*, 833; Fisher Ames to Josiah Quincy, 12 February 1806, Josiah Quincy MSS., LC.

30. Jefferson to John Jay, 9 January 1787, Boyd, *Papers of Thomas Jefferson*, 11: 31; Dudley, *The Naval War of 1812*, 1: xlvii; Jefferson to Barnabas Bidwell, 5 July 1806, Lipscomb and Bergh, *The Writings of Thomas Jefferson*, 11: 116.

31. Jefferson to Secretary of the Navy, 24 October 1805, Jefferson MSS., LC.

32. Notes from Jefferson to Albert Gallatin on "A Bill for Establishing a Naval Militia," December 1805, Jefferson Papers, The New-York Historical Society, New York.

33. Robert Smith to Jefferson, 14 November 1805, Jefferson MSS., LC; Thomas Truxtun to ?, 18 April 1799, Thomas Truxtun Papers, United States Naval Academy Museum, Annapolis, MD.

34. Henry Dearborn to Jefferson, November 1805, Jefferson MSS., LC.

35. *Annals*, 9th Congress, 1st Session, 4 December 1805, 262, 2 January 1806, 327–30, 22 January 1806, 69–70, 25 February 1806, 141; Malone, *Jefferson the President: Second Term*, 513–14, Jefferson to Henry Dearborn, 31 December 1805, Jefferson to William Burwell, 15 January 1806, Jefferson MSS., LC.

36. *Annals*, 9th Congress, 1st Session, 21 April 1806, 1272–73; Jefferson to Robert Smith, 22 April 1806, Jefferson MSS., LC.

37. *Annals*, 10th Congress, 2nd Session, 3 March 1807, 1286–87; Owsley, "Robert Smith," Coletta, *American Secretaries of the Navy,* 1: 82; Robert Smith to Jefferson, 13 January 1808, Jefferson MSS., LC.

38. Jefferson to the Senate and House of Representatives, "Special Message on Gun-Boats," 8 February 1807, Richardson *Messages of the Presidents*, 1: 407–9.

39. Jefferson to Samuel Smith, 30 July 1807, Lipscomb and Bergh, *The Writings of Thomas Jefferson*, 11: 301; "Notes on Consultation, 26 July 1807 to 22 October 1807," Jefferson MSS., LC.

40. Jefferson's Seventh Annual Message, 27 October 1807, Richardson, *Messages of the Presidents*, 1: 413–18.

41. *Annals*, 10th Congress, 1st Session, 16 November 1807, 903; Jefferson to Samuel Smith, 5 November 1807, Jefferson to Robert Smith, 14 January 1808, Jefferson MSS., LC.; Jefferson to William Short, 15 November 1807, Thomas Jefferson Papers, Swem Library, College of William and Mary, Williamsburg, Virginia.

42. Malone, *Jefferson the President: Second Term*, 513–15; *Annals*, 10th Congress, 1st Session, 19 January 1808, 1472–81, 20 January 1808, 1484–86, 26 January 1808, 1509–11; Lawrence Delbert Cress, *Citizens in Arms: The Army and Militia in American Society to the War of 1812* (Chapel Hill: The University of North Carolina Press, 1982), 166–71.

43. Jefferson to Robert Smith, 14 January 1808, Jefferson, MSS., LC; Goldsborough, *Naval Chronicle*, 336.

44. Archibald McBryde to Constituents, 10 May 1810, Cunningham, *Circular Letters*, 2: 708.

Chapter 6
The Politics of Construction:
Realization of Republican Philosophy

1. David Porter to Secretary of the Navy, 12 May 1808, *Letters Received by the Secretary of the Navy: Captains Letters, 1805–61, 1866–85*, RG45, M125; Linda M. Maloney, *The Captain from Connecticut: The Life and Naval Times of Isaac Hull* (Boston: Northern University Press, 1986), 120.

2. Robert Smith to John Gavino, 24 January 1803, Robert Smith to George Harrison, 24 February 1803, *Misc. Letters Sent*; Secretary of the Navy to Samuel Barron, 24 February 1803, Bauer, *The New American State Papers*, 46; Chapelle, *History of the American Sailing Navy*, 182.

3. Robert Smith to George Harrison, 17 March 1803, *Misc. Letters Sent*.

4. Robert Smith to George Harrison, 19 March 1803, 21 March 1803, Robert Smith to ? Greene, 12 April 1803, Robert Smith to Eliphalet Beebe, 25 April 1803, *Misc. Letters Sent*; William F. Trimble, "From Sail to Steam: Shipbuilding in the Pittsburgh Area, 1790–1865," *The Western Pennsylvania Historical Magazine* 58 (April 1975): 152.

5. Jefferson's Third Annual Message, 17 October 1803, Richardson, *Messages of the Presidents*, 1: 348; Secretary of the Navy to John Rodgers and James Barron, 21 December 1803, Knox, *Barbary Powers*, 3: 282–83; "Register of Ships and Officers," National Archives, Washington, D.C., RG45: 171; Jefferson to Secretary of the Navy, 15 June 1804, Jefferson MSS., LC.

6. Robert Smith to Thomas Tingey, 21 December 1803, *Misc. Letters Sent*; Chapelle, *History of the American Sailing Navy*, 192–93; James Leander Cathcart to ?, 30 January 1804, Knox, *Barbary Powers*, 3: 373; "Data on Gunboats Built by the United States, 1804–1808," RG45: AC Box 18, National Archives; Secretary of the Navy to John Lovell, 18 July 1804, "Gunboat Letters," RG45: 173; Jefferson to Robert Smith, 4 July 1804, Jefferson MSS., LC; "Register of Ships and Officers," National Archives, Washington, D.C., RG45: 171; Charles Oscar Paullin, *Commodore John Rodgers: Captain, Commodore and Senior Officer of the American Navy, 1773–1838* (Annapolis, MD: United States Naval Institute Press, 1967), 119.

7. Robert Smith to Daniel Bedinger, 21 December 1803, 4 January 1803, *Misc. Letters Sent*; "Register of Ships and Officers," National Archives, Washington, D.C., RG45: 171; Chapelle, *History of the American Sailing Navy*, 193–94; Secretary of the Navy to John B. Cordis, 18 September 1804, "Gunboat Letters," RG45: 173; "Data on Gunboats," RG45: AC Box 18; John H. Dent to the Secretary of the Navy, 21 October 1811, *Commanders Letters*.

8. "Data on Gunboats," RG45: AC, Box 18; Chapelle, *History of the American Sailing Navy*, 192; Jefferson to Secretary of the Navy, 15 June 1804, Jefferson MSS., LC; Secretary of the Navy to James Barron, 17 February 1804, Knox, *Barbary Powers*, 3: 430.

9. Chapelle, *History of the American Sailing Navy*, 192–93; "Extract from Preble Diary," 30 May 1804, Knox, *Barbary Powers*, 4: 131; McKee, *Edward Preble*, 341; Goldsborough, *Naval Chronicle*, 323; Stephen Cathalan to Robert R. Livingston, 13 February 1804, Knox, *Barbary Powers*, 3: 406; Abraham Gibbs to Edward Preble, 21 February 1804, ibid., 3: 448; Edward Preble to James Leander Cathcart, 18 March 1804, ibid., 3: 501; Sir John Acton (Prime Minister of State, the Two Sicilies) to James Leander Cathcart, 27 March 1804, ibid., 3: 538; Joseph Barnes (consul of Sicily) to Edward Preble, 16 April 1804, ibid., 4: 29; Glenn Tucker, *Dawn Like Thunder, The Barbary Wars and the Birth of the U.S. Navy* (New York: Bobbs-Merrill Company, Inc., 1963), 291.

10. Stephen Decatur to Edward Preble, 30 March 1804, Knox, *Barbary Powers*, 3: 547; Edward Preble to James Leander Cathcart, 1 June 1804, ibid., 4: 141; Edward Preble to Secretary of the Navy, 18 September 1804, ibid., 4: 293–94; Dudley, *The Naval War of 1812*, 1: li; Tucker, *Dawn Like Thunder*, 291.

11. *The Boston Repertory* 12 March 1805; Edward Preble to the Secretary of the Navy, 18 September 1804, Knox, *Barbary Powers*, 4: 295–98; Dudley, *The Naval War of 1812*, 1: li; Chapelle, *History of the American Sailing Navy*, 193; Holloway H. Frost, *We Build a Navy* (Annapolis, MD: United States Naval Institute Press, 1929; reprint, 1940), 174–77.

12. "Register of Ships and Officers," National Archives, Washington, D.C., RG45: 171; Robert Smith to Jefferson, 17 June 1804, 14 September 1804, Jefferson MSS., LC.

13. McKee, *Edward Preble*, 316–17; Chapelle, *History of the American Sailing Navy*, 195–97; Robert Smith to Jefferson, 3 July 1804, Jefferson to Robert Smith, 4 July 1804, Jefferson MSS., LC.

14. Chapelle, *History of the American Sailing Navy*, 195–96; McKee, *Edward Preble*, 317; Secretary of the Navy to John Striker, 25 August 1804, Secretary of the Navy to John Beekman, 24 September 1804, "Gunboat Letters," RG45: 173; "Register of Ships and Officers," National Archives, Washington, D.C., RG45: 171; "List of Ships Built," Josiah Fox MSS., LC.

15. "Register of Ships and Officers," National Archives, Washington, D.C., RG45: 171; Chapelle, *History of the American Sailing Navy*, 196.

16. Chapelle, *History of the American Sailing Navy*, 196–97; "Gunboat *No. 5*," National Archives, RG45: AD Box 45, 1804–05; "Register of Ships and Officers," National Archives, Washington, D.C., RG45: 171.

17. "Register of Ships and Officers," National Archives, Washington, D.C., RG45: 171; "Data on Gunboats," RG45: AC Box 18; J. Twiggs to Josiah Fox, 3 March 1805, Josiah Fox Papers, National Archives, RG45: AC Box 18; "Data on Gunboats," RG45: AC Box 18; Chapelle, *History of the American Sailing Navy*, 197–98.

18. "Register of Ships and Officers," National Archives, Washington, D.C., RG45: 171; John Shaw to Secretary of the Navy, 26 April 1805, *Commanders Letters*; Constance Lathrop, "Vanished Ships," *United States Naval Institute Proceedings* 60 (July 1934): 949.

19. Chapelle, *History of the American Sailing Navy*, 198; Ferrell, *American Diplomacy*, 130; Paullin, *Commodore John Rodgers*, 144–46; John Rodgers to the Secretary of the Navy, 12 July 1805, *Commanders Letters*.

20. "Register of Ships and Officers," National Archives, Washington, D.C., RG45: 171; Secretary of the Navy to Lt. Spriggs, 14 March 1805, "Gunboat Letters," RG45: 173; "Data on Gunboats," RG45: AC Box 18.

21. "Register of Ships and Officers," National Archives, Washington, D.C., RG45: 171; Chapelle, *History of the American Sailing Navy*, 197–98; "Data on Gunboats," RG45: AC Box 18; Nathaniel Fanning to Secretary of the Navy, 1 February 1805, 8 February 1805, 22 March 1805, *Letters Received by the Secretary of the Navy: Miscellaneous Letters, 1801–1884*, RG45, M–124.

22. "Register of Ships and Officers," National Archives, Washington, D.C., RG45: 171; Chapelle, *History of the American Sailing Navy*, 196–97; Secretary of the Navy to Commanders (circular), 9 April 1805, Secretary of the Navy to Haraden, 12 April 1805, Secretary of the Navy to Lt. Spriggs, 14 March 1805, "Gunboat Letters," RG45. 173.

23. Robert Smith to Jefferson, 30 August 1805, Jefferson MSS., LC; Secretary of the Navy to Alexander Murray, 29 January 1808, "Gunboat Letters," RG45: 173.

24. *Statutes at Large*, 2 March 1805, 2: 330; "Register of Ships and Officers," National Archives, Washington, D.C., RG45: 171; Jefferson to De Witt Clinton, 29 January 1805, De Witt Clinton Papers, Rare Book and Manuscript Library, Columbia University, New York; Jefferson to Secretary of the Navy, 13 May 1805, Jefferson MSS., LC.

25. Jefferson to DeWitt Clinton, 29 January 1805, De Witt Clinton Papers, Rare Book and Manuscript Library, Columbia University, New York; "Contracts," RG45: 235, 1: 239, 246; Jefferson to TMR (Thomas Mann Randolph), 13 July 1806, Jefferson MSS., LC.

26. McKee, *Edward Preble*, 88–89, 320–21; Chapelle, *History of the American Sailing Navy*, 199–200; "Ships Contracts," RG45: 235, 1: 239–42; "Gunboat Dimensions," National Archives, RG45: AD Box 43, #17; "Data on Gunboats," RG45: AC Box 18; "Register of Ships and Officers," National Archives, Washington, D.C., RG45: 171.

27. McKee, *Edward Preble*, 320–22; "Ships Contracts," RG45: 235, 1: 246–50; "Contracts for Gunboats, 1805–06," National Archives, RG45: AD Box 45, 1805–07; "Register of Ships and Officers," National Archives, Washington, D.C., RG45: 171; Chapelle, *History of the American Sailing Navy*, 208–9.

28. Jefferson to General Claiborne, 7 July 1804, Jefferson Papers, Coolidge Collection, Massachusetts Historical Society, Boston; "Register of Ships and Officers," National Archives, Washington, D.C., RG45: 171; Jefferson to the Secretary of the Navy, 23 May 1805, Jefferson MSS., LC.

29. Robert Andrue Schweitzer, "The Jeffersonian Congresses: A Quantitative Look, 1801–1813," (M.A. Thesis, Wayne State University, 1975), 86–88; Austin and Clubb, *Political Facts of the United States*, table 3.2, table 2.2.

30. "Register of Ships and Officers," National Archives, Washington, D.C., RG45: 171; Secretary of the Navy to General Henry Carberry, 5 April 1805, "Gunboat Letters," RG45: 173; Schweitzer, "The Jeffersonian Congresses," 86; Robert Smith to Jefferson, 26 May 1805, Jefferson MSS., LC; Aleine Austin, *Matthew Lyon: "New Man" of the Democratic Revolution, 1749–1822* (University Park: The Pennsylvania State University Press, 1981), 134.

31. Chapelle, *History of the American Sailing Navy*, 208–9; Jefferson to Secretary of the Navy, 10 June 1805, Jefferson MSS., LC; Secretary of the Navy to Henry Carberry, 27 May 1805, Secretary of the Navy to John Smith, 11 June 1805, Secretary of the Navy to Henry Carberry, 14 June 1805, Secretary of the Navy to Matthew Lyon, 20 January 1806, "Gunboat Letters," RG45: 173; "Data on Gunboats," RG45: AC Box 18.

32. Matthew Lyon to Secretary of the Navy, 6 January 1806, "Data on Gunboats," *Misc. Letters Received*; John Shaw to Secretary of the Navy, 27 April 1806, 1 August 1806, 4 September 1806, *Commanders Letters*.

33. Chapelle, *History of the American Sailing Navy*, 209–10; Jefferson to Jacob Crowninshield, 12 September 1805, Jefferson MSS., LC; Jefferson's Fifth Annual Message, 3 December 1805, Richardson, *Messages of the Presidents*, 1: 370–76; K. Jack Bauer, "Naval Shipbuilding Programs, 1794–1860," *Military Affairs* 29 (1965): 32; Jefferson to Mr. Bowdoin, 10 July 1806, Jefferson MSS., LC.

34. Circulars from Secretary of the Navy to ..., 22 May 1806; Circular ..., 29 May 1806; Secretary of the Navy to Chauncey and Barron, 27 March 1806, "Gunboat Letters," RG45: 173; "Data on Gunboats," RG45: AC, Box 18.

35. Jefferson to General Staunton, 15 January 1806, Jefferson Papers, Huntington Library; Schweitzer, "The Jeffersonian Congresses," 110–12; Secretary of the Navy to Edward Preble, 10 July 1806, Secretary of the Navy to Stephen Decatur, Jr., 15 July 1806, 24 July 1806, Secretary of the Navy to Samuel Barron, 11 July 1806, Secretary of the Navy to Nathaniel Lyon, John Conell, and Peter Mills, 17 July 1806, Secretary of the Navy to General Henry Carberry 18 July 1806, Secretary of the Navy to John Rodgers, 9 September 1806, 29 September 1806, "Gunboat Letters," RG45: 173; "Register of Ships and Officers," National Archives, Washington, D.C., RG45: 171; Chapelle, *History of the American Sailing Navy*, 218–24; "Ships Contracts," RG45: 235, 1: 274–76, 279, 292–93, 264–71, 277–78, 280–83, 285–86; "Bomb Vessels and Gunboats," no date, housed at end of 1806, Jefferson MSS., LC; "Memoirs of Mrs. John Rodgers," no date, 28, Rodgers Family Papers, NHF-LC.

36. Chapelle, *History of the American Sailing Navy*, 218; Secretary of the Navy to John Conell and Peter Mills, 17 July 1805, "Gunboat Letters," RG45: 173; "Contracts," RG45: 235, 1: 277–78; "Register of Ships and Officers," National Archives, Washington, D.C., RG45: 171; "Data on Gunboats," RG45: AC Box 18.

37. Secretary of the Navy to General Carberry, 10 November 1806, "Gunboat Letters," RG45: 173; John Shaw to Secretary of the Navy, 24 July 1806, 1 August 1806, 15 August 1806, 4 September 1806, *Commanders Letters*.

38. Morton Borden, *Parties and Politics in the Early Republic, 1789–1815* (Arlington Heights, IL: Harlan Davidson, Inc., 1967), 60–61; Secretary of the Navy to Jonathan Mason, 9 June 1806, Secretary of the Navy to Edward Preble, 10 July 1806, Secretary of the Navy to Isaac Hull, 1 April 1806, Secretary of the Navy to Charles

Stewart, 13 April 1807, "Gunboat Letters," RG45: 173; Owsley, "Robert Smith," Coletta, *American Secretaries of the Navy*, 1: 38; Austin and Clubb, *Political Facts of the United States*, table 3.2; McKee, *Edward Preble*, 326–27; "Ships Contracts," RG45: 235, 1: 292–93.

39. Secretary of the Navy to Stephen Decatur, Jr., 10 June 1806, 15 July 1806, "Gunboat Letters," RG45: 173; "Data on Gunboats," RG45: AC Box 18; Schweitzer, "The Jeffersonian Congresses," 110–12; Austin and Clubb, *Political Facts of the United States*, table 3.2.

40. "Ships Contracts," RG45: 235, 1: 279, 274–77; "Data on Gunboats," RG45: AC Box 18; Chapelle, *History of the American Sailing Navy*, 219–20; Maloney, *Isaac Hull*, 120–21.

41. Schweitzer, "The Jeffersonian Congresses," 110–12; Austin and Clubb, *Political Facts of the United States*, tables 2.2, 3.2.

42. "Register of Ships and Officers," National Archives, Washington, D.C., RG45: 171; "Gunboat Dimensions," National Archives, RG45: AD Box 43, #17; Chapelle, *History of the American Sailing Navy*, 220–23.

43. Schweitzer, "The Jeffersonian Congresses," 110–12; "Register of Ships and Officers," National Archives, Washington, D.C., RG45: 171; "Ships Contracts," RG45: 235, 1: 264–71.

44. Jefferson's Diary Notes, 11 July 1806, Jefferson's Cabinet Notes, 5 March 1806, 24 October 1806, Jefferson to Henry Dearborn, 26 April 1806, Henry Dearborn to James Wilkinson, 6 May 1806, Jefferson MSS., LC; Secretary of the Navy to Captains Hull, Preble, Samuel Barron, 20 March 1807, Secretary of the Navy to Isaac Hull, 1 April 1807, Secretary of the Navy to Charles Stewart, 13 April 1807, "Gunboat Letters," RG45: 173.

45. Jefferson to the Senate and House of Representatives, 9 February 1807, Richardson, *Messages of the Presidents*, 1: 407–9; Jefferson to Henry Dearborn, Jefferson to Robert Smith, 6 February 1807, Jefferson to Albert Gallatin, 9 February 1807, Jefferson MSS., LC.

46. Memo from Robert Smith to Jefferson, 1 July 1807, Jefferson MSS., LC; "Statement of the Armaments, Officers, and Crew and distribution of the Naval Force at New Orleans, 3 November 1807," RG45: AD Box 45, 1807.

47. Mary P. Adams, "Jefferson's Military Policy," 133–36, 195–98; Secretary of the Navy to John Beckman, Ingraham and Son, John Striker, Daniel Bedinger, George Harrison, 30 July 1807, Secretary of the Navy to Benjamin Smith, 8 August 1807, "Gunboat Letters," RG45: 173.

48. Jefferson to Henry Dearborn, 7 July 1807, Jefferson MSS., LC; Jefferson to the Masters and other Officers Sailing to and from the Ports of Norfolk and Portsmouth, 8 July 1807, Jefferson to Governor William H. Cabell, 8 July 1807, Lipscomb and Bergh, *The Writings of Thomas Jefferson*, 11: 261–62; Jefferson's "Memorandum of the Preparatory Measures which may be adopted by the Executive in Relation to War," 25 July 1807, Jefferson to Thomas Paine, 6 September 1807, Jefferson MSS., LC; Jefferson's Seventh Annual Message, 27 October 1807, Richardson, *Messages of the Presidents*, 1: 413–18.

49. Secretary of the Navy to Jefferson, 13 January 1808, 26 January 1808, Jefferson to Robert Smith, 14 January 1808, Jefferson MSS., LC; Secretary of the Navy to William Van Deurson, 12 January 1808, "Gunboat Letters," RG45: 173.

50. "Register of Ships and Officers," National Archives, Washington, D.C., RG45: 171; Secretary of the Navy to Alexander Murray, 29 January 1808, Secretary of the Navy to O. H. Perry, 10 March 1808, "Gunboat Letters," RG45: 173.

51. Secretary of the Navy to Thomas Tingey, 18 December 1808, "Gunboat Letters," RG45: 173; "State of the Gunboats," 1 November 1808, Jefferson MSS., LC.

52. Chapelle, *History of the American Sailing Navy*, 224–25; "Register of Ships and Officers," National Archives, Washington, D.C., RG45: 171; Secretary of the Navy to William Bainbridge, 22 March 1808, "Gunboat Letters," RG45: 173; "Ships Contracts," RG45: 235, 1: 302–3; "Data on Gunboats," RG45: AC Box 18.

53. Secretary of the Navy to Isaac Hull, 22 March 1808, "Gunboat Letters," RG45: 173; "Ships Contracts," RG45: 235, 1: 303–6; Chapelle, *History of the American Sailing Navy*, 225; "Data on Gunboats," RG45: AC Box 18; Maloney, *Isaac Hull*, 123.

54. Paullin, *Commodore John Rodgers*, 199; "Register of Ships and Officers," National Archives, Washington, D.C., RG45: 171; Chapelle, *History of the American Sailing Navy*, 225; "Ships Contracts," RG45: 235, 1: 307–12, 316–19; Secretary of the Navy to John Rodgers, 22 March 1808, circular from Secretary of the Navy, 6 April 1808, "Gunboat Letters," RG45: 173; Secretary of the Navy to George Harrison, 20 August 1807, *Misc. Letters Sent*.

55. Chapelle, *History of the American Sailing Navy*, 203, 225; "Register of Ships and Officers," National Archives, Washington, D.C., RG45: 171; Secretary of the Navy to Alexander Murray, 22 March 1808, "Gunboat Letters," RG45: 173; Secretary of the Navy to Messrs. Riddle and Bird, *Misc. Letters Sent*.

56. Chapelle, *History of the American Sailing Navy*, 225; "Register of Ships and Officers," National Archives, Washington, D.C., RG45: 171; Secretary of the Navy to Sam Evans, 22 March 1808, "Gunboat Letters," RG45: 173.

57. Chapelle, *History of the American Sailing Navy*, 225; "Register of Ships and Officers," National Archives, Washington, D.C., RG45: 171; Secretary of the Navy to Stephen Decatur, 22 March 1808, Secretary of the Navy to Theodore Armistead, 16 April 1808, "Gunboat Letters," RG45: 173.

58. Chapelle, *History of the American Sailing Navy*, 225–26; Robert Smith to Nathaniel Ingraham and Son, 4 September 1806, *Misc. Letters Sent*; "Register of Ships and Officers," National Archives, Washington, D.C., RG45: 171; "Ships Contracts," RG45: 235, 1: 312–14; Secretary of the Navy to Ingraham and Son, 2 June 1808, "Gunboat Letters," RG45: 173; "Petition from the State of South Carolina to William Jones, Secretary of the Navy, 1813," National Archives, RG45: AC Box 18.

59. Alan D. Watson, *Wilmington: Port of North Carolina* (Columbia: University of South Carolina Press, 1992), 42; Chapelle, *History of the American Sailing Navy*), 226; "Register of Ships and Officers," National Archives, Washington, D.C., RG45: 171; Secretary of the Navy to Benjamin Smith, 22 March 1808, "Gunboat Letters," RG45: 173; Secretary of the Navy to Mr. [William] Blackledge, 28 January 1808, to Benjamin Smith, 4 June 1808, *Misc. Letters Sent*; Robert Smith to Thomas Tingey, 26 July 1808, *Letters Sent by the Secretary of the Navy to Commandants and Navy Agents, 1808–1865*, RG45, M441; Thomas Gautier to the Secretary of the Navy, 22 May 1809, Gautier Papers, SHC-UNC.

60. Secretary of the Navy to Thomas Tingey, 6 February 1808, *Letters Sent to Commandants and Navy Agents*; Sarah McCulloh Lemmon, *Frustrated Patriots: North Carolina and the War of 1812* (Chapel Hill: The University of North Carolina Press, 1973), 41; Hugh Campbell to Thomas Gautier, 21 September 1811, Thomas Gautier to the Secretary of the Navy, 12 April, 1809, 30 May 1809, 5 October 1809, Gautier Papers, SHC-UNC.

61. Secretary of the Navy to John Rodgers, 2 July 1808, "Gunboat Letters," RG45: 173; "Ships Contracts," RG45: 235, 1: 348–55.

62. Chapelle, *History of the American Sailing Navy*, 226; Robert Smith to Jefferson, 21 January 1809, Jefferson MSS., LC; Secretary of the Navy to the Senate, 25 May 1809, *ASP*, 193; Secretary of the Navy to the House of Representatives, 8 June 1809, *ASP*, 199; Secretary of the Navy to the Senate, 13 December 1810, *ASP*, 229; William Jones to the Senate, 18 March 1814, *ASP*, 306.
63. Schweitzer, "The Jeffersonian Congresses," 110–12; Austin and Clubb, *Political Facts of the United States*, table 3.2.
64. Schweitzer, "The Jeffersonian Congresses," 110–12; Austin and Clubb, *Political Facts of the United States*, table 3.2.
65. Schweitzer, "The Jeffersonian Congresses," 110–12.

Chapter 7
Prewar Operations: Defense and Other Diverse Duties

1. Mahan, *Influence of Sea Power*, 1: 22-76; Paolo Coletta, *The American Naval Heritage in Brief*, 2nd ed. (Washington, D.C.: University Press of America, Inc., 1980), 2.
2. Secretary of the Navy to John Lovell, 18 July 1804, Secretary of the Navy to John B. Cordis, 18 September 1804, "Gunboat Letters," RG45: 173; Isaac Chauncey to the Secretary of the Navy, 26 December 1805, *Commanders Letters*; "Register of Ships and Officers," National Archives, Washington, D.C., RG45: 171; Isaac Chauncey to the Secretary of the Navy, 20 December 1805, 26 December 1805, *Misc. Letters Sent*; Claude G. Bowers, *Jefferson in Power* (Boston: Houghton Mifflin Company, 1936), 266.
3. David F. Long, *Sailor-Diplomat: A Biography of Commodore James Biddle, 1783–1848* (Boston: Northeastern University Press, 1983), 30; Robert Smith to Jefferson, 30 August 1805, Jefferson to Robert Smith 18 September 1805, Jefferson MSS., LC; Secretary of the Navy to Gunboat Commanders, 17 April 1805, "Gunboat Letters," RG45: 173; "Squadron under Commodore Rodgers — Division of gunboats under Isaac Hull," 27 April 1805, National Archives, RG45: DB Box 155, 1805; Allen, *Our Navy and the Barbary Corsairs*, 224–26; Cooper, *History of the Navy*, 1: 265–66.
4. Paullin, *Commodore John Rodgers*, 162.
5. "Naval Force of Tunis," 1803, Jefferson MSS., LC; Daniel Todd Patterson to Robert E. Griffith, 25 May 1802, Daniel Todd Patterson Papers, NHF-LC; Ray W. Irwin, *The Diplomatic Relations of the United States with the Barbary Powers, 1776–1816* (Chapel Hill: University of North Carolina Press, 1931), 138–39.
6. Paullin, *Commodore John Rodgers*, 166; *Statutes at Large*, 2 March 1805, 2: 330; Jefferson's Cabinet Notes, 19 July 1806, 24 October 1806, Jefferson MSS., LC.
7. Robert Smith to Jefferson, 19 December 1806, Jefferson MSS., LC.
8. Malone, *Jefferson the President: Second Term*, 231–34, 243; John Shaw to the Secretary of the Navy, 22 August 1806, *Commanders Letters*.
9. John Shaw to the Secretary of the Navy, 19 September 1806, 3 October 1806, 10 October 1806, W. C. C. Claiborne to John Shaw, 7 October 1806, *Commanders Letters*.
10. John Shaw to the Men of his Squadron, 9 October 1806, John Shaw to Commanders Read and Patterson, 24 October 1806, John Shaw to the Secretary of the Navy, 22 August 1806, 10 October 1806, 31 October 1806, *Commanders Letters*.

11. Jefferson's Cabinet Notes, 24 October 1806, Jefferson MSS., LC; Malone, *Jefferson the President: Second Term*, 246–47; Adams, *History of the United States*, 819; Thomas P. Abernathy, *The Burr Conspiracy* (New York: Oxford University Press, 1954), 154–55; John Shaw to the Secretary of the Navy, 29 November 1806, *Commanders Letters*; James Ripley Jacobs, *Tarnished Warrior: Major-General James Wilkinson* (New York: The Macmillan Company, 1938), 230–31.

12. John Shaw to the Secretary of the Navy, 20 November 1806, *Commanders Letters*.

13. Jacobs, *Tarnished Warrior*, 229–30; Adams, *History of the United States*, 815; John Smith (of Ohio) to N. Evans, 25 January 1808, John Smith MSS., LC; John Shaw to the Secretary of the Navy, 24 December 1806, *Commanders Letters*; Secretary of the Navy to Andrew Gregg, Chairman, Committee on the Naval Peace Establishment, 16 December 1805, Dudley, *The Naval War of 1812*, 1: 4.

14. Adams, *History of the United States*, 814; Malone, *Jefferson the President: Second Term*, 247–48; James Wilkinson to Jefferson, 21 October 1806, Jefferson MSS., LC; Matthew L. Davis, *Memoirs of Aaron Burr* (1836; reprint, Freeport, NY: Books for Libraries Press, 1970), 2: 382.

15. Thomas Truxtun to Jefferson, 10 August 1806, Jefferson MSS., LC; Ferguson, *Truxtun of the "Constellation,"* 244–45.

16. Milton Lomask, *Aaron Burr: The Conspiracy and Years of Exile, 1805–1836* (New York: Farrar, Straus, Giroux, 1982), 176–78; Jefferson's Cabinet Notes, 24 October 1806, 25 October 1806, Jefferson MSS., LC; Robert Smith to Jefferson, 22 December 1806, Bauer, *The New American State Papers*, 1: 203–5.

17. Lomask, *Aaron Burr*, 180–82; James Wilkinson to Jefferson, 12 November 1806, Jacobs, *Tarnished Warrior*, 232–33.

18. John Shaw to the Secretary of the Navy, 9 December 1806, 15 December 1806, W. C. C. Claiborne to John Shaw, 1 December 1806, *Commanders Letters*; Jefferson to the Secretary of the Navy, 23 December 1806, Jefferson MSS., LC.

19. John Shaw to the Secretary of the Navy, 12 January 1807, *Commanders Letters*; W. C. C. Claiborne to James Wilkinson, 19 January 1807, Dunbar Rowland, *Official Letter Books of W. C. C. Claiborne, 1801–1816* (Jackson, MS: State Department of Archives and History, 1917), 4: 100–101.

20. Lomask, *Aaron Burr*, 212, 222–23; "Biography of John Shaw," no author, no date, 8, John Shaw Papers, NHF-LC; "Newspaper Clipping," Morse Family Papers, LC; Leonard W. Levy, *Jefferson and Civil Liberties, The Darker Side* (Chicago: Ivan R. Dee, Inc., 1963), 83–84; Joseph Nicholson to Jefferson, 22 March 1808, Joseph Nicholson Papers, LC.

21. John Shaw to the Secretary of the Navy, 28 May 1807, *Commanders Letters*; Robert Smith to David Lewis, 11 May 1807, *Misc. Letters Sent*.

22. Paullin, *Commodore John Rodgers*, 187–88.

23. Leonard Guttridge and Jay D. Smith, *The Commodores* (New York: Harper and Row, 1969), 137; Stephen Decatur to Robert Smith, 12 July 1807, 27 August 1807, *Letters Received by the Secretary of the Navy: Captain's Letters, 1805–61, 1866–85*, RG45, M125; George E. Davies, "Robert Smith and the Navy," *Maryland Historical Magazine* 14 (December 1919): 314–19; Owsley, "Robert Smith," Coletta, *American Secretaries of the Navy*, 1: 86–87.

24. Paullin, *Commodore John Rodgers*, 188–90.

25. Jefferson, "Anas," 28 July 1807, Ford, *The Writings of Jefferson*, 1: 415; Mary P. Adams, "Jefferson's Military Policy," 202–20.

26. David F. Long, *Nothing Too Daring: A Biography of Commodore David Porter, 1780–1843* (Annapolis, MD: United States Naval Institute Press, 1970), 40, 43, 52;

David Porter to the Secretary of the Navy, 26 June 1808, *Commanders Letters*; David Porter to John Henley, 2 July 1810, John Henley Papers, Nimitz Library, United States Naval Academy.

27. Porter to Secretary of Navy, 1 January 1810, 4 May 1810, *Commanders Letters*; Porter to John Henley, 2 July 1810, Henley Papers, Nimitz Library.

28. Michael B. Carroll to John Henley, 20 June 1810, Michael B. Carroll to Secretary of the Navy, 5 July 1810, 28 July 1810, John Shaw Papers, NHF-LC; Henry Demis to the District Court of Orleans, 9 October 1810, Brugman Privateer Papers, The Historic New Orleans Collection, New Orleans, LA; Jane Lucas de Grummond, *Baratarians and the Battle of New Orleans* (Baton Rouge: Louisiana State University Press, 1961), 12–15; Udolpho Theodore Bradley, "The Contentious Commodore: Thomas ap Catesby Jones of the Old Navy, 1788–1858" (Ph.D. dissertation, Cornell University, 1933), 25–26.

29. Paul Hamilton to Hugh Campbell, 22 January 1811, *Letters Sent to Officers*; Hugh Campbell to the Secretary of the Navy, 18 July 1812, Dudley, *The Naval War of 1812*, 1: 195–97.

30. Lyle Saxon, *Lafitte the Pirate* (New Orleans, LA: Robert L. Crager and Company, 1950), 25–26.

31. Long, *Nothing Too Daring*, 43–45; Louis Martin Shears, *Jefferson and the Embargo* (New York: Octagon Books, 1978), 90–91; Jefferson to Robert Smith, 14 February 1808, Lipscomb and Bergh, *The Writings of Thomas Jefferson*, 11: 439–40.

32. Jefferson to Robert Smith, 14 February 1808, Jefferson to Albert Gallatin, 14 February 1808, Lipscomb and Bergh, *The Writings of Thomas Jefferson*, 11: 439–40; Robert M. Johnstone, Jr., *Jefferson and the President: Leadership in the Young Republic* (Ithaca, NY: Cornell University Press, 1978), 275; Levy, *Jefferson and Civil Liberties*, 112–13.

33. Jefferson to Secretary of the Navy, 16 July 1808, Lipscomb and Bergh, *The Writings of Thomas Jefferson*, 12: 93; Jefferson to the Secretary of the Navy, 9 August 1808, ibid., 12: 121.

34. Albert Gallatin to Jefferson, 28 December 1808, Jefferson MSS., LC; John Dent to the Secretary of the Navy, 28 February 1808, P. C. Wederstrandt to the Secretary of the Navy, 13 June 1808, 8 July 1808, 15 July 1808, John Smith to the Secretary of the Navy, 11 August 1808, John Dent to the Secretary of the Navy, 2 April 1808, 30 November 1808, 23 December 1808, *Commanders Letters*; Secretary of the Navy to Lieutenant Samuel Elbert, 2 May 1808, Dudley, *The Naval War of 1812*, 1: 35–36.

35. David Porter to John Henley, 8 July 1808, John Henley Papers, Nimitz Library; David Porter to the Secretary of the Navy, 26 June 1808, 26 August 1808, 24 September 1808, 16 March 1809, 25 March 1809, 1 April 1809, Benjamin Reed to David Porter, 19 February 1808, *Commanders Letters*.

36. David Porter to the Secretary of the Navy, 15 February 1809, 19 February 1809, *Commanders Letters*; Long, *Nothing Too Daring*, 43–44.

37. Albert Gallatin to Jefferson, 29 July 1808, Jefferson MSS., LC; Jefferson to Albert Gallatin, 19 August 1808, Jefferson Papers, The New-York Historical Society, New York.

38. Jefferson to Gallatin, 14 February 1808, Jefferson MSS., LC; Paullin, *Commodore John Rodgers*, 198–99; Malone, *Jefferson the President: Second Term*, 601–2.

39. John Shaw to the Secretary of the Navy, 6 January 1809, Sam Evans to the Secretary of the Navy, 12 March 1808, 26 March 1808, 15 April 1808, 22 June 1808, 25 July 1808, 9 September 1808, 2 December 1808, *Commanders Letters*.

40. John Randolph to Richard Kidder Randolph, 8 April 1810, John Randolph MSS., LC; Jefferson to James Kerr, 31 March 1809, Jefferson MSS., LC; Andrew Butler to Thomas Sumter, 14 January 1808, Thomas Sumter MSS., LC; Benjamin Stoddert to John Rutledge, John Rutledge Papers, SHC-UNC.
41. Charles Goldsborough to John Rodgers, to David Porter, 24 April 1809, *Letters Sent to Officers*; Paul Hamilton to Isaac Chauncey, 14 September 1811, *Letters Sent by the Secretary of the Navy to Commandants and Navy Agents, 1808–65*, RG45, M441.
42. David Porter to the Secretary of the Navy, 26 December 1808, *Commanders Letters*.
43. David Porter to the Secretary of the Navy, 26 December 1808, 5 April 1809, lieutenants on station to David Porter, 23 February 1809, *Commanders Letters*; Secretary of the Navy to Porter, 26 December 1808, John Henley Papers, Nimitz Library.
44. Porter to Louis Alexis, 8 July 1809, 9 July 1809, Porter to the Secretary of the Navy, 25 August 1809, *Commanders Letters*; Long, *Nothing Too Daring*, 52–55.
45. Long, ibid., 47–48.
46. Edmund Pendleton Gaines to George Washington Campbell, 22 April 1809, George Washington Campbell MSS., LC; Robert Smith to David Holmes, 21 December 1810, Robert Smith MSS., LC; James Wilkinson to David Porter, 12 May 1809, David Porter to James Wilkinson, 1 September 1809, *Commanders Letters*; Long, *Nothing Too Daring*, 48–50.
47. David Porter to the Secretary of the Navy, 27 July 1809, 29 December 1809, 10 January 1810, *Commanders Letters*; "Gunboats on the Mississippi River," RG45: AF, Box 64, 1810; "Statement of Lt. Thomas ap Catesby Jones Concerning Engagement on Lake Borgne on 14 December 1814," 12 March 1815, National Archives, RG45: HJ, Box 181, 1814–15.
48. David Porter to P. C. Wederstrandt, 12 March 1810, Morse Family Papers, LC; "Biography of John Shaw," no author, no date, 8, John Shaw Papers, NHF-LC; John Shaw to Commander, Balize Division," 3 May 1812, "John Shaw Papers, NHF-LC.
49. John Shaw to the Secretary of the Navy, 21 December 1813, John Shaw MSS., LC; Goldsborough, *Naval Chronicle*, 327.
50. Richard Wheeler, *In Pirate Waters* (New York: Thomas Y. Crowell Company, 1969), 52–53; Paul Hamilton to John Shaw, 14 February 1811, *Letters Sent to Officers*.

Chapter 8
The Legacy: A Lesson Unlearned

1. Adams, *History of the United States*, 1331–33; Symonds, *Navalists and Antinavalists*, 194; William Crawford to Charles Tait, 12 October 1814, Charles Tait Papers, Tait Family Collection, State of Alabama, Department of Archives and History, Montgomery.
2. Jefferson's Eighth Annual Message, 8 November 1808, Richardson, *Messages of the Presidents*, 1: 439–44; Jefferson to the Senate and House of Representatives, 6 January 1809, Jefferson MSS., LC.
3. Return Jonathan Meigs, Jr., to A. Brown, 2 May 1809, Return Jonathan Meigs, Jr., Papers, State Library of Ohio, Columbus; Robert Walsh to Nicholas Biddle, 11 July 1809, Reginald C. McGrane, ed., *The Correspondence of Nicholas Biddle: Dealing*

with National Affairs, 1807–1844 (Boston: Houghton Mifflin Company, 1919), 6; Symonds, *Navalists and Antinavalists*, 134, 143; *Annals*, 23 January 1809, 10th Congress, 2nd session, 328–31; ibid., 18 January 1809, 1095–96; ibid., 26 January 1809, 1184–85; ibid., 31 January 1809, 1808.

4. *Annals*, 11th Congress, 1st session, 25 April 1810, 1963–77; Symonds, *Navalists and Antinavalists*, 143–46.

5. Goldsborough, *Naval Chronicle*, 326–27; Frank L. Owsley, "Paul Hamilton," Coletta, *American Secretaries of the Navy*, 1: 95; Paul Hamilton to Joseph Anderson, 6 June 1809, *ASP*, 194; Adams, *History of the United States*, 119.

6. *Statutes at Large*, 12th Congress, 1st session, 30 March 1812, 699; Nathaniel Macon, to ? Jones, 7 January 1812, Nathaniel Macon MSS., LC; Paul Hamilton to Morton Waring, 11 May 1812, 19 May 1812, Paul Hamilton Papers, South Caroliniana Library, University of South Carolina, Columbia; Paul Hamilton to John Rodgers and Stephen Decatur, 21 May 1812, Paul Hamilton to Charles Gordon, 23 June 1812, *Letters Sent to Officers*.

7. E. B. Potter and J. R. Fredland, *The United States and World Sea Power* (Englewood Cliffs, NJ: Prentice-Hall, Inc. 1955), 238; Edward K. Eckert, "William Jones: Mr. Madison's Secretary of the Navy," *Pennsylvania Magazine of History and Biography* 96 (April 1972): 168; Edward K. Eckert, *The Navy Department in the War of 1812* (Gainesville: University of Florida Press, 1973), 14; William James, *The Naval History of Great Britain* (London: Macmillan and Company, 1902), 5: 456; Irving Brant, *James Madison, Commander in Chief* (Indianapolis, IN: The Bobbs-Merrill Company, Inc., 1961), 6: 39.

8. Dudley, *The Naval War of 1812*, 1: 115; Dean R. Mayhew, "Jeffersonian Gunboats in the War of 1812," *American Neptune* 42 (April 1982): 149; Cooper, *History of the Navy*, 116–18; Mahan, *War of 1812*, 2: 165–67; Sam Kello to James H. Rochelle, 17 March 1813, James H. Rochelle Papers, William R. Perkins Library, Duke University; Adams, *History of the United States*, 807.

9. Hulbert Footner, *Sailor of Fortune: The Life and Adventures of Commodore Barney, USN* (New York: Harper & Brothers, 1940), 267–71; Mayhew, "Jeffersonian Gunboats in the War of 1812," 111–12; Cooper, *History of the Navy*, 134–35.

10. Cooper, *History of the Navy*, 135–36; Mayhew, "Jeffersonian Gunboats in the War of 1812," 112; Footner, *Sailor of Fortune*, 274–75.

11. Footner, *Sailor of Fortune*, 277–79; Milton S. Davis, "The Capture of Washington," *United States Naval Institute Proceedings* 63 (June 1937): 843–44; Theodore Roosevelt, *The Naval War of 1812* (New York: G. P. Putnam's Sons: 1882), 290–91; Cooper, *History of the Navy*, 136; Alexander Cochrane to His Royal Highness, 3 September 1814, Alexander Cochrane Papers, NHF-LC.

12. Davis, "The Capture of Washington," 845–48; John Wayles Eppes to Francis Eppes, 30 September 1814, John Wayles Eppes MSS., LC; Thomas L. Spragins to Melchizedek Spragins, 24 October 1814, Melchizedek Spragins Papers, William R. Perkins Library, Duke University.

13. Secretary of the Navy to Isaac Chauncey, 31 August 1812, Dudley, *The Naval War of 1812*, 1: 297–301; Secretary of the Navy to Thomas Macdonough, 28 September 1812, ibid., 1: 319–20; Charles Goldsborough to Daniel Dobbins, 15 September 1812, *Misc. Letters Sent*; Max Rosenberg, *The Building of Perry's Fleet on Lake Erie, 1812–1813* (Harrisburg: Pennsylvania Historical and Museum Commission, 1950), 47.

14. C. S. Forester, *The Age of Fighting Sail: The Story of the Naval War of 1812* (Garden City, NY: Doubleday and Company, Inc., 1956), 154–59.

15. Richard Dillon, *We Have Met the Enemy: Oliver Hazard Perry, Wilderness Commodore* (New York: McGraw-Hill Book Company, 1978), 61; Rosenberg, *Building Perry's Fleet*, 26–27.

16. Oliver H. Perry to William Jones, 27 December 1813, *ASP*, 294–97; Mahan, *War of 1812*, 2: 98–99; Roosevelt, *The Naval War of 1812*, 249–56; C. S. Forester, *The Age of Fighting Sail: The Story of the Naval War of 1812* (Garden City, NY: Doubleday and Company, Inc., 1956), 182–87.

17. Thomas Macdonough to Paul Hamilton, 20 December 1812, Dudley, *The Naval War of 1812*, 1: 370–71; Harrison Bird, *Navies in the Mountains: The Battles on the Waters of Lake Champlain and Lake George* (New York: Oxford University Press, 1962), 271–74; Roosevelt, *The Naval War of 1812*, 259–61.

18. Bird, *Navies in the Mountains*, 287–92, 298–99; Thomas Macdonough to the Secretary of the Navy, 23 November 1813, *Commanders Letters*; Forester, *The Age of Fighting Sail*, 234.

19. George R. Clark, William O. Stevens, Carroll S. Alden, and Herman F. Krafft, *A Short History of the United States Navy* (Philadelphia: J. B. Lippincott Company, 1911), 191; Roosevelt, *The Naval War of 1812*, 340–42, 351–56; Waldo H. Heinrichs, Jr. "The Battle of Plattsburg — The Losers," *American Neptune* 21 (January 1961): 53–56; Bird, *Navies in the Mountains*, 306.

20. "Muster Rolls of the Officers and Men Attached to the New York Navy Yard and the Gunboat Flotilla Based at New York: 1813–1815," *United States Navy Yard, New York*, Nimitz Library; Mayhew, "Jeffersonian Gunboats in the War of 1812," 106–8; *Log of U.S.S. Gunboat No. 6*, 19 May 1814, 27–28 May 1814, National Archives, RG24, M1030a.

21. Mahan, *War of 1812*, 2: 194–97; Mayhew, "Jeffersonian Gunboats in the War of 1812," 112–14; Donald R. Hickey, *The War of 1812: A Forgotten Conflict* (Urbana: University of Illinois Press, 1989), passim.

22. "Statement of Lt. Thomas ap Catesby Jones Concerning Engagement on Lake Borgne on 14 December 1814," 12 March 1815, National Archives, RG45: HJ Box 181, 1814–15; John Shaw to James Wilkinson, 12 September 1812, "British Troops Landed in New Orleans in 1815," John Shaw Papers, NHF-LC; Robert J. Hanks, "' … the Ruinous Folly of a Navy,'" *America Spreads Her Sails*, ed. Clayton R. Barrow, Jr. (Annapolis, MD: Naval Institute Press, 1973), 3–6; Wilbur S. Brown, *The Amphibious Campaign for West Florida and Louisiana* (Tuscaloosa: University of Alabama Press, 1969), 78–81; Cooper, *History of the Navy*, 142–45.

23. Brown, *The Amphibious Campaign*, 81; Battle of New Orleans Sesquicentennial Commission, *Battle of New Orleans Sesquicentennial Celebration, 1815–1965* (Washington, D.C.: Government Printing Office, 1965), 46–47; Frank L. Owsley, Jr., *Struggle for the Gulf Border Lands: The Creek War and the Battle of New Orleans, 1812–1815* (Gainesville, University of Florida Press, 1981), 140.

24. Forester, *The Age of Fighting Sail*, 267–69; Owsley, *Struggle for the Gulf*, 139–40; Daniel Patterson to William Jones, 22 November 1813, 7 December 1813, 21 January 1814, 31 January 1814, *Commanders Letters*; Paul Hamilton to John Shaw, 25 September 1812, William Jones to Daniel Patterson, 18 October 1813, *Letters Sent to Officers*.

25. Roosevelt, *The Naval War of 1812*, 293; Millis, *Arms and Men*, 56; Mayhew, "Jeffersonian Gunboats in the War of 1812," 117.

26. *Statutes at Large*, 12th Congress, 2nd session, 3 March 1813, 2: 821; ibid., 13th Congress, 3rd session, 27 February 1815, 3: 218.

27. Benjamin Crowninshield to Alexander Murray, 18 March 1815, Benjamin Crowninshield to George Harrison, 18 March 1815, Benjamin Crowninshield to

John Cassin, 9 March 1815, *Letters Sent to Commandants and Navy Agents*; Benjamin Crowninshield to Robert Henley, Hugh Campbell, John Dent, Bernard Henry, Joshua Barney, John Creighton, Jacob Lewis, 9 March 1815, Benjamin Crowninshield to Hugh Campbell, 10 March 1815, 29 March 1815, Benjamin Crowninshield to John Creighton, 20 March 1815, *Letters Sent to Officers*.

28. Goldsborough, *Naval Chronicle*, 326–27; *Niles National Register*, 20 May 1815, vol. 8, no. 12, p. 215; "Statement of the progress made in executing the instructions of the Secretary of the Navy of 14th February last," RG45: AY Box 122, 1813–15.

29. D. L. Clinch to R. Butler, 2 August 1816, "Operation, Negro Fort," National Archives, RG45: HJ Box 181, 1816; James W. Covington, "The Negro Fort," *Gulf Coast Historical Review* 5 (Spring 1990): 80–81.

30. Dudley W. Knox, "A Forgotten Fight in Florida," *United States Naval Institute Proceedings* 62 (April 1936): 507; Covington, "The Negro Fort," 81.

31. Knox, "A Forgotten Fight in Florida," 507–8; Covington, "The Negro Fort," 81–82.

32. D. L. Clinch to R. Butler, 2 August 1816, "Operation, Negro Fort," National Archives, RG45: HJ Box 181, 1816; Knox, "A Forgotten Fight in Florida," 512–13; Covington, "The Negro Fort," 83, 86–87. Covington gives the date of the attack as 25 July, whereas Dudley and the letter cited above give the date as 27 July 1816.

33. M. Robertson to John Rodgers, 15 September 1817, National Archives, RG45: AY Box 122, 1817; Covington, "The Negro Fort," 83; Chapelle, *History of the American Sailing Navy*, 355; Edward K. Eckert, "Early Reform in the Navy Department," *American Neptune* 33 (October 1973): 240; Smith Thompson to Congress, *ASP*, 3 December 1822, 804; George F. Emmons, *The Navy of the United States, From the Commencement, 1753 to 1853, with a Brief History of Each Vessel's Service and Fate as Appears upon Record* (Washington, D.C.: Gideon and Company, 1853), 22–23.

34. *Federal Gazette* (Baltimore, MD) 22 January 1806; Jefferson to Wilson Cary Nicholas, 6 December 1804, Ford, *The Writings of Jefferson*, 10: 124; William Plumer, 8 November 1804, *Memorandum*, 188; Emmons, *The Navy of the United States*, 23; Samuel Eliot Morison, *The Oxford History of the American People* (New York: Oxford University Press, 1965), 371; editorial, *Washington Federalist* 11 March 1807; Thomas Truxtun to Timothy Pickering, 8 December 1807, Timothy Pickering Papers, Massachusetts Historical Society; William Augustus Fales, "An Oration Pronounced at Lenox, July 4, 1807" (Pittsfield, PA: Phinehas Allen, 1807), 16, *Early American Imprints*, series II, no. 12535.

35. Leiner, "The 'Whimsical Phylosophic President' and His Gunboats," 252–53; Joseph Tarbell to the Secretary of the Navy, 7 December 1810, David Porter to the Secretary of the Navy, 7 September 1808, 13 July 1808, Charles Gordon to the Secretary of the Navy, 1 March 1813, *Commanders Letters*; McKee, *A Gentlemanly and Honorable Profession*, 156–57; William Jones to John Dent, 18 November 1814, William Jones to Alexander Murray, 7 May 1814, Paul Hamilton to Sam Evans, 11 September 1811, *Letters Sent to Officers*.

36. Thomas Gautier to the Secretary of the Navy, 9 August 1808, Thomas Gautier Papers, UNC-SHC; Symonds, *Navalists and Antinavalists*, 219–35.

37. Robert W. Tucker and David C. Hendrickson, *The Empire of Liberty: The Statecraft of Thomas Jefferson* (New York: Oxford University Press, 1990), 224–25; George F. Buker, *Swamp Sailors: Riverine Warfare in the Everglades, 1835–1842* (Gainesville, University of Florida Press, 1975), passim; Potter and Nimitz, *Sea Power*, 231–32, 275–311; Russell F. Weigley, *The American Way of War: A History of United States Military Strategy and Policy* (Bloomington: Indiana University Press, 1973), 170–78.

38. Thomas Gautier to John Dent, 29 March 1813, Thomas Gautier Papers, UNC-SHC.

Bibliography

Manuscript Collections

William Bainbridge Papers. Naval Historical Foundation Collection, Library of Congress, Washington, D.C.

Burwell Bassett MSS. Library of Congress, Washington, D.C.

Bayard Family MSS. Library of Congress, Washington, D.C.

Bayard Papers, MS. 109. Manuscripts Division, Maryland Historical Society Library, Baltimore.

Breckinridge Family MSS. Library of Congress, Washington, D.C.

Brugman Privateer Papers. The Historic New Orleans Collection, New Orleans, Louisiana.

William Burwell MSS. Library of Congress, Washington, D.C.

George Washington Campbell MSS. Library of Congress, Washington, D.C.

De Witt Clinton Papers. Rare Book and Manuscript Library, Columbia University, New York.

Alexander Cochrane Papers. Naval Historical Foundation Collection, Library of Congress, Washington, D.C.

John Wayles Eppes MSS. Library of Congress, Washington, D.C.

Josiah Fox MSS. Library of Congress, Washington, D.C.

Josiah Fox Papers. National Archives, Washington, D.C.

Albert Gallatin Papers. The New-York Historical Society, New York.

Thomas Gautier Papers. Southern Historical Collection, Library of the University of North Carolina at Chapel Hill.

Paul Hamilton Papers. South Caroliniana Library, University of South Carolina, Columbia.

John Henley Papers. Nimitz Library, United States Naval Academy, Annapolis, MD.

H.M.S. Penguin Orderbook. Nimitz Library, United States Naval Academy, Annapolis, MD.

Thomas Jefferson MSS. Library of Congress, Washington, D.C.

Thomas Jefferson Papers. Manuscripts Division, Special Collections, University of Virginia Library, Charlottesville.

Thomas Jefferson Papers. Swem Library, College of William and Mary, Williamsburg, Virginia.

Thomas Jefferson Papers. Coolidge Collection, Massachusetts Historical Society, Boston.

Thomas Jefferson Papers. Henry E. Huntington Library, San Marino, California.

Thomas Jefferson Papers. The New-York Historical Society, New York.

Thomas Jefferson Papers. Rare Books and Manuscripts Division, The New York Public Library, Astor, Lenox and Tilden Foundation, New York City, New York.

Thomas Jefferson Papers. William R. Perkins Library, Duke University, Durham, North Carolina.

Thomas Jefferson Papers. Virginia Historical Society, Richmond.

Walter Jones Papers. Virginia Historical Society, Richmond.

Benjamin Henry Latrobe Papers, MS 2009. Manuscripts Division, Maryland Historical Society Library, Baltimore.

Nathaniel Macon MSS. Library of Congress, Washington, D.C.

Return Jonathan Meigs, Jr., Papers. State Library of Ohio, Columbus.

Morse Family Papers. Library of Congress, Washington, D.C.

Joseph H. Nicholson MSS. Library of Congress, Washington, D.C.

Daniel Todd Patterson Papers. Naval Historical Foundation Collection, Library of Congress, Washington, D.C.

Timothy Pickering Papers. Massachusetts Historical Society, Boston.

Edward Preble MSS. Library of Congress, Washington, D.C.

Josiah Quincy MSS. Library of Congress, Washington, D.C.

John Randolph MSS. Library of Congress, Washington, D.C.

John Randolph Papers. Manuscripts Division, Special Collections, University of Virginia Library, Charlottesville.

John Randolph Papers. Virginia Historical Society, Richmond.

James H. Rochelle Papers. William R. Perkins Library, Duke University, Durham, NC.

Rodgers Family Papers. Library of Congress, Washington, D.C.

John Rutledge Papers. Southern Historical Collection, Library of the University of North Carolina at Chapel Hill.

John Shaw MSS. Library of Congress, Washington, D.C.

John Shaw Papers. Naval Historical Foundation Collection, Library of Congress, Washington, D.C.

John Smith (Ohio) MSS. Library of Congress, Washington, D.C.

John Cotton Smith MSS. Library of Congress, Washington, D.C.

Robert Smith MSS. Library of Congress, Washington, D.C.

Samuel Harrison Smith MSS. Library of Congress, Washington, D.C.

Smith Family Papers. Library of Congress, Washington, D.C.

Melchizedek Spragins Papers. William R. Perkins Library, Duke University, Durham, NC.

Thomas Sumter MSS. Library of Congress, Washington, D.C.

Charles Tait Papers, Tait Family Collection. State of Alabama, Department of Archives and History.

John Taylor Papers. William R. Perkins Library, Duke University, Durham, NC.

Thomas Truxtun Papers. Naval Academy Museum, United States Naval Academy, Annapolis, MD.

United States Navy Yard, New York. "Muster Rolls of the Officers and Men Attached to the New York Navy Yard and the Gunboat Flotilla Based at New York: 1813-1815," Nimitz Library, United States Naval Academy, Annapolis, MD.

Public Documents and Published Collections

Ames, Fisher. *Works of Fisher Ames*. 2 vols. Edited by William B. Allen. Boston: Seth Ames, 1854; reprint ed. Indianapolis, IN: Liberty Classics, 1983.

Bauer, K. Jack. *The New American State Papers: Naval Affairs*. 10 vols. Wilmington, DE: Scholarly Resources Inc., 1981.

Bayard, James A. "The Papers of James A. Bayard, 1796-1815." Edited by Elizabeth Donnan. *Annual Report of the American Historical Association for the Year 1913*. Washington, D.C.: 1915.

Biddle, Nicholas. *The Correspondence of Nicholas Biddle: Dealing with National Affairs, 1807-1844*. Edited by Reginald C. McGrane. Boston: Houghton Mifflin Company, 1919.

Carter, Clarence Edwin, ed. *The Territorial Papers of the United States*. 27 vols. Washington, D.C.: Government Printing Office, 1934–69.

Claiborne, W. C. C. *Official Letterbooks of W. C. C. Claiborne, 1801-1816*. 6 vols. Edited by Dunbar Rowland. Jackson, MS: State Department of Archives and History, 1917.

Cunningham, Noble E., Jr., ed. *Circular Letters of Congressmen to their Constituents, 1789-1829*. Chapel Hill: University of North Carolina Press for the Institute of Early American History and Culture, Williamsburg, Virginia, 1978.

Dudley, William S., ed. *The Naval War of 1812: A Documentary History*. 2 vols. to date. Washington, D.C., Naval Historical Center: Government Printing Office, 1985-.

Gallatin, Albert. *The Writings of Albert Gallatin*. 3 vols. Edited by Henry Adams. Philadelphia, PA: J. B. Lippincott Company, 1879; reprint ed. New York: Antiquarian Press, 1960.

Jefferson, Thomas. *The Papers of Thomas Jefferson*. 25 vols. to date. Edited by Julian P. Boyd. Princeton, NJ: Princeton University Press, 1950-.

_____. *The Writings of Jefferson*. 10 vols. Edited by Paul Leicester Ford. New York: G. P. Putnam's Sons, 1892-1899.

_____. *The Writings of Thomas Jefferson*. 20 vols. Edited by Andrew A. Lipscomb and Albert Ellery Bergh. Washington, D.C.: The Thomas Jefferson Memorial Association, 1903-1904.

_____. *The Writings of Thomas Jefferson*. 8 vols. Edited by H. A. Washington. Washington, D.C.: Taylor and Maury, 1853-1854.

Knox, Dudley W., ed. *Naval Documents Related to the United States Wars with the Barbary Powers*. 6 vols. Washington, D.C.: Government Printing Office, 1939-1944.

Latrobe, Benjamin Henry. *The Correspondences and Miscellaneous Papers of Benjamin Henry Latrobe*. 3 vols. Edited by John C. Van Horne and Lee W. Formwalt. New Haven: Yale University Press, 1984-1988.

Monroe, James. *The Writings of James Monroe*. 8 vols. Edited by Stanislaus Murray Hamilton. New York: G. P. Putnam's Sons, 1900; reprint ed., New York: AMS Press, 1969.

Paine, Thomas. *The Complete Writings of Thomas Paine*. Edited by Philip S. Foner. New York: The Citadel Press, 1945.

Pitt, William. *The Correspondence of William Pitt*. 2 vols. Edited by Gertrude Selwyn Kimball. New York: The Macmillan Company, 1906; reprint ed., New York: Kraus Reprint Company, 1969.

Plumer, William. *Memorandum of the Proceedings in the United States Senate, 1803-1807*. Edited by Everett Somerville Brown. New York: Macmillan Company, 1923.

Richardson, James D., ed. *A Compilation of the Messages and Papers of the Presidents, 1789-1897*. 10 vols. Washington, D.C.: Government Printing Office, 1896-1899.

Smith, Robert. "Some Papers of Robert Smith, Secretary of the Navy 1801-1809 and Secretary of State 1809-1811." Edited by Bernard C. Steiner. *Maryland Historical Magazine* 20 (January 1925):139-150.

U.S. Congress. *Annals of the Congress of the United States*. 42 vols. Washington, D.C.: Gales and Seaton, 1834-1856.

_____. *American State Papers: Documents, Legislative and Executive of the Congress of the United States: Class VI, Naval Affairs*. 6 vols. Edited by Walter Lowrie and Walter S. Franklin. Washington, D.C.: Gales and Seaton, 1832.

_____. *The Public Statutes at Large of the United States of America*. 86 vols. to date. Boston: Charles C. Little and James Brown, 1845-.

U.S. Department of the Navy. "Contracts for Gunboats, 1805-1806." National Archives, RG45: AD Box 45, 1805-07.

_____. "Data on Gunboats Built by the United States, 1804-1808." National Archives, RG45: AC Box 18.

_____. "Gunboat Dimensions." National Archives, RG45: AD Box 43, #17.

_____. "Gunboat Letters." National Archives, RG45: 173.

_____. "Gunboat *No. 5*." National Archives, RG45: AD Box 45, 1804-05.

_____. "Gunboats on the Mississippi River." National Archives, RG45: AF Box 64, 1810.

_____. "Letters Received by the Secretary of the Navy: Captains' Letters, 1805-1861, 1866-1885." National Archives microfilm series no. RG45, M125.

_____. "Letters Received by the Secretary of the Navy from Commanders, 1804-1886." National Archives microfilm series no. RG45, M147.

_____. "Letters Received by the Secretary of the Navy: Miscellaneous Letters, 1801-1884." National Archives microfilm series no. RG45, M124.

_____. "Letters Sent by the Secretary of the Navy to Commandants and Navy Agents, 1808-1865." National Archives microfilm series no. RG45, M441.

_____. "Letters Sent by the Secretary of the Navy to Officers, 1798-1868." National Archives microfilm series no. RG45, M149.

_____. Log of *U.S.S. Gunboat No. 6*. National Archives microfilm series no. RG24, M1030a.

_____. Log of *U.S.S. Gunboat No. 32*. National Archives microfilm series no. RG24, M1030a.

_____. Log of *U.S.S. Gunboat No. 71*. National Archives microfilm series no. RG24, M1030a.

_____. Log of *U.S.S. Gunboat No. 81*. National Archives microfilm series no. RG24, M1030a.

_____. "Miscellaneous Letters Sent by the Secretary of the Navy, 1789-1886." National Archives microfilm series no. RG45, M209.

_____. "Operation, Negro Fort." National Archives, RG45: HJ Box 181, 1816.

_____. "Petition from the State of South Carolina to William Jones, Secretary of the Navy, 1813." National Archives, RG45: AC Box 18.

_____. "Register of Ships." National Archives, RG45: 171.

_____. "Ship Contracts." National Archives, RG45: 235

_____. "Squadron under Commodore John Rodgers — Division of Gunboats under Isaac Hull, 27 April 1805." National Archives, RG45: DB Box 155, 1805.

_____. "Statement of Lt. Thomas ap Catesby Jones Concerning the Engagement on Lake Borgne on 14 December 1814." 12 March 1815, National Archives, RG45: HJ Box 181, 1814-15.

_____. "Statement of the Armaments, Officers, and Crew and Distribution of the Naval Force at New Orleans, 3 November 1807." National Archives, RG45: AD Box 45, 1807.

_____. "Statement of the Progress Made in Executing the Instructions of the Secretary of the Navy of 14th February Last." National Archives, RG45: AY Box 122, 1813-15.

Newspapers

The Boston Repertory, Boston, Massachusetts.
Federal Gazette, Baltimore, Maryland.
National Intelligencer and Washington Advertiser, Washington, D.C.
Niles National Register, Baltimore, Maryland.
Providence Gazette, Providence, Rhode Island.
Washington Federalist, Washington, D.C.

Books and Dissertations

Abernathy, Thomas P. *The Burr Conspiracy*. New York: Oxford University Press, 1954.

Adams, Henry. *John Randolph*. Boston: Houghton, Mifflin & Company, 1882.

————. *Life of Albert Gallatin*. Philadelphia, PA: J. B. Lippincott, 1879; reprint ed., New York: Peter Smith, 1943.

————. *History of the United States of America*. New York: Charles Scribner's Sons, 1891; reprint ed., New York: Literary Classics of the United States, Inc., 1986.

Adams, James Truslow, ed. *Jeffersonian Principles*. Boston: Little, Brown, and Company, 1928.

Adams, Mary P. "Jefferson's Military Policy With Special Reference to the Frontier: 1805-1809." Ph.D. dissertation, University of Virginia, 1958.

Albion, Robert G. *Makers of Naval Policy, 1798-1947*. Annapolis, MD: Naval Institute Press, 1980.

Allen, Gardner W. *Our Navy and the Barbary Corsairs*. Boston: Houghton Mifflin, 1905; reprint ed., 1967.

Ambler, Charles Henry. *Thomas Ritchie; A Study in Virginia Politics*. Richmond, VA: Bell Book and Stationery Company, 1913.

Anderson, Dice Robins. *William Branch Giles: A Study in the Politics of Virginia and the Nation from 1790-1830*. Menasha, WI: George Banta Publishing Company, 1914; reprint ed., Gloucester, MA: Peter Smith, 1965.

Armstrong, Thom M. *Politics, Diplomacy and Intrigue in the Early Republic*. Dubuque, IA: Kendall/Hunt Publishing Company, 1991.

Austin, Aleine. *Matthew Lyon: "New Man" of the Democratic Revolution, 1749-1822*. University Park: The Pennsylvania State University Press, 1981.

Austin, Erik W. and Clubb, Jerome M. *Political Facts of the United States Since 1789*. New York: Columbia University Press, 1986.

Balinky, Alexander. *Albert Gallatin*. New Brunswick, NJ: Rutgers University Press, 1958.

Bartlett, Joseph. "An Oration Delivered at Biddleford, 4 July 1805." Saco, ME: William Weeks, 1805. *Early American Imprints*. Series II, no. 7956.

Bemis, Samuel Flagg. *Jay's Treaty; A Study in Commerce and Diplomacy*. Knights of Columbus, 1923; reprint ed., New Haven: Yale University Press, 1962.

Bidwell, Barnabas. "An Address to the People of Massachusetts." Boston: Adams and Rhoades, 1804. *Early American Imprints*. Series II, no. 5871.

Bird, Harrison. *Navies in the Mountains; The Battles on the Waters of Lake Champlain and Lake George*. New York: Oxford University Press, 1962.

Borden, Morten. *Parties and Politics in the Early Republic, 1789-1815*. Arlington Heights, IL: Harlan Davidson, Inc., 1967.

Bowers, Claude. *Jefferson in Power*. Boston: Houghton Mifflin Company, 1936.

Bradley, Udolpho Theodore. "The Contentious Commodore: Thomas ap Catesby Jones of the Old Navy, 1788-1858." Ph.D. dissertation, Cornell University, 1933.

Brant, Irving. *James Madison: Commander in Chief*. 6 vols. Indianapolis, IN: The Bobbs-Merrill Company, Inc., 1941-61.

Brown, Wilbur. *The Amphibious Campaign for West Florida and Louisiana*. Tuscaloosa: University of Alabama Press, 1969.

Bryant, Samuel W. *The Sea and the States*. Samuel Bryant, 1947; reprint ed., New York: Thomas Y. Crowell Company, 1967.

Buker, George E. *Swamp Sailors: Riverine Warfare in the Everglades, 1835-1842*. Gainesville: University of Florida Press, 1975.

Cassell, Frank A. *Merchant Congressman in the Young Republic: Samuel Smith of Maryland*. Madison: University of Wisconsin Press, 1971.

Caldwell, Lynton K. *The Administrative Theories of Hamilton and Jefferson*. New York: Russell and Russell, Inc., 1964.

Chapelle, Howard I. *History of the American Sailing Navy*. New York: Bonanza Books, 1949.

Clark, George R., Stevens, William O., Alden, Carroll S., and Krafft, Herman F. *A Short History of the United States Navy*. Philadelphia, PA: J. B. Lippincott Company, 1911.

Coletta, Paolo. *The American Naval Heritage in Brief*. 2nd. ed. Washington, D.C.: University Press of America, Inc., 1980.

Cooney, David M. *A Chronology of the U.S. Navy: 1775-1965*. New York: Franklin Watts, Inc., 1965.

Cooper, James Fenimore. *History of the Navy of the United States of America*. Cooperstown: H & E Phinney, 1848.

Coxe, Tench. "Thoughts on the Subject of Naval Power in the United States of America and on Certain Means of Encouraging and Protecting their Commerce and Manufacturing." Philadelphia, PA, 1806. *Early American Imprints*. Series II, no. 10223.

Crackel, Theodore J. *Mr. Jefferson's Army, Political and Social Reform of the Military Establishment, 1801-1809*. New York: New York University Press, 1987.

Cress, Lawrence Delbert. *Citizens in Arms: The Army and Militia in American Society to the War of 1812*. Chapel Hill: The University of North Carolina Press, 1982.

Cunningham, Noble E., Jr. *The Process of Government under Jefferson*. Princeton: Princeton University Press, 1978.

Davis, Matthew L. *Memoirs of Aaron Burr*. 1836; reprint ed., New York: Books for Libraries Press, 1970.

De Camp, L. Sprague. *The Ancient Engineers*. New York: Ballatine Books, 1963.

De Grummond, Jane Lucas. *The Baratarians and the Battle of New Orleans*. Baton Rouge: Louisiana State University Press, 1961.

Dillon, Richard. *We Have Met the Enemy: Oliver Hazard Perry, Wilderness Commodore*. New York: McGraw-Hill Book Company, 1978.

Dodd, William E. *The Life of Nathaniel Macon*. New York: Burt Franklin, 1908; reprint ed., 1970.

Eckert, Edward K. *The Navy Department in the War of 1812*. Gainesville: University of Florida Press, 1973.

Emmons, George F. *The Navy of the United States. From the Commencement 1753 to 1853; with a Brief History of Each Vessel's Service and Fate as Appears upon Record*. Washington, D.C.: Gideon and Co., 1853.

Erney, Richard Alton. *The Public Life of Henry Dearborn*. Ph.D. dissertation, Columbia University, 1957; New York: Arno Press, 1979.

Fales, William Augustus. "An Oration Pronounced at Lenox, July 4, 1807." Pittsfield, PA: Phinehas Allen, 1807. *Early American Imprints*. Series II, no. 12535.

Ferrell, Robert. *American Diplomacy*. 3rd. ed. New York: W. W. Norton and Company, 1975.

Ferguson, Eugene S. *Truxtun of the "Constellation"*. Baltimore, MD: Johns Hopkins Press, 1956.

Footner, Hulbert. *Sailor of Fortune: The Life and Adventures of Commodore Barney, USN*. New York: Harper & Brothers, 1940.

Forester, C. S. *The Age of Fighting Sail: The Story of the Naval War of 1812*. Garden City, NY: Doubleday and Company, Inc., 1956.

Fowler, William M. *Jack Tars and Commodores*. Boston: Houghton Mifflin Company, 1984.

Frost, Holloway H. *We Build a Navy*. Annapolis, MD: United States Naval Institute Press, 1929; reprint ed., 1940.

Garland, Hugh A. *The Life of John Randolph of Roanoke*. New York: D. A. Appleton and Company, 1851.

Gleaves, Albert. *James Lawrence: Captain, United States Navy Commander of the "Chesapeake"*. New York: G. P. Putnam's Sons, 1904.

Glinczanka, Agnieszka and Paszkowski, Josef, eds. *Korespondencja; 1798-1817*. Wydawniczy: Panstwowy Instytut, 1976.

Goldsborough, Charles. *The United States Naval Chronicle*. Washington, D.C.: James Wilson, 1824.

Guttridge, Leonard, and Smith, Jay D. *The Commodores*. New York: Harper and Row, 1969.

Hamlin, Talbot. *Benjamin Henry Latrobe*. New York: Oxford University Press, 1968.

Hanks, Robert J. "' … the Ruinous Folly of a Navy.'" In *America Spreads Her Sails*, pp. 3-20. Edited by Clayton R. Barrow, Jr. Annapolis, MD: Naval Institute Press, 1973.

Harlow, Ralph Volney. *The History of Legislative Methods in the Period before 1825*. New Haven: Yale University Press, 1917.

Henrich, Joseph G. "The Triumph of Ideology: The Jeffersonians and the Navy, 1779-1807." Ph.D. dissertation, Duke University, 1970.

Hickey, Donald R. *The War of 1812*. Urbana: University of Illinois Press, 1989.

Hitsman, J. MacKay. *The Incredible War of 1812*. Toronto: University of Toronto Press, 1965.

Horsman, Reginald. *The Causes of the War of 1812*. New York: A. S. Barnes and Company, 1962.

Irwin, Ray W. *The Diplomatic Relations of the United States with the Barbary Powers, 1776-1816*. Chapel Hill: University of North Carolina Press, 1931.

Jacobs, James Ripley. *Tarnished Warrior: Major-General James Wilkinson*. New York: The Macmillan Company, 1938.

James, William. *The Naval History of Great Britain*. 6 vols. London: Macmillan and Company, 1902.

Jefferson, Thomas. *Notes on the State of Virginia*. Philadelphia, PA: Prichard and Hall, 1788.

Johnson, Allen, ed. *Dictionary of American Biography*. New York: Charles Scribner's Sons, 1928.

Johnstone, Robert M., Jr. *Jefferson and the Presidency: Leadership in the Young Republic*. Ithaca, NY: Cornell University Press, 1978.

Jordan, Weymouth T. *George Washington Campbell of Tennessee, Western Statesman*. Tallahassee: Florida State University, 1955.

Lemmon, Sarah McCulloh. *Frustrated Patriots: North Carolina and the War of 1812*. Chapel Hill: The University of North Carolina Press, 1973.

Levy, Leonard. *Jefferson and Civil Liberties; The Darker Side*. Chicago: Ivan R. Dee, Inc., 1963.

Lewis, Emanuel Raymond. *Seacoast Fortifications of the United States*. 2nd. ed. Annapolis, MD: Leeward Publications, Inc., 1979.

Lomask, Milton. *Aaron Burr: The Conspiracy and Years of Exile, 1805-1836*. New York: Farrar, Straus, Giroux, 1982.

Long, David F. *Nothing Too Daring; A Biography of Commodore David Porter, 1780-1843*. Annapolis, MD: Naval Institute Press, 1970.

_____. *Sailor-Diplomat; A Biography of Commodore James Biddle, 1783-1848*. Boston: Northeastern University Press, 1983.

Lossing, Benson J. *The Story of the United States Navy*. New York: Harper and Brothers, 1880.

Lynch, William O. *Fifty Years of Party Warfare*. Indianapolis, IN: The Bobbs-Merrill Company, Inc., 1931; reprint ed., Gloucester, MA: Peter Smith, 1967.

Mahan, Alfred Thayer. *The Influence of Seapower Upon History*. Privately printed, 1890; reprint ed., New York: Sagamore Press, Inc., 1957.

_____. *Sea Power and its Relation to the War of 1812*. 1905; reprint ed., New York: Haskell House Publishers, Ltd., 1969.

Malone, Dumas. *Jefferson and His Time*. 6 vols. Boston: Little, Brown, and Company, 1948-1981.

Maloney, Linda M. *The Captain from Connecticut: The Life and Naval Times of Issac Hull*. Boston: Northeastern University Press, 1986.

McCaughey, Robert A. *Josiah Quincy, 1772-1864: The Last Federalist*. Cambridge: Harvard University Press, 1974.

McDonald, Forrest. *The Presidency of Thomas Jefferson*. Lawrence: University of Kansas Press, 1976.

McKee, Christopher. *Edward Preble*. Annapolis, MD: Naval Institute Press, 1972.

_____. *A Gentlemanly and Honorable Profession: The Creation of the U.S. Naval Officer Corps, 1794-1815*. Annapolis, MD: Naval Institute Press, 1991.

Middlekauf, Robert. *The Glorious Cause*. Oxford: Oxford University Press, 1982.

Millis, Walter. *Arms and Men: A Study of American Military History*. New York: G. P. Putnam's Sons, 1956.

Morison, Samuel Eliot. *Harrison Gray Otis, 1765-1848*. Boston: Houghton Mifflin Company, 1969.

_____. *The Oxford History of the American People*. New York: Oxford University Press, 1965.

Morse, John T. *Thomas Jefferson*. Boston: Houghton, Mifflin and Company, 1898.

New Orleans Sesquicentennial Commission. *Battle of New Orleans Sesquicentennial Celebration, 1815-1965*. Washington, D.C.: Government Printing Office, 1965.

Owsley, Frank L., Jr. "Paul Hamilton." In *American Secretaries of the Navy*. 2 vols. Edited by Paolo Coletta. Annapolis, MD: Naval Institute Press, 1980, 1:93-98.

_____. "Robert Smith." In *American Secretaries of the Navy*. 2 vols. Edited by Paolo Coletta. Annapolis, MD: Naval Institute Press, 1980, 1:77-90.

_____. *Struggle for the Gulf Borderlands: The Creek War and the Battle of New Orleans, 1812-1815*. Gainesville: University of Florida Press, 1981.

Palmer, Michael. *Stoddert's War: Naval Operations During the Quasi-War with France, 1799-1801*. Columbia: University of South Carolina Press, 1987.

Paullin, Charles Oscar. *Commodore John Rodgers: Captain, Commodore and Senior Officer of the American Navy: 1773-1838*. Annapolis, MD: Naval Institute Press, 1967.

_____. *Paullin's History of Naval Administrations, 1775-1911*. Annapolis, MD: Naval Institute Press, 1968.

Perkins, Bradford. *The First Rapproachment: England and the United States: 1795-1805*. London: Cambridge University Press, 1955.

Peterson, Merrill D. *Thomas Jefferson and the New Nation*. London: Oxford University Press, 1970.

Potter, E. B. and Fredland, J. R. *The United States and World Sea Power*. Englewood Cliffs, NJ: Prentice-Hall, Inc. 1955.

Potter, E. B. and Nimitz, Chester W. *Sea Power: A Naval History*. Englewood Cliffs, NJ: Prentice-Hall, Inc., 1960.

Prentiss, Henry Putnam. *Timothy Pickering as the Leader of New England Federalism, 1801-1815*. Reprint ed. New York: Da Capo Press, Inc., 1972.

Rayner, B. L. *Sketches of the Life, Writings, and Opinions of Thomas Jefferson*. New York: A. Francis and W. Boardman, 1832.

Roosevelt, Theodore. *The Naval War of 1812*. New York: G. P. Putnam's Sons, 1882; reprint ed., Annapolis, MD: Naval Institute Press, 1987.

Rosenberg, Max. *The Building of Perry's Fleet on Lake Erie, 1812-1813*. Harrisburg: Pennsylvania Historical and Museum Commission, 1950.

Saxon, Lyle. *Lafitte the Pirate*. New Orleans: Robert L. Crager and Company, 1950.

Shalhope, Robert E. *John Taylor of Caroline; Pastoral Republican*. Columbia: University of South Carolina Press, 1980.

Schachner, Nathan. *Thomas Jefferson: A Biography*. New York: Appleton-Century-Crofts, 1951.

Schlesinger, Arthur M. *History of American Presidential Elections, 1798-1968*. New York: Chelsea House Publishers and McGraw-Hill Book Company, 1971.

Schweitzer, Robert Andrue. "The Jeffersonian Congresses: A Quantitative Look, 1801-1813." M.A. thesis, Wayne State University, 1975.

Shears, Martin. *Jefferson and the Embargo*. New York: Octagon Books, 1978.

Smelser, Marshall. *The Democratic Republic, 1801-1815*. New York: Harper and Row, 1968.

Spaulding, E. Wilder. *His Excellency George Clinton*. Port Washington, NY: Ira Friedman, Inc., 1964.

Spivak, Burton. *Jefferson's English Crisis*. Charlottesville: University of Virginia Press, 1979.

Sprout, Harold, and Sprout, Margaret. *The Rise of American Naval Power*. Princeton, NJ: Princeton University Press, 1946.

Stagg, J. C. A. *Mr. Madison's War: Politics, Diplomacy, and Warfare in the Early Republic, 1783-1830*. Princeton: Princeton University Press, 1983.

Stanly, John. "Letter to His Constituents." Washington, D.C.: 1803. *Early American Imprints*. Series II, no. 5097.

Stapleton, Darwin H. *The Engineering Drawings of Benjamin Henry Latrobe*. New Haven: Yale University Press, 1980.

Symonds, Craig. *Navalists and Antinavalists; The Naval Policy Debate in the United States, 1785-1827*. Newark: The University of Delaware, 1980.

Tucker, Glenn. *Dawn Like Thunder; The Barbary Wars and the Birth of the U.S. Navy*. Indianapolis, IN: Bobbs Merrill, 1963.

Tucker, Robert W., and Hendrickson, David C. *Empire of Liberty: The Statecraft of Thomas Jefferson*. New York: Oxford University Press, 1990.

Tucker, Spencer C. *The Jeffersonian Gunboat Navy*. Columbia: University of South Carolina Press, 1993.

Wade, Arthur. "Artillerists and Engineers: The Beginnings of American Seacoast Fortifications, 1794-1815." Ph.D. dissertation, Kansas State University, 1977.

Walters, Raymond, Jr. *Albert Gallatin: Financier and Diplomat.* New York: MacMillan Company, 1957.

Watson, Alan D. *Wilmington: Port of North Carolina.* Columbia: University of South Carolina Press, 1992.

Weigley, Russell F. *The American Way of War: A History of United States Military Strategy and Policy.* Bloomington: Indiana University Press, 1973.

Westfall, Richard S. *The Construction of Modern Science: Mechanisms and Mechanics.* New York: John Wiley and Sons, 1971.

Wheeler, Richard. *In Pirate Waters.* New York: Thomas Y. Crowell Company, 1969.

Whitaker, Arthur Preston. *The Mississippi Question, 1795-1803.* New York: D. Appleton-Century Company for the American Historical Association, 1934.

White, Leonard D. *The Jeffersonians.* New York: Macmillan Company, 1951.

Wright, Louis, and Macleod, Julia H. *The First Americans in North Africa: William Eaton's Struggle for a Vigorious Policy Against the Barbary Pirates, 1790-1805.* Princeton: Princeton University Press, 1945.

Zahniser, Marvin R. *Charles Cotesworth Pinckney, Founding Father.* Chapel Hill: University of North Carolina Press for the Institute of Early American History and Culture at Williamsburg, Virginia, 1967.

Articles

Aldridge, Alfred Owen. "Thomas Paine's Plan for a Descent on England." *William and Mary Quarterly* 14 (January 1957): 74-84.

Balinky, Alexander. "Albert Gallatin, Naval Foe." *Pennsylvania Magazine of History and Biography* 82 (July 1958): 293-304.

Bauer, K. Jack. "Naval Shipbuilding Programs, 1794-1860." *Military Affairs* 29 (Spring 1965): 29-40.

Cooke, Mary Lewis, and Lewis, Charles Lee. "An American Naval Officer in the Mediterranean, 1802-1807." *United States Naval Institute Proceedings* 47 (July-December 1941): 1533–39.

Covington, James W. "The Negro Fort." *Gulf Coast Historical Review* 5 (Spring 1990): 79-91.

Davies, George E. "Robert Smith and the Navy." *Maryland Historical Magazine* 14 (December 1919): 305–22.

Davis, Milton S. "The Capture of Washington." *United States Naval Institute Proceedings* 63 (June 1937): 830–50.

Eckert Edward K. "Early Reform in the Navy Department." *American Neptune* 33 (October 1973): 231–45.

_____. "William Jones: Mr. Madison's Secretary of the Navy." *Pennsylvania Magazine of History and Biography* 96 (April 1972): 167–82.

Ferguson, Eugene. "Mr. Jefferson's Dry Dock." *American Neptune* 11 (April 1954): 108–14.

Hamilton, J. G. de Roulhac. "The Pacificism of Thomas Jefferson." *Virginia Quarterly Review* 31 (Summer 1955): 606–20.

Heinrichs, Waldo H., Jr. "The Battle of Plattsburg — The Losers." *American Neptune* 21 (January 1961): 42–56.

Howland, Felix. "The Blockade of Tripoli, 1801-1802." *United States Naval Institute Proceedings* 63 (July-December 1937): 1702–4.

Knox, Dudley W. "A Forgotten Fight in Florida." *United States Naval Institute Proceedings* 62 (April 1936): 507–13.

Lathrop, Constance. "Vanished Ships." *United States Naval Institute Proceedings* 60 (July 1934): 949–52.

Leiner, Frederick C. "The 'Whimsical Phylosophic President' and His Gunboats." *American Neptune* 43 (October 1983): 245–66.

Macleod, Julia H. "Jefferson and the Navy: A Defense." *Huntington Library Quarterly* 3 (1944–45): 153–84.

Mayhew, Dean R. "Jeffersonian Gunboats in the War of 1812." *American Neptune* 42 (April 1982): 101–17.

Moran, Charles. "Commodore Preble's Sicilian Auxiliaries." *United States Naval Institute Proceedings* 65 (January-June 1939): 80–82.

Norton, Paul F. "Jefferson's Plans for Mothballing the Frigates." *United States Naval Institute Proceedings* 82 (July 1956): 736–41.

Paullin, Charles Oscar. "Naval Administration Under Secretaries of the Navy Smith, Hamilton, and Jones, 1801-1814." *United States Naval Institute Proceedings* 32 (December 1906): 1289-1328.

Smith, Gene A. "A 'Perfect State of Preservation': Thomas Jefferson's Dry Dock Proposal." *Virginia Cavalcade* 39 (Winter 1990): 118–28.

_____. "'For the Purposes of Defense': Thomas Jefferson's Naval Militia." 53 *American Neptune* (Winter 1993): 30-38.

_____. "U.S. Navy Gunboats and the Slave Trade in Louisiana Waters, 1808-1811." *Military History of the West* 23 (2) (Fall 1993): 135–47.

Trimble, William F. "From Sail to Steam: Shipbuilding in the Pittsburgh Area, 1790-1865." *The Western Pennsylvania Historical Magazine* 58 (April 1975): 147–67.

Tucker, Spencer C. "Mr. Jefferson's Gunboat Navy." *American Neptune* 43 (April 1983): 135–41.

Index